THE NATIONAL TRUST

HISTORICAL ATLAS OF BRITAIN

Prehistoric to Medieval

THE NATIONAL TRUST

HISTORICAL ATLAS OF BRITAIN

Prehistoric to Medieval

GENERAL EDITOR: NIGEL SAUL

SUTTON PUBLISHING
IN ASSOCIATION WITH
THE NATIONAL TRUST

Published in Association with National Trust Enterprises Ltd
First published in the United Kingdom in 1994 by Alan Sutton Publishing Limited,
an imprint of Sutton Publishing Limited · Phoenix Mill · Thrupp · Stroud ·
Gloucestershire · GL5 2BU

First published in paperback in 1997 by Sutton Publishing Limited

British Library Cataloguing in Publication Data
A catalogue record for this book is available from the British Library.

ISBN 0–7509–0313–9 (cased)
ISBN 0–7509–1679–6 (paper)

Library of Congress Cataloging in Publication Data

The National Trust historical atlas of Britain: prehistoric to medieval Britain / general
editor, Nigel Saul.
        p.   cm.
    ISBN 0–7509–0313–9: $55.00
    1. Great Britain–Historical geography–Maps.   2. Great Britain–Civilization–To
1066–Maps.   3. Great Britain–Civilization–Medieval period, 1066–1485–Maps.
4. National Trust (Great Britain).   5. Great Britain–Antiquities.   I. Saul, Nigel.
II. National Trust (Great Britain).   III. Title: Historical atlas of Britain.   IV. Title:
Prehistoric to medieval Britain.
G1812.21.S1N3 1993 <G&M>
911'.41–dc20
                                                                                          92–46029
                                                                                                CIP
                                                                                               MAP

*Cover illustrations: top: View of the stones at Avebury with the sun emerging from
behind a tree at dawn (National Trust Photographic Library/David Norton);
bottom: Fountains Abbey showing the Cellarium and the Guest House at dusk
(National Trust Photographic Library/Matthew Antrobus); back: Cuddy's Crag
under snow (National Trust Photographic Library/Charlie White)*

 ALAN SUTTON™ and SUTTON™ are the trade
marks of Sutton Publishing Limited

Typeset in 10/14pt Sabon.
Typesetting and origination by
Sutton Publishing Limited.
Printed in Hong Kong by
Midas Printing Limited.

CONTENTS

PART I: PREHISTORY *by Roger Mercer*

PART II: ROMAN AND EARLY MEDIEVAL BRITAIN *by Philip Dixon*

PART III: MEDIEVAL BRITAIN
by Nigel Saul

LIST OF MAPS

PART I

PART II

PART III

ABBREVIATIONS

E   east

W   west

N   north

S   south

km   kilometres

K   000 (thousands)

NT   National Trust

NTS   National Trust for Scotland

PREFACE

The writing of this historical atlas has presented the co-authors with both a challenge and an opportunity. The challenge has been to use maps as a medium for the presentation of the social and cultural history of prehistoric and medieval Britain; the opportunity, to take advantage of the properties of the National Trust to convey something of the flavour of British society in the period under review.

The atlas format has a number of attractions. It can highlight the connection between geography and history; it can facilitate the discussion of complex archaeological data; and it can suggest insights and possibilities which words by themselves cannot. But it also carries with it a number of difficulties. First, and most obviously, a map cannot easily convey the process of chronological change. It presents a snapshot of one moment in time, not a moving picture of a process of evolution. For that evolutionary process to be captured what is needed is not one but a series of maps of each topic, and given the constraints of space and cost that is not always possible. Secondly – and this is a particular problem for the Middle Ages – the atlas format cannot properly do justice to the fluidity of boundaries. Boundaries in the modern sense scarcely existed in the Middle Ages. There were only vaguely defined border areas where one ruler's authority faded imperceptibly into another's. This was the case on England's northern frontier for most of the period; it was also the case in the congeries of competing lordships that made up medieval Ireland. Because of these difficulties we have chosen to focus our attention on those aspects of the past which gain most from cartographic treatment – that is, chiefly, the social, economic and demographic. Politics have not been ignored. They have been introduced as and where necessary to provide background to the discussion. But except in the case of central events like the Viking invasions or the Norman Conquest they have not been placed centre-stage.

The prominence given to the properties of the National Trust and National Trust for Scotland accords well with this emphasis. The Trusts have in their ownership a remarkable collection of properties which illustrate the changing character of life in these islands from the earliest times to the present day. From the prehistoric period come Avebury and Cissbury, from the Roman period Chedworth villa, and from the medieval, to name but some of the most famous properties, Fountains, Bodiam and Ightham Mote. These are without exception monuments of vital importance to a proper understanding of the social or religious history of their respective periods. Some of them – Bodiam, for example – have been studied and written about for three-quarters of a century or more. Others, like Ightham, while relatively little studied in the past, have been the subject of detailed investigation since passing into Trust ownership. Others again – notably the prehistoric sites like Avebury – have barely been investigated at all, because investigations cannot be carried out without excavation, and the Trusts, seeing themselves primarily as conservation bodies, are reluctant to sanction excavation work on their sites. Sometimes we have to be content to admire a monument without knowing all that we would like to know about its past.

As a result of the gaps and limitations in our knowledge it has not always been possible in this book to give every property the attention that it deserves. Some properties figure prominently in its pages, others much less so, those of prehistoric origin least of all. Some unevenness of treatment is probably inevitable under the circumstances. Nevertheless it has been the authors' aim throughout to make maximum use of Trust properties in illustrating their arguments; and where this has not been possible, as in the discussion of prehistory, a list is appended of Trust properties of comparable date to those discussed, so that the Trusts' riches in this area can be appreciated.

It is probably fair to say that the Trusts' greatest strength in their pre-modern holdings are to be found in their collection of medieval secular and domestic buildings – manor-houses like Ightham and Old Soar, parsonages like those at Alfriston and Muchelney, and clothiers' dwellings such as those at Lacock. There are abbeys and priories in the Trusts' care as well – most obviously, Fountains: but, of course, there are no cathedrals and only one parish church. To overlook cathedrals and churches just because they do not belong to either of the Trusts would be to leave a major lacuna in our coverage of a period in which, from the seventh century, the essential framework of belief was provided by the Church. Thus, where necessary, and particularly in coverage of the late Middle Ages, use has been made of major monuments (mainly churches) which lie outside the Trusts' own resources.

All three authors would like to acknowledge the co-operation of Margaret Willes and the staff of the National Trust in London, and of Alan Sutton Publishing Ltd who came to the rescue of this venture at an earlier stage of its life. The editor would like to acknowledge comments and suggestions that he has received from Christopher Dyer, Anthony Goodman and Caroline Barron. He would also like to thank Rosemary Prudden of Alan Sutton's for her careful, and cheerful, work in producing the book.

NIGEL SAUL

PART I

PREHISTORY

ROGER MERCER

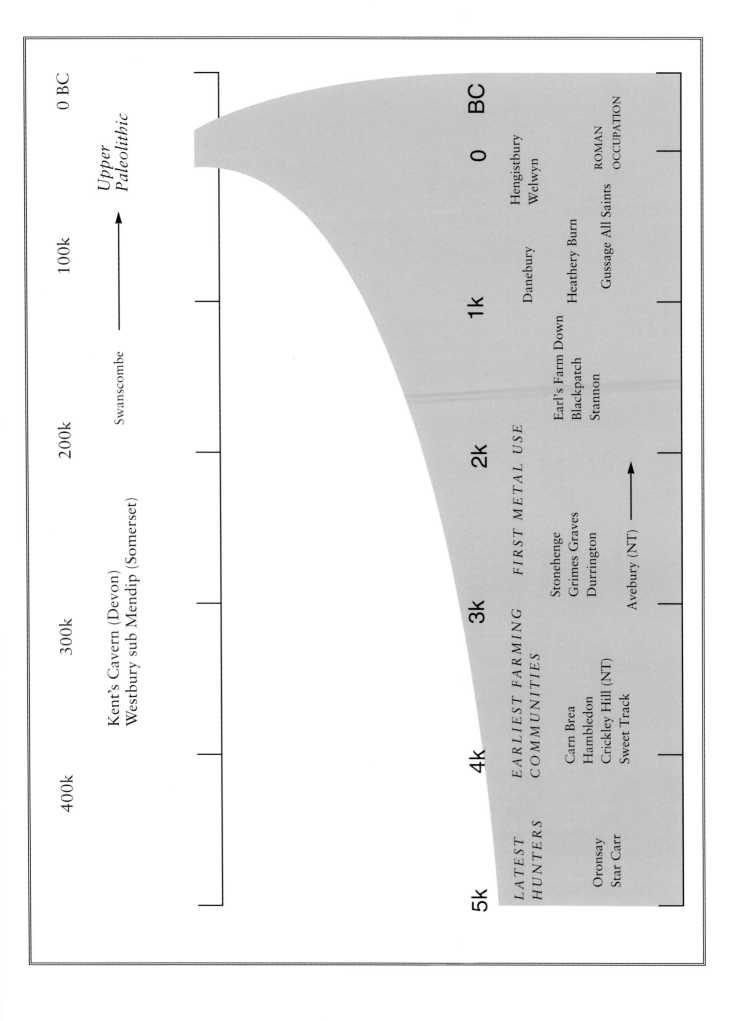

I
THE EARLIEST OCCUPATION OF BRITAIN BY MAN

THE EARLIEST HUNTERS (THE PALEOLITHIC OR 'OLD STONE AGE' PERIOD)

The earliest known occupation of the British Isles probably took place some time around 400,000 years ago, during a period of interglacial climatic relaxation. The evidence for Man's presence at so distant a time is scanty to say the least; and what evidence there is comes chiefly from just two sites – Kent's Cavern, near Torquay, and a cave in a modern limestone quarry at Westbury-sub-Mendip in Somerset. At the latter site simple struck flakes and a finished cutting-tool were located in deposits of silt and conglomerate created by weathering of, and water deposition from, the surrounding limestone rock. Only Man could have made the tools; and he has ineradicably registered his presence for us by their manufacture.

At Kent's Cavern a layer of conglomerate limestone near the floor of the cave contained remains of animals including cave bear and sabre-tooth cat. Alongside these were traces of a crude stone-working industry producing simple 'hand axes' manufactured by very powerful blows administered by smashing one heavy stone block against another. Archaeologists term this very basic shattering of stones to produce tools of a rudimentary nature 'Early Acheulian', after the site at St Acheul in the Somme Valley of France which was first studied in the mid-nineteenth century.

Some 200,000 years later, after a further period of glaciation, a second interglacial period, known as the Hoxnian (after an important site at Hoxne (Suffolk) can be identified. Important deposits from this period have been revealed by gravel quarrying at Swanscombe (Kent). From the lowest levels come massive flakes and cores worked by powerful swinging blows of stone upon stone producing 'cleavers' and 'choppers' of flint. It is likely that this activity was carried on by a pre-sapiens human forerunner. In the same area substantial mammal remains were found – of deer, rhinoceros, wild

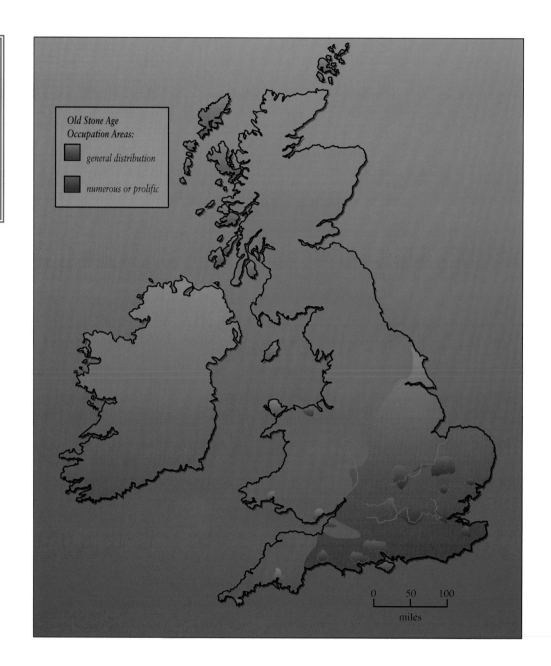

MAP 1: GENERAL
DISTRIBUTION OF OLD
STONE AGE OCCUPATION
AREAS IN BRITAIN

*Stone tools provide the main
surviving body of evidence,
usually incorporated with river
gravels but also in cave
deposits.*

Old Stone Age
Occupation Areas:

general distribution

numerous or prolific

0   50   100

miles

oxen, bear and straight-tusked elephant (now extinct) – and the conclusion must be drawn that this human forerunner subsisted by hunting. But doing so could not have been easy with the rudimentary instruments that he had at his disposal.

Following the end of the last Ice Age, some time between 12,500 and 8000 BC, the animals and plants upon which Man subsisted re-established themselves, and Man himself rapidly appeared in their wake. The environment in which he lived was a harsh one of treeless steppe, inhabited by mammoth, woolly rhino, wild horse and giant deer. Human groups survived by the specialized hunting of these migratory fauna as they moved to and from the brief summer grazings revealed by the seasonal release of tracts of land from the grip of the ice. For some of the time these human groups lived in caves. Indeed, it is as 'cavemen' that they are often known, because it is in such settings that deposits have survived and have yielded information about them. But, equally, during the summer months at least, they would have been mobile in their

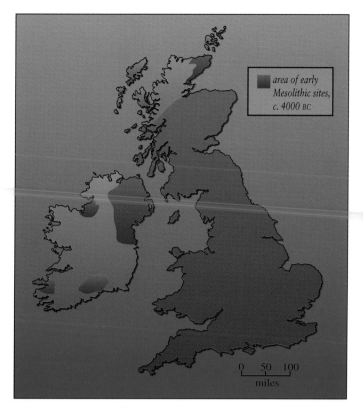
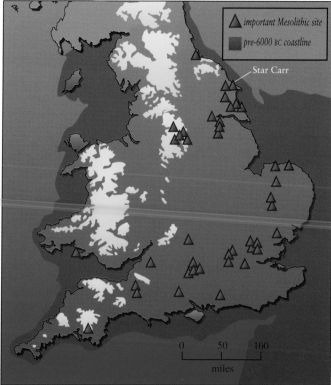

symbiotic attachment to the herds of reindeer and horse upon which they depended – not only for their food, but for a whole range of other materials (fat, tallow, sinew, bone, skin) that were essential to their economy. The tools which they used to cut up and strip these animals were generally of stone – 'burins', or engravers, in the early part of the period, and more elaborate ones with an elongated cutting edge later; with the passage of time, their tools became more sophisticated and more effective (map 1).

THE LATEST HUNTERS (THE MESOLITHIC PERIOD)

With the final passing of the ice from the land surface of Britain an extremely rapid series of environmental changes took place which were to change the British landscape from one dominated by tundra-type conditions to one where substantial tracts of land were covered by pine, birch and alder forest. This – in geological terms – catastrophic change brought with it an equally important transformation from the point of view of Man. As a result of the unlocking of vast quantities of water from the shrinking polar ice-caps there was a gradual rise in sea level that was to inundate the vast tracts of land covered by what is now the North Sea. By roughly 6000 BC the land-bridge linking Britain with the continent of Europe was broken, and Britain became an island.

With this change came others that were to require fundamental adjustments by Man. The newly developing closed landscape of woodland and scrub (and the absence of the mosses and lichens that form the staple diet of reindeer) led to the progressive diminution of the reindeer and horse herds that had formed the main quarry of the Late

MAP 2: THE DISTRIBUTION OF EARLY MESOLITHIC SITES IN BRITAIN
The map on the left shows the area of the British Isles colonized by the end of the Mesolithic era (c. 4000 BC). The one on the right shows some of the more important sites in England; among them Star Carr (North Yorkshire), set against the pre-6000 BC shoreline.

SWANSCOMBE (Kent) The layers of alternating loam and river gravel within which the deposits at Swanscombe have been located

Paleolithic hunters. Their place in the food chain was taken by other ungulate species such as elk, red deer and aurochs (wild cattle) – animals of much subtler organizational patterns which for substantial parts of the year spent their lives moving and grazing in small groups or singly. Without doubt, this in turn demanded different approaches to, and implements for, hunting, and probably a different social organization and seasonal adjustment of that organization in order to obtain a living from these resources. Having said this, the ambient vegetation also provided a range of food resources which had not been available in earlier 'glacial' regimes, and doubtless these (roots, stems, leaves and fruit) formed an important element of the diet of these newly developed communities. But in these chilly northern climes it is doubtful if any group could have subsisted even in the medium term without the concentrated resources of protein and carbohydrate that are only available in the form of animal products. Not only were such animal products – fats, sinew, gut, bone, antler, skin and blood – vital for sustenance but also for raw materials wherewith to produce hunting weapons, tools and to fulfil a multi-tude of other purposes.

In hunting these elusive and alert animals, two new developments were required, and therefore, in the fullness of time, met. One was a more damaging armature point to inflict a wound that, if not deadly, would tear the animal's flesh to promote an

STAR CARR (North Yorkshire)
Platform of timber laid down to
consolidate the ground beside a
prehistoric lake in order to provide a
firm footing for specialized hunting
groups

unsustainable loss of blood. The other, in order to locate the animal as it rushed, injured and panicked, through the brush, was the dog. Both dog and the new arrowpoints are located at what is probably still the most important site of the Early Mesolithic yet to be excavated in Britain, Star Carr, set in the Vale of Pickering in North Yorkshire.

The effectiveness (and risks) of this style of hunting are perhaps best illustrated by the skeleton of an elk of *c.* 7000 BC found in what at the time may have been a quagmire, near Poulton-le-Fylde (Lancashire). The animal – to judge by lesions still visible on its bones – had been wounded at least three times and had made its escape. Finally it was wounded again but eluded its hunters only to drown in the bog into which it was pursued. This remarkable find is an indication not only of the reality of hunting life in the period, but also, poignantly, of the risks of *over-hunting*, if one animal could be engaged by hunters at least four times in its short life.

As well as bow and arrow these hunters used barbed hunting spears (looking rather like harpoons) with which to lance their quarry and stone maces and 'mattocks' which may have been a ready means of despatch for fallen animals.

The terrain in which the struggle for survival was carried on tended to be the higher ground on the edge of fen or 'carr' lands in which birds and fish teemed. Star Carr (North Yorkshire) is an example of a site found in such a habitat. In some parts of the British Isles, notably in Scotland, sites on islands and by the coast also tended to be settled. One such site – and a very informative one at that – has been identified at Oronsay in the Inner Hebrides. Here the remains of 'shell-middens', clustering around the ancient shore-line some 10 m above present high tide, betray the presence of a community that inhabited the site some 4–5,000 years BC. They were a people that supported themselves by hunting. Grey seal provided the bulk of their meat intake, but red deer also seem to have been eaten. There are signs, indeed, that deer from two quite distinct populations were hunted; one presumably was native to the island, while the other was hunted on the mainland nearby. The implication is that sea-borne hunting expeditions went in search of game and came back laden with venison.

Oronsay in the Mesolithic period would have borne little resemblance to the treeless, windswept island of today. Alder, birch and hazel were then plentifully present, and willow grew in sheltered locations. Bearing in mind the juxtaposition of marine resource, light woodland and fresh water, and the availability of deer and seal, present-day marginal areas like this island would have been highly attractive to the early hunting and gathering populations that frequented them.

'Hunting, Shooting and Fishing'

Star Carr is situated near the east end of the Vale of Pickering some 5 miles (8 km) south of Scarborough. It was discovered by the cleaning of a field drain, and excavation began in 1949 and continued until 1951. From analyses of the animal bone it seems that a minimum of 75 animal carcasses were represented on the site (26 red deer, 12 elk, 17 roe deer, 16 aurochs and 4 wild pig). The occupation took place on a mat of birch and other timber laid down to consolidate the boggy lake-edge. The bone and other evidence would suggest that the site was probably in use during the spring–autumn segment of the year, and radio-carbon dating suggests a date c. BC 7,500. In winter the occupying group (which may have comprised hunters only and not 'dependants') may have migrated to the coastlands to exploit the broader range of resources available there. The group certainly stockpiled antler for the production of tools and their most striking output was a series of barbed points (fifty-four in all) manufactured on red deer antler. Two clusters of stone beads and three amber beads (as well as perforated teeth) must represent some kind of cosmetic enhancement, just possibly necklaces broken or discarded. Large quantities of flint of greyish/blue colour, imported from the Yorkshire Wolds immediately to the south, were worked to produce cutting, scribing and scraping tools to enable the cleaning of skins, the cutting of sinew and the working of antler. The site saw the production of a new type of tool – a highly effective and easily maintained flint axe, sharpened by simple transverse blows to produce a virgin flake edge and a discarded sharpening flake. The importance of the axe is the capacity it offered for the alteration and use of the increasingly wooded environment surrounding the site comprising birch trees and some pine, alder, hazel and willow. Also found at Star Carr were the remains of one animal which was the key to the hunter's successful exploitation of the fleet of foot quarry – the dog. This domesticate is thus present in north-west Europe by the middle of the eighth millennium BC. The hunting that the dogs engaged in was conducted by spear and bow and arrow. The barbed spears made of antlers have already been mentioned briefly. The archery is represented by 246 tiny blunted-back points (blunted to facilitate hafting), none showing any sign of use for their final deadly purpose.

II
THE ADVENT AND DEVELOPMENT OF FARMING COMMUNITIES

It has been seen how the energetic and developed societies in Britain in the Early and Later Mesolithic periods survived by exploiting a wide range of resources. Over time there is evidence, in the form of the vastly increased number of sites, of a rapid increase of population which was a reflection of people's success in taming the environment of post-glacial Britain. This very success may have bred its own insecurity, creating a need to enhance 'productivity' in order to retain the *status quo*. By 4500 BC the means of that enhancement were freely and widely available in north-west Europe – in farming, in our sense of the word, with all its paraphernalia of husbanded domesticated stock and crops.

By 4500 BC it is clear that farming communities had begun to be established over wide tracts of Britain. The evidence lies incontrovertibly in the bones of their domestic-ated animals and in the carbonized seeds and fossil pollens of their crops – mainly wheat and barley.

Farming, however, is not just about husbanding crops and animals. It is inextricably linked to the organization of the landscape in a way that earlier populations would have found quite incomprehensible. At one level it intensifies productivity by harnessing the genetic development of animals and plants: thus a system of calendrical notation has to be called into being to enable the events of the farming cycle to be sited appropriately in time. At another level, it encourages the development of veterinary skills, primitive soil sciences and a knowledge of meteorology, without which cultivation of the soil can hardly be carried on. Most important of all, however, it requires people to settle down. Where there are crops, land has to be enclosed, tilled, planted, weeded, guarded, weeded again, harvested – and then the product stored in conditions conducive to its survival for a year or more. Communities that are to achieve this have to stay in one place. While the possibility cannot be denied of small groups moving off (for example, to upland summer pasture) for periods, the inherent stability that this demands leads to profound changes in social and architectural organization.

Accumulation is very much 'the name of the game' for the farmer. His (and his wife's) pre-occupation must be with the growth of the herd, the increase in the area of land under cultivation and the husbanding of those herds and lands to improve and conserve their quality. These factors dictate that the creation of wealth and resources will run beyond any single human life-span and that the 'investment' (of labour, skill or surplus production) by one generation may well operate to the benefit of another. As a consequence, just as the transmission of genetic qualities is a key factor in the life of animals, so the passage of hereditary accumulation (or 'wealth') must have become of critical importance in human communities. Furthermore the demarcation of ground and the understanding of 'whose land was whose' would have required definition in an altogether more sophisticated way. Disputes over territorial possession and heredity would have been inevitable. Archaeologists believe that such considerations may lie at the root of the development of *monuments* – often colossal structures set in the landscape whose purpose was clearly to impress and to act as a focus for communal activity both in their construction and in their consequent use and alteration (map 3).

The availability of social and production surpluses enabled a further development to occur at this time throughout Britain (and indeed, western Europe). The requirement for edge tools (particularly, but not only, axes), for clearance, construction and carpentry, demanded access to large-scale resources of top-quality stone raw material for their manufacture. All over Britain, from the Shetland Islands to Cornwall and from East Anglia to North Wales, resources of stone of suitable working qualities together with flint were located and exploited by 'open-cast' quarrying as well as by mining (map 6). Such mining and quarrying continued for nearly 2,000 years, until finally the advent of widespread metal use rendered it obsolescent. During that long period changes took place in its operating methods. These changes probably reflect broader social changes which took place in the years before 2500 BC. It seems certain that mining became more complex in both organization and method, while the distribution of the product, often located at very considerable distances from the quarry-source, also became more sophisticated and complex; simple patterns of exchange, in other words, gave way to what appear to be entrepreneurial ones wherein products seem to be moved in numbers to entrepôt locations, whence they were then redistributed.

This greater complexity seems generally to reflect broader trends in society as we move closer to 2500 BC. The evidence would suggest that astonishing concentrations of human effort were possible at this time to allow the construction of monuments of grandiose conception and execution. Silbury Hill in Wiltshire close to the Avebury henge complex would have required, it has been calculated, nine million 'man-hours' for its construction whereas the principal phase of Stonehenge (see p. 19) may have taken more than thirty million. Naturally we have no means of knowing how long these vast projects took, but they are inconceivable without very large numbers of people being organized, controlled and supplied for long periods of time. This suggests strongly the concentration of power into relatively few hands within each region of the country with the emergence, from the necessarily segmented groups of the earliest farmers about a thousand years before, of very large cohesive political groupings. It also suggests substantial population growth, which in turn proclaims the success of this first phase of farming in Britain.

All this was not without its price, however. More and more evidence is emerging, in the form of traces of 'dust-bowl' type developments, of early third millennium BC landscape degradation almost certainly brought about by over-cropping, over-grazing and over-felling that de-stabilized the subtle and precarious balance that always prevails in any heavily exploited landscape.

CARN BREA (Cornwall)
Pattern of post-holes of a Neolithic house set directly behind the stone enclosing wall of the fortress

CARN BREA

Set 2.5 km to the south of Redruth (Cornwall), a low granite hill is crowned by the locally characteristic 'tors' or granite outcrops. The whole hilltop is surrounded by a series of ramparts of varying type, some being massive stone walls constructed from boulders assembled from the surrounding hillside, while others comprise a dug ditch with a revetted 'dump' rampart set behind it. Complex entrances lead through these ramparts at various points. Set on the east summit of the hill, clearly visible today, is a small 2 acre enclosure formed by a wall of boulders, many weighing in excess of 2–3 tons that join granite outcrops to form a complete circuit.

Excavations that had taken place in the 1890s had produced large quantities of Neolithic pottery and tools, the distribution of which focused upon this eastern summit enclosure. Excavations conducted between 1970 and 1973 revealed this enclosure to be an enclosed settlement site dating to between 3900 and 3400 BC. As such it was the first Neolithic village to be recognized in Britain (although two other very similar sites have now been recognized in similar locations on Helman Tor near Lostwithiel and possibly at Rough Tor (NT) also in Cornwall).

CARN BREA (Cornwall)
The collapsed Neolithic wall composed of mighty boulders hauled in from the surrounding countryside

Set within the 2 acre enclosure at Carn Brea was a series of fourteen or more platforms created by the careful clearance of stone which was then used to revet their forward and rearward edges. Upon the platforms were found ubiquitous traces of what appeared to be timber house-structures with working areas, hearths and pits for storage. On the basis of the number of structures, and of the nature of the task involved in constructing the enclosure wall, a population of the settlement of *c.* 100–150 people has been suggested.

Sadly the extremely acid and abrasive nature of the soil at Carn Brea (and at Helman Tor) denied to archaeologists any trace of bone, antler, or other organic substance, so that little could be said about the subsistence economy of the village. Nevertheless substantial excavation outside the enclosure on the hilltop produced evidence of the clearance of stone into heaps and the hoe-cultivation of substantial areas, presumably for the cultivation of cereals. Furthermore, excavation of parts of the outer defensive system on the hill indicated that this too was Neolithic in date. This outer defensive complex provided a corral of about 11 acres which would have been ideal for penning of cattle. The cattle dung would have fertilized the ground to be sown in spring and harvested at the end of the summer during which time the beasts would have grazed the rich grass growing in the valleys of the surrounding rivers.

Whatever the precise nature of the economy, it must have provided the site with a firm foundation of wealth, for the settlement at Carn Brea was a key location in the development of communication and exchange in Cornwall (and indeed far beyond). The enclosure must have been a centre for the production and 'export' of axes

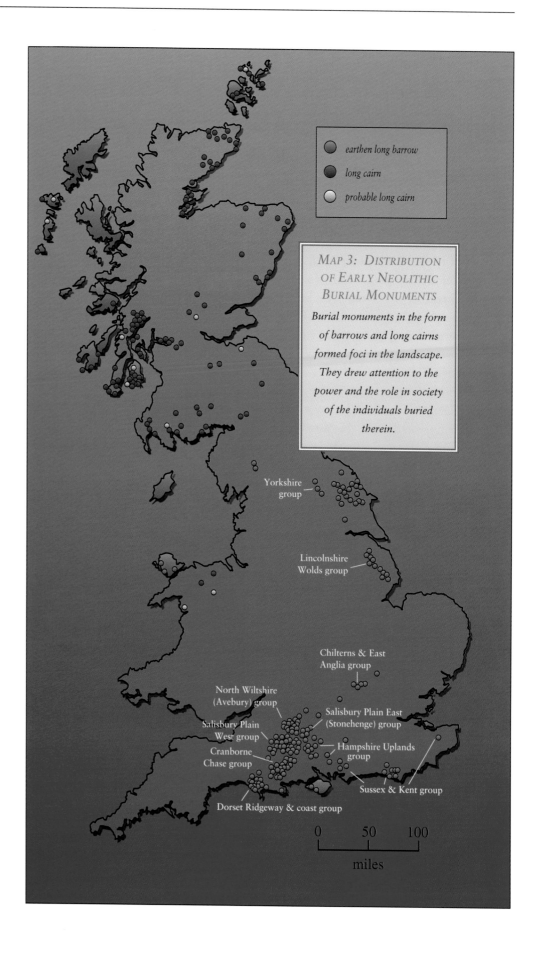

earthen long barrow

long cairn

probable long cairn

MAP 3: DISTRIBUTION
OF EARLY NEOLITHIC
BURIAL MONUMENTS

*Burial monuments in the form
of barrows and long cairns
formed foci in the landscape.
They drew attention to the
power and the role in society
of the individuals buried
therein.*

Yorkshire
group

Lincolnshire
Wolds group

Chilterns & East
Anglia group

North Wiltshire
(Avebury) group

Salisbury Plain East
(Stonehenge) group

Salisbury Plain
West group

Hampshire Uplands
group

Cranborne
Chase group

Sussex & Kent group

Dorset Ridgeway & coast group

0   50   100

miles

manufactured on rock quarried in the Camborne area – edge-grinding stones, incomplete axes, roughouts and completed axes have all been located on the site. As importantly, however, flint was used extensively on the site. Nearby Cornish beaches must have been combed for the valued pebbles, but in addition fresh nodular flint as well as completed flint axes were imported to the site from far to the east, the nearest possible source being at Beer on the Dorset/Devon border.

As a substitute for flint, chert was also extensively used, a material again finding its origins in north Devon and Dorset. In addition, it has also become clear that *all* of the pottery used at Carn Brea was also imported from what appears to have been a specialized manufacturing centre sited in the present-day parish of St Keverne, nearly 30 km to the south in the Lizard peninsula.

Carn Brea was thus an entrepôt. It was a settled community probably of relatively high prestige and of considerable wealth, able to command resources from a wide range of origins, many at a great distance.

Carn Brea has one other vital insight to offer. Every timber structure on the site had been burnt; and all over the site, but especially close to the likely site of the entrance of the enclosure, hundreds of finely worked leaf-shaped flint (and chert) arrowheads were found, some of which were scorched by fire. Additionally, there were signs that the enclosure wall had been deliberately slighted. Since 1970 evidence has become increasingly available that the pressures of territorialism and accumulated 'wealth', as well as the concentration of population in defined centres, led to the jealousy and fear that found their outcome in war. There is little doubt that some time in the middle of the fourth millennium BC this settlement was attacked by massed archers and burnt with considerable fury. As far as archaeologists can tell, it was never reoccupied.

HAMBLEDON HILL AND CRICKLEY HILL

Hambledon Hill is an enormous site on a clover-leaf-shaped hilltop 8 km north-west of Blandford Forum (Dorset), quite differently set and designed from Carn Brea. The two sites are, however, broadly contemporary and, along with sites like Crickley Hill (Gloucestershire), Hembury (Devon), which was also destroyed by archery attack, and Maiden Castle (Dorset) formed part of a network of contact in terms of the same axe, flint and pottery products (map 4).

The focus of the site at Hambledon Hill is a 9 hectare enclosure defined by what was a low revetted chalk-filled rampart – the chalk extracted from a discontinuous line of quarry pits (a 'causewayed ditch') set immediately to its outer side. The function of the enclosure remains unclear in its entirety, but apparently at an early phase in its life it became closely linked with the disposal of human dead – an activity associated with a considerable degree of ceremonial. The evidence for this was found in a series of pits in the enclosure which contained artefacts that could not conceivably have constituted domestic rubbish or accidental losses. For example, there was imported pottery, some of it from the the specialized production centre in the Lizard peninsula (Cornwall): at least three complete vessels of this highly prestigious ware were found. There were also axes from Cornwall (some from precisely those sources controlled by Carn Brea) and from other places of origin, including the other side of the English Channel. Red deer antler (always shed and not culled), selected fossils and selected groups of flint

HAMBLEDON HILL (Dorset)
A ceremonial deposit of organic debris on the ditch floor of the causewayed enclosure

13

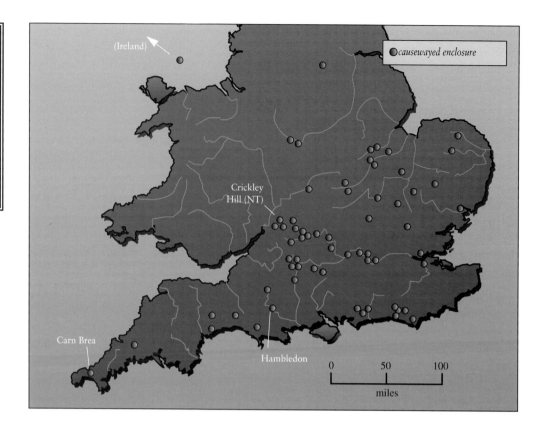

implements as well as grinding stones manufactured on a glauconite sandstone from near Sidmouth (Devon), all figured as selected and specialized groups of objects within these pits.

The excavator believed these curious groups to be ceremonial deposits placed in the pits to accompany the 'excarnation' (or open air exposure) of human bodies – a rite still observed in Tibet and India. His evidence for this came, not from the interior where no human remains left exposed could ever be expected to survive, but from the ditches of this main focal enclosure. Here were found considerable quantities of human skeletal debris, often small elements completely disarticulated but also intact human skulls which, when in skeletal condition, had been placed carefully in the bottom of the ditch. Perhaps most significantly an entire cadaver had been dragged into the ditch by dogs (their teeth marks were all over the bones) and dismembered there. The provenance of the cadaver and skeletons is unknown.

What is particularly interesting about the skeletal evidence from the main enclosure at Hambledon is that there is a very high proportion of children's and adolescents' bones. Sixty per cent of the skeletal material relates to young people under fifteen years of age – such as would be expected of a primitive subsistence farming community. When we come to look at the deposits of bodies and fragments of bodies in the contemporary long barrows, however, we shall see that this proportion is precisely reversed. Indeed two long barrows flank the main enclosure at Hambledon. Alongside the human bone in the ditch of the main enclosure is a very considerable mass of animal bone representing what appears to be rather wasteful and extravagant feasts. The great bulk of the bone (over 70 per cent) is of cattle – domesticated cattle, a smaller beast than wild aurochs of earlier periods, while pig and sheep as well as dogs and a very few wild species form the balance of the assemblage. Extravagant as the feasting may have been, it appears to have been sustained by the consumption of the surplus cows and a few bulls from a very substantial herd oriented towards milk production. As cattle were in all likelihood a prime measure of wealth as well as a means of sustenance at the period, the maintenance of this long cycle (eight to ten years) of production (at a lower rate) makes more sense than the short cycle (two to three years) of higher protein yielding meat production.

Set 800 m south-east of the main enclosure is a smaller enclosure 2 acres in extent which had a radically different function. It too was surrounded by a causewayed ditch and timber-revetted chalk rampart and within it were found pits containing what *does* appear to be random domestic debris, together with other features that suggest domestic occupation – thus perhaps, in a very different environment, forming a parallel for the eastern summit enclosure at Carn Brea. Yet this settlement (perhaps like that at Carn Brea) appears to have been highly specialized with the same extravagant feasting diet sustained by its occupants and with other features (like skulls in the ditch) that reflect closely the more macabre activities being pursued at the main enclosure. Was this some kind of priestly settlement for those who served the 9 hectare necropolis that dominated the hill?

Whether or not this was the case, after the site had been in use for some time, a great outer enclosure, enclosing some 60 hectares, was constructed enclosing the whole clover-leaf of the hill – the largest early prehistoric enclosure known in Europe. At first univallate, and rebuilt at least once in that state, the southern flank of the site was ultimately reinforced by two further concentric ditches and banks to form a formidable defensive obstacle. Shortly after the period of this reinforcement the site was attacked (like Carn Brea) and these ramparts with their timber and hurdling façades set afire over a length of at least 120 m. As the timber revetment burned, so scorched chalk from the body of the rampart poured into the ditch burying the bodies of three young men. One of these casualties, shot in the lungs by a leaf arrowhead, may have been carrying a very young child whom he crushed with his forward fall. Once again, after this catastrophe there is no sign that the site was reoccupied.

HAMBLEDON HILL (Dorset)
The skeleton of a young man killed by arrow-shot during the final destruction of the great Neolithic enclosure complex at Hambledon

15

CRICKLEY HILL (Gloucestershire)
The base of the final Neolithic
rampart and southern entrance from
outside, showing (centre) roadway
and postholes of the largest Neolithic
house

The site at Crickley Hill (Gloucestershire), which is owned by the National Trust, is equally indicative of the situation briefly described at Hambledon Hill. Here too there was an elaborate and repeatedly refurbished rampart system within which ceremonial functions were performed. However, the residential as well as the ceremonial character of the enclosure is indicated by the rows of linearly disposed rectangular houses uncovered by Philip Dixon in his recent excavations. An interesting sidelight on the history of the site is afforded by the strong probability that occupation was abruptly terminated by a violent attack of the sort that ended occupation at Carn Brea. After an interval of about 1,000–1,500 years, however, the site was re-occupied, though not as a habitation, and in the Iron Age it was used as a hill-fort.

THE SWEET TRACK (Somerset)
A carefully constructed linear
platform or causeway running for
nearly 2 km across the Somerset fens

THE SWEET TRACK

From around 4000 BC the area now known as the Somerset Levels was becoming increasingly wet. Farmers moving in this fen margin environment began to build wooden linear platforms or trackways to facilitate access to a series of islands of firm ground (now known as 'burtles'). They may well have farmed these islands but, given the extraordinarily rich environment of the fens, with its populations of fish and fowl, hunting could have been an equal attraction. The tracks became waterlogged and were gradually engulfed by peat growth.

The earliest track discovered so far, which seems anyway to have replaced an earlier one on roughly the same route, is known as the Sweet Track. It was built in the winter of 3807–6 BC, or shortly thereafter – as we are able to tell by the astounding advances made in tree-ring and radio-carbon dating. This date may be considered the first absolutely firm one in British prehistory.

The purpose of the track would appear to have been to provide a firm plank walkway raised above the water. The structure comprises a foundation of rails held in place by pegs upon which was piled peat as a support for the superstructure of planks that formed the walkway. The ends of the planks were prevented from lateral movement by long vertical pegs driven into the substructure and the deposits beneath. Different woods were selected for different purposes, so that for the hard-worn walkway planks oak was selected while the pegs were mainly of hazel or alder.

The trackway was bound to be a focus beside which objects could be lost or concealed. An unused flint axe and an axe of jadeite were placed alongside the track, as were fine pottery bowls – objects that might suggest votive offering rather than careless loss. Wooden pins and a wooden dish as well as leaf arrowheads, one with part of its haft still adhering to it, represent the kinds of object, rare elsewhere, that such circumstances can produce.

The greatest interest lies in the timber of the track itself, however. The careful use of oak (which splits evenly and is hard) for planking, and other woods for specific purposes, indicates that we are dealing with foresters and carpenters of no mean ability. The quality of working (all, of course, carried out using stone tools) is of very high calibre. Perhaps the most surprising aspect, however, is the evidence even at this early stage for *husbanding* timber by coppicing or pollarding trees to encourage the multiple growth of long straight rods suitable for a multitude of uses. Such activity suggests a degree of control and care exercised within woodland that indicates that the farmers' impact upon the landscape was, at least in certain areas, very considerable indeed and probably irreversible.

STONEHENGE

It is Stonehenge that in many ways provides the focus of earlier British prehistory. It is unique and yet its relevance is general. It spans, in its construction, an enormous period of time (from about 3000–1000 BC). It is of compulsive interest to both academic and layman alike, and it lies at the centre of one of the most extraordinary areas in Britain, portraying the development of our landscape as it has been affected by Man through time.

There is little doubt now that the monument began its life as early as 3000 BC when what was essentially a circular causewayed ditch was dug, 115 m in diameter, with an internal bank, and with a single entrance to the north-east. Inside the bank lay a ring of fifty-six holes (first noticed by John Aubrey in the seventeenth century by virtue of the differential growth of lusher grass over them), which almost certainly originally held upright timbers which were later withdrawn – human cremations being placed in many instances in the consequent voids. Again almost certainly, other concentric rings existed nearer the centre of this enclosure that are now incomprehensible as a result of later disturbance. Outside the entrance stood an unworked block of sarsen stone weighing some 25 tons, known now as the Heel Stone.

STONEHENGE (Wiltshire)
The ring of great sarsen stones

Probably around 2200 BC the conception of Stonehenge was revolutionized and major steps taken to enhance its impressiveness. The entrance to the ditched enclosure, which had probably been at least partly recut, was widened (by backfilling one ditch butt) in order to be accurately aligned upon the contemporary midsummer sunrise/midwinter sunset. This achieved, an Avenue (NT) of two parallel ditches with external bank was laid out over a distance of more than 500 m to the northeast towards the River Avon and four 'station stones' of largely unworked sarsen were set at four points just within the bank of the enclosure. All this appears to have been in preparation for the importation to the site, ultimately probably from Pembrokeshire at a distance of some 320 km, of pillars of volcanic tufa, myolite and spotted dolerite, most of which occur around Carn Meini in the Prescelly Mountains. Almost certainly these pillars, very finely worked, had been used in another monument before their appearance on the site at Stonehenge – a monument comprising some uprights with lintels set atop.

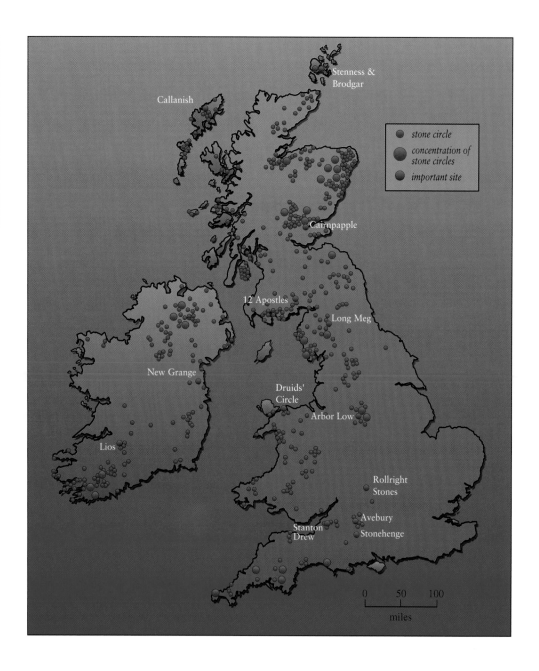

MAP 5: THE
DISTRIBUTION OF STONE
CIRCLES IN THE BRITISH
ISLES, c. 3000–2500 BC

*Note the heavy concentrations
in western England, Scotland
and Southern and Northern
Ireland. Only the most
important sites are named.*

With their appearance on the site work began on setting them into holes – the Q and R holes – but then there was a change of plan. The project was abandoned when it was two-thirds finished; the bluestones were temporarily removed from the site, and the Q and R holes backfilled.

At this juncture, shortly before 2000 BC, a total of seventy-four great sarsen blocks were imported to the site probably from the Marlborough Downs 25 km to the north. Thirty blocks comprising the uprights of an outer circle of orthostats, each member weighing over 25 tons, were dressed precisely to size with their form incorporating a tapered effect, the pillars widening slightly as they rise from the ground to compensate for the effects of perspective. Twenty-nine lintels were also formed by hand mauling with complex jointings and with a true curve to both internal and external surface to respect the circularity of this monument. A further ten uprights (each weighing up to 50 tons) were erected to form the central horseshoe of

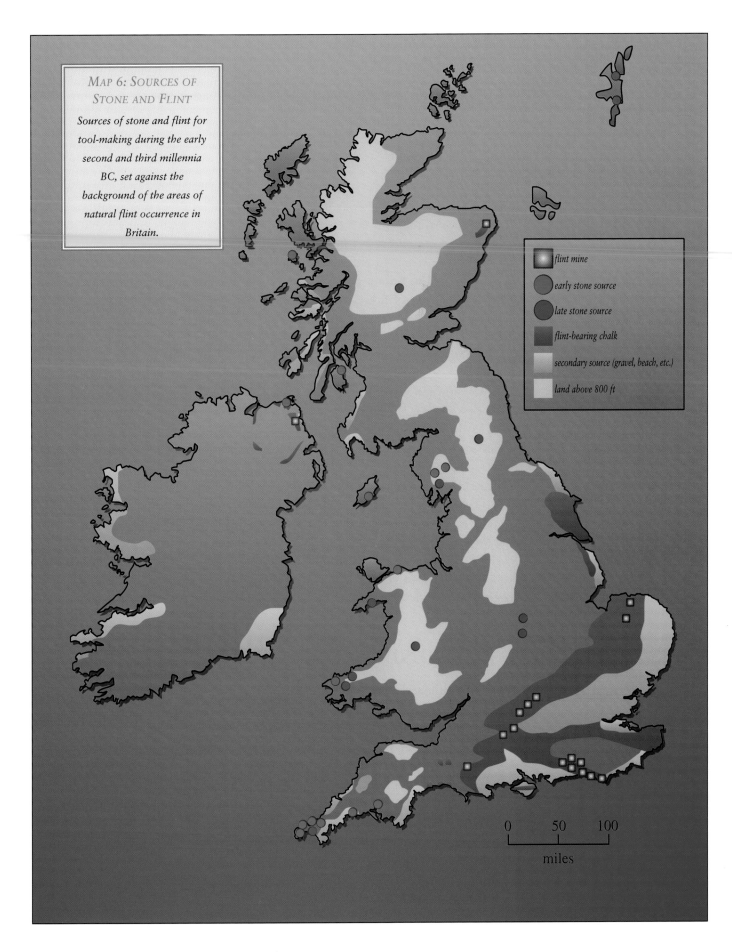

MAP 6: SOURCES OF
STONE AND FLINT

Sources of stone and flint for
tool-making during the early
second and third millennia
BC, set against the
background of the areas of
natural flint occurrence in
Britain.

flint mine

early stone source

late stone source

flint-bearing chalk

secondary source (gravel, beach, etc.)

land above 800 ft

0   50   100

miles

trilithons, with five lintels weighing up to 25 tons set atop these once again with complex jointings and all-over dressing.

Ergonomic estimates suggest that the first phase at Stonehenge (ditch, Aubrey holes and Heel Stone) would have taken about 11,000 man hours, the second abortive stage (Q and R holes) 360,000 man hours and the third (sarsen) stage 1.75 million man hours. Yet on top of these quantum leaps in labour input we have to add the absolutely colossal input required for stone-dressing, particularly in the sarsen stage – the dressing possibly taking a further 25–28 million man hours.

These are megalomanic figures and, of course, render Stonehenge stupendously unique. Whose conception was it? Who wielded the influence and wealth to render feasible such a conception? The answers to these questions remain elusive. One statement we can, however, now make with some confidence: there is no need to suppose the existence of external forces or architects on the grounds that 'nothing like this existed in Britain before'. The jointing mechanisms at Stonehenge are very plainly based upon timber jointing techniques. There are a number of technical arguments that suggest very strongly that the timber circles at Durrington Walls (Wiltshire) and on a number of other sites were lintelled structures that form a perfectly good pedigree for Stonehenge. We even know, from Durrington, that the replacement of posts (through rotting?) was frequent. The megalomanic leap came when the decision was made to build a new circle of uprights and lintels that would last for ever.

When the sarsen phase had come to an end – and this included two great portal stones set each side of the entrance to the enclosure, one of which, the 'Slaughter Stone' survives prostrate – the bluestones were brought back on to the site and erected in two rings of sockets – the Y and Z holes. However, this project was also abandoned before completion (like the Q and R holes phase) and about 1500 BC the bluestones were moved into the setting reflecting both the sarsen horseshoe and the ring that they are to be found in today.

About 1100 BC the Avenue ditch appears to have been recut and redefined with the bank refreshed with material thence derived. This brought to an end the 2,000-year-long sequence of development on this extraordinary and very sacred site.

MINING ACTIVITY IN BRITAIN

The mining of flint, like the quarrying of stone, commenced in Britain, as we have seen, at almost the same time as organized farming – a situation which was the case in most of northern and western Europe. Probably the earliest mining complexes to have been identified are a group in Sussex – at Blackpatch, Harrow Hill and Cissbury (NT) (map 6). These, along with a number of similar sites, date from roughly between 4000 and 3500 BC. They are all rather small, and at Cissbury, the largest, the number of shafts did not exceed a hundred. Around 2500 BC, however, the nature of mining activity changed, and the scale of the complexes appears to have become larger. One good example of such a complex is Easton Down (Wiltshire); but easily the most famous is that known as Grimes Graves (Norfolk).

The flint mine complex at Grimes Graves was vast, with over 50 acres under activity and nearly five hundred shafts known to have been dug. A variety of mining techniques and practices have been identified on the site, affording evidence that miners adapted

 Neolithic axe factory

relative frequency (%) distribution of axes:
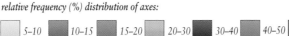
5–10   10–15   15–20   20–30   30–40   40–50   50–60   60–70

their methods to changing circumstances. The deepest shafts were on a truly massive scale. In one shaft excavated in the early 1970s it was calculated that approximately 1,000 tons of chalk were excavated from a bell-shaped shaft, 13 m deep and 12 m in diameter at the surface, before the desired layer of floorstone was reached. This mass of material was evacuated by means of a series of platforms and ladders, and it was estimated that a party of twelve workers would have taken five to six months to finish the task (although traces of weathering at intermittent stages in the great chalk dump beside the shaft may suggest that the process was interrupted). Only then was an estimated 8 tons of flint recovered from the floor of the shaft and galleries. Unlike the earlier mines in Sussex, there is some evidence to suggest that after preliminary working into 'blanks' of raw material, this product was then transported from the site to other locations where it was worked up to create the final product, although some finished working and tool production certainly occurred on the site.

The scale of the activity at Grimes Graves was prodigious. An estimate based upon experimental flint working suggests that from the 8 tons of flint that are known to have been extracted from one relatively unproductive shaft something like 5–10,000 axes could have been manufactured (and many more smaller implements). Thus five hundred known shafts on the site could have produced, over the life span of the site of five hundred years, some 5 million axes – and furthermore, Grimes Graves was not the only factory site in production (map 7). Of course, the kind of heavy engineering that was undertaken at Avebury and Stonehenge, as well as the normal demands of farming at a time of increasing land intake, would have required massive use of edge-tools of which this figure is but one register.

In trying to visualize the level of activity at Grimes Graves in the third millennium BC we need to think not only of the output from the mines but also of the input – input in cordage, timber, protective clothing (the notion of miners working naked in a flint mine, shown in some reconstruction drawings, is a bizarre one) and perhaps,

MAP 7: AXE FACTORIES IN THE NEOLITHIC PERIOD

The map on the left shows the distribution of axes which were made at the factory at Penmaenmawr in North Wales. The other two maps show the distribution of axes which were transported from western manufacturing centres to distribution points in the east. Prospecting expeditions may have been sent by eastern communities into the Highland zone to bring back tools which they could not supply for themselves.

most graphically, the all-important red deer antlers from which the picks were made that enabled the digging to go forward. In the one shaft excavated at Grimes Graves in 1971 over one hundred antler picks were found discarded on the floor of the shaft. Many others must have been broken or made blunt during the excavation of the shaft. Hundreds of antlers must have been consumed by the mining every year, yet almost every example was naturally cast by its parent animal. Furthermore deliberate selection took place with left-hand antlers favoured as more amenable to the right-handed pickman. In order to obtain quantities of this order of cast antler with such confidence it is difficult to resist the conclusion that the careful and very successful management of red deer was taking place in the locality of the mines. Such a conclusion placed alongside that from the Sweet Track helps to fill out for us the degree of intensity and the scale of land management in the broadest sense achieved by these early farming groups.

The exploitation of the mine complex at Grimes Graves continued until *c.* 1800 BC, by which time the production of metal tools must have been rendering its product less attractive. However, the scale of that metal production is perhaps indicated by the scale of that which it replaced.

DURRINGTON WALLS AND AVEBURY

By the middle of the third millennium BC the scale and complexity of social undertakings in Britain appears to have become much greater. The clearest evidence of this is provided by the great earthwork enclosures of southern England, of which the largest known lies at Avebury (NT), while the most fully excavated is near Stonehenge, at Durrington Walls, in central Wiltshire (map 8).

Durrington Walls comprises a massive enclosure 380 m x 320 m in *internal* dimensions surrounded by a ditch up to 7 m deep and 13 m wide. In total, 49,000 cubic metres of chalk (weighing 85,000 tons) would have had to be dug to create this ditch, with the material carried across a wide berm to be piled 3 m high to form a bank. To create this vast enclosure it has been suggested some 90,000 man days of work would have been required. Clearly there are major implications here for our understanding of the size of population of central Wessex in the period. An operation so ambitious could hardly have been undertaken without the mobilization of massive resources in manpower and materials.

In a sense, however, the crude scale of ditch and bank are themselves dwarfed by the scale of activity on the inner platform of the site. During the excavations undertaken in the late 1960s two great timber rings were located on the platform. Geophysical survey carried out since then has indicated that there may be as many as thirty-five more within the whole enclosure. These timber rings are complex in structure and of unknown function. The southern circle started life as four concentric rings of timber posts surrounding a central setting approached from the south-east through a timber façade with timbers of graded height approaching the highest at the axial point of entrance to the circle.

The second phase of this ceremonial setting saw it rendered altogether more massive with oaken posts often nearly 2 m in diameter. While an attempt seems to have been made to follow the original setting, the conception was new with six concentric rings with no known central feature. So massive were the posts (weighing, in many instances, probably more than 5 tons) that the only practicable way to get them upright was by digging ramps into the earth-fast post-sockets into which the posts could be tipped into a half upright position. With the post hauled into upright position the ramp was quickly backfilled with chalk and rammed (345 red deer antler picks were found discarded in these rammed fillings – see Grimes Graves). In order to 'tip' the uprights into the ramps there has to be a very close relationship between the length of ramp and the length of post; thus we have a good index as to how high the timber posts originally were. The circle is built upon a gentle slope and it would appear that an attempt was made to produce an upper level for the post-tops that was truly horizontal. It may be that this very clear effort was for the emplacement of timber lintels. If so, then Durrington southern circle phase 2, built about 2300 BC, may be a timber prototype for the extraordinary developments at Stonehenge that were to take place one to two hundred years later.

The function of the site is, of course, more difficult to suggest. That its broad function was ceremonial is perhaps generally accepted, but beyond this broad conclusion we are faced with a range of factors concerning the disposition and nature of artefacts on the site, suggesting specialized, and carefully controlled, deposition. The very unusual emphasis upon pork consumption evidenced by the animal bone assemblage from the site might suggest feasting based upon that creature of such admirable fecundity.

The other, northern circle was set 120 m north of the circle just described. It was far less well preserved and it appears to comprise a single timber ring with four great uprights set within it. It too was approached through a timber screen set to the southwest through which led an avenue of posts. It seems to have been built at much the same time as the second phase of the southern circle.

Avebury is of course an even mightier monument set at the foot of the Marlborough Downs. It has been relatively little touched by the excavator, and our knowledge of it is a good deal more sketchy. The location had long been hallowed by the presence nearby of the causewayed enclosure (see Hambledon Hill) at Windmill Hill (NT). Moreover, by 2750 BC work had commenced upon the largest man-made mound in Europe at Silbury Hill set just to the south of the site. This astonishing monument, which may well have taken well over a century to complete, consumed over 9 million man hours and was, on completion, a stepped mound in revetted chalk, shining white to an incredible height of 40 m. Its function is unknown, but its completion may have marked the beginning of the construction of the Avebury monument itself.

The building of the bank and ditch at Avebury was probably undertaken at a date parallel with the definition of the enclosure at Durrington. It was, however, an altogether greater undertaking. The enclosed area is some 350 m in diameter with a ditch that was between 7 and 10 m deep and 21 m wide at the surface while its consorting bank must have stood originally as much as 7 m high. Well over 1.5 million man hours must have been expended in its construction. There is every likelihood that, were sufficiently extensive and scientific excavations to take place at Avebury, timber circles like those discovered at Durrington might be located there. However that might be, at a date of around 1900 BC these possible settings were replaced by two inner circles, and possibly a third which was abandoned at an early stage, and then one great outer circle (the largest in Britain) of (probably originally) some hundred massive undressed stones weighing in many instances over 50 tons. The two inner circles exhibited some twenty-

AVEBURY *(Wiltshire)*
The avenue of great megaliths which
forms a ceremonial approach to the
circles of sarsen stones

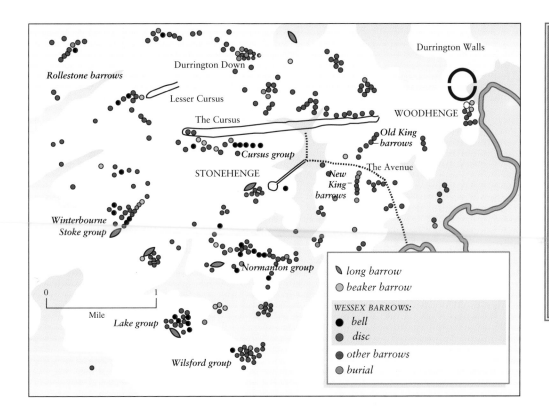

MAP 8: THE STONEHENGE AREA

The great series of circles sits at the centre of a complex ritual landscape peppered with barrow cemeteries and ceremonial 'avenues'. The barrows are of varying construction with some of simple mounds (bowl barrows), some enclosed by ditches (bell barrows) and others more in the form of enclosures related to the earlier henge tradition (disc and saucer barrows).

five to thirty massive stones each, together with inner rectangular settings rather like the layout at Durrington north circle.

As if this astonishingly grandiose conception were not enough, two long avenues of stones (and possibly, it now seems, a third) were erected leading away from the monument to the south-west and south-east (and possibly to the north). The layout of these avenues is only known in detail in one instance, the south-easterly West Kennet Avenue, which joined the great Avebury monument to another stone circle on Overton Hill (christened, if that is the word, 'The Sanctuary' by William Stukely, the great eighteenth-century antiquary). This monument is itself of three phases with two preceding timber circle complexes succeeded by a stone circle built when the avenue reached the site. It can be suggested that other structures remain to be discovered at the other end of the other avenue(s?).

III
THE COMING OF
METAL, 2500–1500 BC

On the face of it the arrival of metal, while providing a welcome new material for edge-tools, need not have presaged very much in the way of social and economic change. The fact that it did resulted partly from changes already under way, and partly from the precise nature of metal production. Each of these factors needs briefly to be considered in turn.

From what has already been said it will be apparent that between 3000 and 2500 BC the structure of society in Britain had been changing rapidly. Population had grown, based upon an advanced farming economy. At the same time power had become more centralized so that the initially segmented farming population became welded into larger geographical and demographic groups capable of a far greater concentration of resources. This enabled both industrial enterprises and public monuments of a far greater scale to be undertaken, often situated in focal rather than the earlier marginal locations. These substantial power concentrations created leadership groups which felt a desire to mark themselves apart from the generality of the population. It is in this critical period between 3000–2500 BC that the first single burials, often of males, begin to appear, sometimes furnished with prestigious objects – objects of jet and amber as well as beautifully produced axes, arrow/javelin heads of flint and flint knives. Right from the onset of farming, as we have seen at Hambledon Hill and Carn Brea, exotic objects had conferred prestige upon the holder; but the trend to associate this prestige with, often male, individuals appears to be a development of this somewhat later period.

With the creation of an energized demand for 'exotica' – a development that was happening simultaneously all over western and central Europe – it was inevitable that routes of 'trade' would be opened up and that the search for novel materials would be active. One of the first such 'novelties' to reach Britain was a fashion for possessing finely made and beautifully decorated pottery vessels which, evidence now suggests, were associated with the drinking of fermented liquids manufactured using cereals and honey – a sort of mead. These vessels, known to archaeologists as 'beakers', began to be made here in clear imitation of continental prototypes by about 2500 BC. It is at this stage that many of the networks or channels of communication were established and within two or three hundred years a whole range of exotic objects, in a variety of materials, were flowing along them.

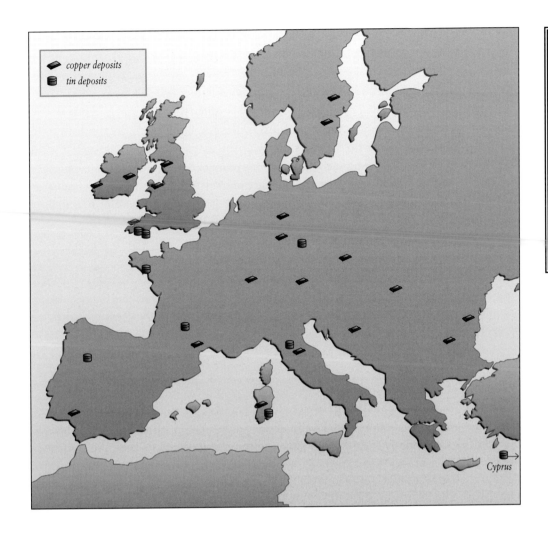

Available in eastern Europe for at least two millennia by 2500 BC had been the technology to locate minerals that, when subjected to more or less complex processes of heating, would produce droplets of beautifully coloured and easily worked copper. By and large this technology had not penetrated northern and western Europe until it was 'sucked in' by the demand for exotic objects. The same technology (broadly speaking) had produced the ability to melt and hammer-work gold.

By 2500 BC, the first objects of gold and copper were being imported into Britain and it was probably not long after this date that specialists were on hand to locate likely ore-producing deposits and rivers in Britain. All the objects manufactured here or imported were essentially trinkets or occasionally copper knives. None of them was ever utilitarian (indeed many when found in the graves appear never to have been used at all), and the only impact they would have had on the 'ordinary farmer in the field' would have been to provide him with 'taxes' to pay over by way of tribute to the élite.

Naturally, metalsmiths were anxious to feed the wonder with which such objects were beheld, and very rapidly over the approximate period 2500–2000 BC objects became larger, more intricate, and 'three-dimensional' – all leading to the desire for improvements in the casting process. Bivalve moulds were quickly introduced, but as these became longer and more intricate the problem became one of how to improve the flow of the metal within them. There were severe limitations to the prehistoric smiths' ability to reach very high temperatures, and the smiths chose instead to alter the constitution of the metal, to make it run better – by the addition of tin recovered from alluvial deposits in rivers and probably discovered during exploration for gold. Tin added to copper, in the proportions 10–90 parts, produces an alloy that we know as bronze which not only flows more evenly in the mould but also produces a somewhat harder end-product.

For Britain this development comprised an extraordinary opportunity. Tin is a rare metal found at relatively few locations in Europe. Britain, however, in its south-western peninsula, presented one of the richest sources of tin available (map 9). Henceforward Britain became effectively bound to European developments as a principal supplier of this staple. Furthermore it will be immediately apparent that channels of communication became ever more complex and sophisticated as the need developed to deliver guaranteed supplies of two metals in broadly the appropriate ratio.

The established hierarchies in Britain, on the basis of the same wealth that had built Durrington Walls and somewhat later Stonehenge, were able to command the services of the finest craftsmen of the age. Initially these men seem to have had their contacts with Brittany but gradually, with other influences from Germany and the Rhineland, an individual insular style emerged. It was the products of these craftsmen, often of immense virtuosity, that accompanied the inhumations and cremations that lie beneath the cemeteries of round barrows that surround Stonehenge as well as barrows in East Anglia, Yorkshire, the Derbyshire Peak and Lowland Scotland – all focusing upon previously established (pre-2500 BC) centres of wealth and influence (map 8).

None of this panoply could have been possible, however, without the healthy functioning of the basic power-plant of prehistoric economy – farming. During the period between 2500 and 1800 BC we are sadly lacking in evidence for farming practice, but from about 1700 BC onwards it appears that climatic improvement led to farms being extended often within field patterns that were clearly laid out again under a measure of centralized control. These 'farmscapes' were extended into upland areas which have often never been cultivated since – thus allowing their survival to the present day. This massive extension of farming, all over Britain, must again presuppose a major demographic expansion. The by-product of this expansion was an increase in the level of wealth which after 1700 BC made possible the extension of bronze tools to a far broader spectrum of the population. Weapon-smiths furnished the requirements not only of the individual but of the small war band – providing rapiers, javelins, stabbing-spears and such like on demand. In this 'democratization' of warfare may be found the end of the ancient centres of control established prior to 2500 BC which tend to disappear from the archaeological record around this time.

BARROW CEMETERIES

Among the most distinctive monuments to survive from the early metalworking period of prehistory are the round 'barrow' burials. Barrows – whether round or long in shape – represent the climax of a long period of increasing elaboration in the interment ceremonies of prominent individuals in southern British society from 3000 BC to shortly after 1500 BC. Surviving examples of barrows are to be seen in a variety of environments, notably the Cotswolds in Gloucestershire and the chalk downlands of Wiltshire.

One of the most rewarding sites of this kind to have been excavated is that at Earl's Farm Down, in an area rich in prehistoric remains 6 km from Stonehenge to the east of Amesbury on the slope of Beacon Hill. Two barrows have been excavated here – a reminder that they often appear not singly but in groups that are termed 'cemeteries'. Of the pair, the one

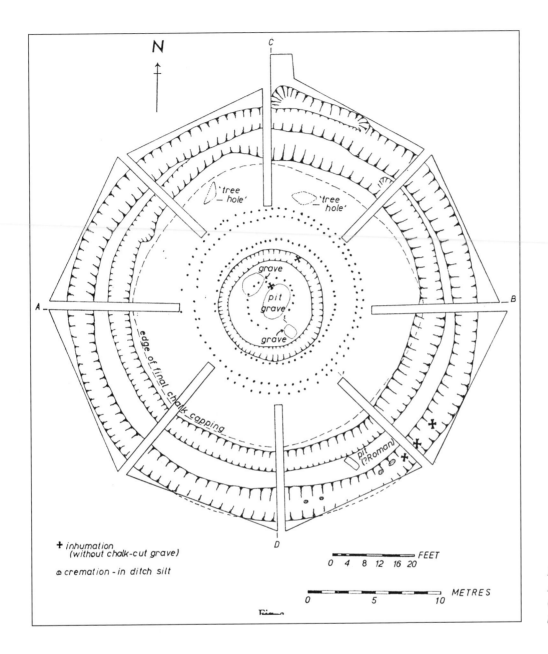

N

tree hole

tree hole

grave

pit grave

grave

A —

— B

edge of final chalk-capping

pit (?Roman)

C

D

✝ inhumation
 (without chalk-cut grave)

⊕ cremation - in ditch silt

FEET
0 4 8 12 16 20

METRES
0   5   10

EARL'S FARM DOWN, AMESBURY, G71 (Wiltshire) Ground-plan of the excavated barrow

known as G71 is the more interesting and instructive to consider in the present context.

The earliest monument to occupy its site was a tiny ring-ditch enclosure without any causeway giving access to the interior. The scale of the monument was minuscule, the ditch being only 0.5 m deep and 0.3 m wide at the base and the whole monument only 6.9 m in diameter. The ditch, such as it was, appears to have been deliberately refilled from its inner side, while in the interior of the enclosure an arc of stakes had stood for some time. The grave associated with this monument was disrupted by later developments but residual bone found scattered in other contexts suggested the presence of an adult male. No associated cultural material was located, but there would be little hesitation in suggesting that the burial dated to well before 2500 BC.

Using this diminutive monument as a focus, and presumably after some lapse of time, a second monument was built – this time a mound with a ring-ditch around it. The vagueness of the earlier remains may well account for the slight eccentricity of this second phase which was built in two phases. First, an oval grave pit was dug and an adult male burial was interred therein probably contained within a wooden gabled shelter. Around the pit, which appears to have been immediately backfilled with its own chalk, three concentric rings of stakes were erected which may have supported fencing. It was at some time after this stage that the barrow was thrown up over the whole – its material derived partly from its surrounding ditch, but the body of the mound being formed of stripped turf presumably drawn from an altogether wider area. Encasing this circular turf-stack was a revetment of chalk and flint derived from the ring-ditch, beneath which was located part of a beaker pot. A radio-carbon date of about 2500 BC was obtained for the wooden structure in the grave pit.

After the lapse of a further substantial period and at a radio-carbon date of roughly 2000 BC this low mound was flattened, and on the new surface a whole new series of rituals took place. A substantial fire was laid on this platform, within which apparently the cremation of human remains took place. The ashes were almost certainly removed from the site and washed to get rid of the charcoal: they may be represented by two deposits of cremated material (in washed condition) – one an inurned cremation deposit within which were located parts of one child and one adolescent. Four other inhumations – a woman and three children – were located in this central area, one associated with a vessel, a late derivative beaker form in the broad native British tradition known to archaeologists as a food vessel.

Over these deposits, after the completion of the ceremonies indicated, a further turf-stack was built which was then capped with white chalk extracted from the ditch – thus creating a brilliant white mound, wonderfully striking, and very different from the dark brown drum of the earlier phase. It is likely that this final monument on the site, built six to seven hundred years after the first, remained a familiar landmark in the area for a long time to come.

BRONZE AGE AGRICULTURE: BLACK-PATCH (EAST SUSSEX) AND STANNON DOWN (CORNWALL)

By 1500 BC the climate had improved to such an extent that areas of hillside, mountain and moor were being occupied that have seldom if ever been used for farming since. A happy consequence of their subsequent neglect has been the preservation intact of agricultural landscapes of this period in various parts of Britain. In southern England sites as distinct as Blackpatch, Alfriston (East Sussex) – an unenclosed platform settlement in the South Downs – and Stannon Down, a plateau settlement near Camelford on Bodmin Moor, Cornwall, can be dated to this period. At Blackpatch (radio-carbon dated to c. 1300 BC) the house group excavated comprised five small round houses, the largest being no more than 8 m in diameter. The houses are entered on their south-east sides via substantial timber porches which open outwards into a subdivided farmyard with paling fences defining smaller areas, probably for livestock retention. Within the buildings are pits for storage and settings of posts for timber uprights for racks, looms and other internal furnishings. Intricate examination of the distribution of artefacts on the floors of the houses has suggested to the excavator a differential function for the five buildings that make up this farm-cluster and the examination of ethnographically comparative examples would support this notion. In the domestic quarters, the loom, a vertical structure about 2–3 m

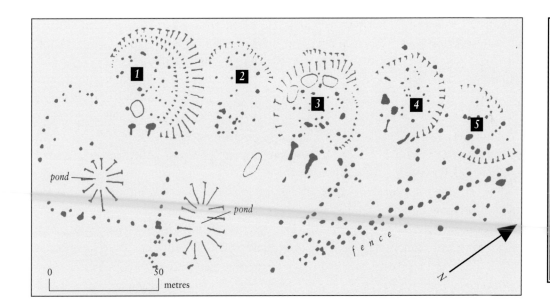

The settlement areas as
revealed by excavation, with
an interpretation made on the
basis of finds and structural
remains.

1. compound head's wife's house, also
used for food preparation
2. animal shelter
3. compound head's house,
also used for storage and crafts
4. reliant relative's house
5. animal shelter

long, was placed against the wall opposite the door so that light would play onto it. The storage pits were against the wall in the darkest part of the house, while the hearth was in the entrance to the house with an activity area for the working of bone and other raw materials set around it. Not all the buildings conformed to this pattern, however, and of the five in the excavated farm-cluster two may have been animal-byres, while the three houses may have had differential social and sexual connotations. The human population envisaged for the farm is a partial extended family of ten or more people. Other sites, very similar in date, form, and location to Blackpatch, have produced ample evidence of the importance on these sites generally of weaving, and the plentiful sheep bone indicates whence the raw material for this activity came. Cattle bone is also plentiful from some sites of this period, and the sex and age distribution of the remains would suggest the culling of the uneconomic element of dairy-oriented herds. Barley is usually the most common crop to survive on these upland sites, and the systems of small fields within which the crops were grown are linked to the settlements with drove roads to allow the passage of animals into the farmstead without risk of damage to crops.

Often these fields have been ploughed on a hillslope for so many seasons that massive soil erosion has set up a downslope movement of soil to create large banks (or lynchets) of soil at the lower limit of each ploughed area. The scatter of pottery and flintwork on the surface of the fields almost certainly means that domestic and farmyard refuse were being dumped there for manuring purposes.

At Stannon Down on Bodmin Moor, 6 km south-east of Camelford and close to Rough Tor (NT) (map 11), another village of round houses was excavated in very different circumstances from Blackpatch. Here a total of nineteen round houses of altogether larger dimensions was found among a small pattern of tiny linear strips of cultivated ground, almost gardens, totalling no more than 2 or 3 acres. Whatever was grown here could only have been the merest light supplement to the diet of a large community – judging by the number and size of the houses – and the economy was probably one based principally on stock rearing of cattle for meat and milk, and sheep (again partly for wool to judge by the remains of looms and their appurtenances on the site).

What is clear at Stannon and on other sites in the area, is that the fields had been in use for some time before the presently surviving houses were built. Elsewhere the

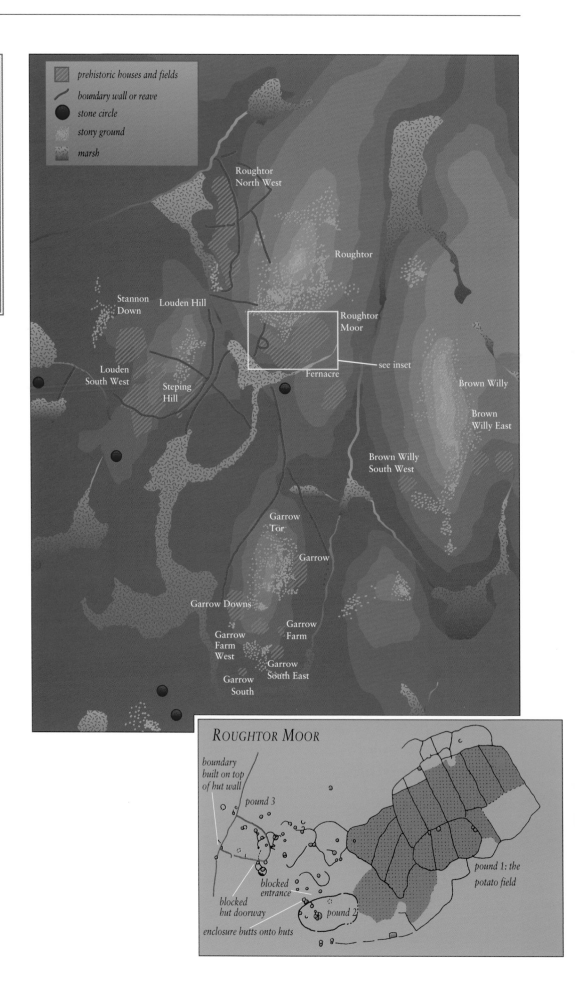

MAP 11: ROUGHTOR (NT) AND ITS ENVIRONMENT (CORNWALL)

Roughtor and Stannon lie close to each other on Bodmin Moor, and between them they exhibit settlements of different type and function within one prehistoric landscape. Roughtor is morphologically similar to Carn Brea, discussed above (p. 11).

prehistoric houses and fields
boundary wall or reave
stone circle
stony ground
marsh

Roughtor North West

Roughtor

Stannon Down

Louden Hill

Roughtor Moor

see inset

Louden South West

Fernacre

Brown Willy

Steping Hill

Brown Willy East

Brown Willy South West

Garrow Tor

Garrow

Garrow Downs

Garrow Farm

Garrow Farm West

Garrow South East

Garrow South

ROUGHTOR MOOR

boundary built on top of hut wall

pound 3

pound 1: the potato field

blocked entrance

blocked hut doorway

enclosure butts onto huts

pound 2

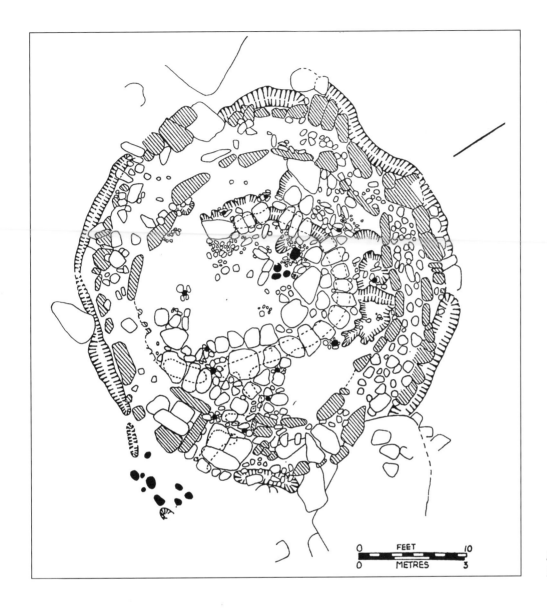

STANNON DOWN (Cornwall)
Plan of hut circle 3

lynchets of previously existing fields were heightened to furnish an enclosure within which houses were then built.

The impression over a wide area of Britain is of intensive farming activity being brought to spatial limits that were seldom, if ever, again attained. Within this area, however, the range of micro-environmental circumstances was so wide as to produce complex cultural, social and economic variation.

This long and vibrant period was brought to an end by a fundamental change that occurred around the year 1000 BC. Archaeologists have tended to attribute this change to 'climatic deterioration'. Certainly it does appear that rainfall increased, but this may have been only one factor, along with the erosion of upland arable and changing social and economic conditions, that led to the abandonment of upland arable land and its cognate settlements. A general intensification of arable agriculture in river valleys seems to be signalled by massive erosion deposits there in the period after 1000 BC with the uplands given over to less productive grazings. Whatever the precise pattern of change, productivity must have broadly been retained to allow the extraordinary wealth of *cultural* activity that we see in the succeeding period.

IV
THE LATE METAL-USING SOCIETIES, 1500 BC–AD 43

By about 1200 BC the optimum climatic phase that had permitted the expansion and prosperity of British agriculture between 1800 and 1200 BC was beginning to fail. Evidence from the record of changing vegetation, furnished by waterlogged deposits capable of preserving fossil material, informs us that climatic change was leading to cooler summers and a greater degree of precipitation. This is a particularly significant development in an oceanic country like Britain, with its high proportion of land between 500 ft and 1500 ft above sea level.

There can be no doubt that the farmed area of upland contracted at this time. The question remains – did this lead to a diminution in general productivity? One is tempted to say yes. Yet at this time Britain was able to attract, absorb and reproduce new technological impulses from the continent of Europe that demanded new techniques of bronze-working to produce the means of improved woodworking and other domestic activities, as well as totally new modes of fighting and warfare. Such demands do not come from impoverished societies. They come from societies in the throes of successful adaptation to change, but we know disappointingly little of the practice and development of agriculture at this period. What we do know is that by 600 BC, when our picture begins to clear, a number of new crops (beans, oats) and animals (Shorthorn cattle) were being regularly cultivated and husbanded, while at the same time techniques of cultivation and storage were being improved.

During this period the archaeologist is largely reliant upon the evidence of 'hoards' – often substantial collections of metalwork that have been found 'hidden' – comprising largely weapons but also metalworking tools, vessels and other finery. The hoards portray a sector of society where the panoply of war was of the greatest significance but also where communal drinking and feasting vessels, items of personal adornment, horse harness and even vehicle fittings occur. All of these items form part of a 'kit' that one might well associate with the kind of society later described in the British (or Danish) context in *Beowulf* or more or less contemporarily (*c.* 800 BC?) by Homer in his epic description of the Trojan Wars. It is possible that the contracting availability of good land together with a growing deficit of other resources (including tin and copper themselves) may well have promoted the generation of local 'big men', who with an armed following preyed on the local farming population and protected it from predation. As well as of the weaponry, we are beginning to know a little more of the circular strongholds within which these 'big men' lived, and there is evidence too of the development of hill-forts from around 1200 BC onwards all over the country.

So the foundation is laid for the final phase of British prehistory. From around 600 BC climatic improvement began to take place, allowing a further growth of prosperity and probably also of population. The local 'big men' became more and more ambitious in their pretensions to fortified residences and centres of power. The development of elaborate defensive schemes is one of the principal features of British prehistoric structures from about 600 BC up to about 100 BC. Another focal concern is the development of weaponry.

From around 600 BC shortage of copper and tin, social changes, and the breakdown in inter-regional communication fostered by the fragmented nature of society, combined to encourage the large-scale adoption of iron – a metal that had been known and, indeed, already in use for certain specialized purposes for several hundred years. The working of iron is a wholly different technology from the production of bronze. It relies upon the large-scale production and supply of charcoal in order to create the greater heat required to smelt iron ore. Because *molten* iron was a phenomenon unknown in prehistory (and, indeed, until the late medieval period), *all* iron work in prehistory was produced by hammering (forging) malleable iron converted from iron ore in very hot conditions. This, of course, was a wholly different process from casting, and as a result weapon and tool forms changed completely at this time. The production of intricate ornament or flowing decoration was, however, almost impossible in forged iron (or wrought iron), and consequently such ornamental pieces as shields, scabbards and sword hilts, continued to be produced in bronze.

This latter consideration is of some importance, as it was after about 500 BC that the first great art style of British prehistory emerged. Its origins are complex, but are probably to be found in the classical civilizations of Greece, Etruria and Rome that were active from 600 BC onwards. The most beautiful objects were manufactured, drawing on a rich decorative vocabulary. They were commissioned, of course, largely by the élite. The vast majority of the population continued to live in ordinary round houses, similar to those that their predecessors had occupied since at least 1500 BC – although the general trend was for these houses to become larger, in the style of the houses of the 'big men'. These 'big men' themselves were in the process of being brought under the control of 'bigger men' still, to the point where once again, as had occurred between 2000 and 1500 BC, whole regions were brought under the control of hierarchies that began again to offer the prospect of state-like societies.

After about 100 BC it is possible to observe the progressive abandonment of local power centres for regional ones and the emergence of truly royal households controlling 'states' the size of East Anglia (the Iceni), Hampshire and part of Sussex (the Atrebates), and Dorset (the Durotriges). This trend was reinforced by alliances formed with peoples on the near European mainland whom Caesar called the Belgae. The élites that dominated these late-prehistoric societies were rich and powerful, and they flaunted their wealth by importing wines and a host of other luxuries from abroad. Evidence of their

Two Hoards of *c.* 700 BC: Heathery Burn and Watford

Much of our evidence for the enigmatic developments that occurred during the first half of the first millennium BC has been deduced from metalwork located in 'hoards' – a generalized term relating to otherwise unassociated groups of metal, sometimes with a scrap component, located apparently randomly although very often in 'watery places' – for example, by lakes, rivers and former morasses. A mighty leap in the rate of their deposition seems to take place after about 1000 BC, with an even steeper acceleration at about 750 BC. Hundreds of examples have been found, of which two will suffice – both from after 750 BC.

One was located (rather unusually) in a cave destroyed by quarrying during the last century at Heathery Burn near Stanhope in County Durham. An astounding range of objects of gold, jet (lignite), iron and, predominantly, bronze were located here in a massive deposit that may or may not all be of one date. Particularly suggestive were the iron tyres and nave bands of a wagon which may have formed part of a prince's hearse. Many other finds were evocative of a princely household. There was a conical bronze bucket in which liquor would have been served, and personal ornaments including pins and bronze attachments for clothing, jet bracelets, gold ornaments and items for personal grooming like tweezers and razors for depilation. Weapons abounded – spears and swords as well as elements of the harness of a horse. Here indeed can be appreciated the wealth of finery that would have belonged to a prince living in the great ring-forts now known to have existed in the Thames Valley area and in Yorkshire at about this date.

A hoard of broadly similar date, but found in rather different (and more typical) circumstances, is that discovered accidentally in 1960 during the construction of a factory near Watford, Hertfordshire. The location was waterlogged at the time of the discovery. The hoard comprised a range of axes and chisels which might pass muster as the stock-in-trade of a smith but also included fragments of five swords (two complete but broken), ten or eleven spearheads, a group of objects reflecting sword-belt-furniture and other aspects of sword harness, and a magnificent beaten bronze vessel. The condition of the objects and their apparent burial in a pit 'off the beaten track' might suggest their deliberate concealment as a pool of scrap for an itinerant smith. The existence of copper ingots in the hoard could well support this suggestion.

As at Heathery Burn (and with the exception of the vessel) all the bronzes were found to contain a high proportion of lead, an adulteration introduced to improve further the running quality of the molten metal. It is significant that the vessel is not so adulterated because it was worked in the solid, and the mechanical qualities of the metal would only have been adversely affected by such adulteration.

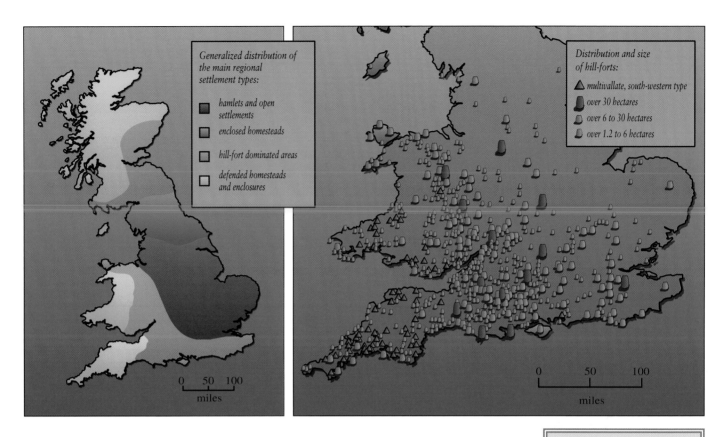

MAP 12: SETTLEMENT
TYPES IN BRITAIN FROM
THE FIFTH TO THE
SECOND CENTURIES BC

*The map on the left shows
how types can be correlated
with particular regions, while
the one on the right analyses
the size and distribution of
hill-forts in south-western and
western Britain.*

life-style has been uncovered on a number of sites, notably at Heathery Burn (Durham), Danebury (Hampshire), Welwyn (Hertfordshire) and Gussage All Saints (Dorset). Of these probably the first in importance is Danebury.

DANEBURY

Danebury, some 5 km north-west of Stockbridge (Hampshire), is one of the most mightily impressive hilltop settlements in England. The first defended enclosure there was built around 550 BC, at a time when the construction of defended sites was becoming more common everywhere in Britain (map 12). The defences protected a hilltop area of 5.3 hectares. This was subdivided by some four or five roadways which remained of consistent alignment throughout the period of five hundred years during which the site was occupied. The continuity indicated by this must be set against the necessarily divisive influence of archaeologists' attempts to perceive change during that long occupation. It is reinforced by two other factors of importance. Firstly, as will be shown, the basic house design remained the same same throughout the period – the familiar one of simple round houses. And secondly, population remained roughly static throughout, at between 200 and 350 souls with possibly a somewhat higher figure in the earlier part of the period .

The earlier stages of the hill-fort's life saw a timber-revetted rampart built round the hilltop fronted by a relatively small, probably U-sectioned, ditch. This small-scale defence was penetrated by a single carriageway entrance about 4 m wide. The lifespan of such a defence, with the propensity of the frontal timbers to rot, cannot have been very long – say thirty to fifty years – and indeed there is evidence that it was bolstered

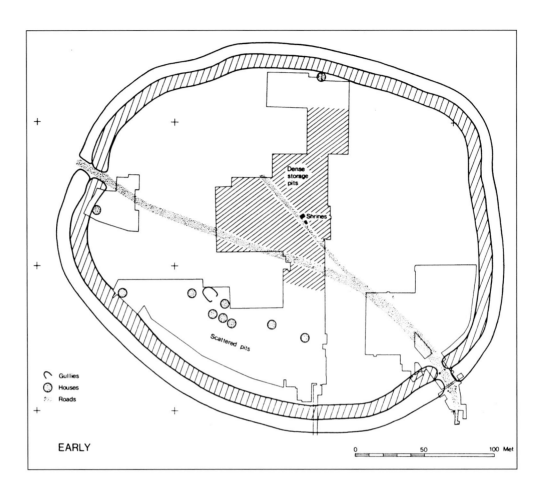

DANEBURY (Hampshire)
Simplified plans of the settlement:
on the left, as it was in the early
period (fifth century BC*). The*
granaries have not been included

on the inner side after an interval. This broadening of the rampart assisted with the redesign of the gate to produce an 'inward barbican' behind a widened (9 m and now dual) carriageway fronted by double gates. This gate-structure was refurbished several times over a period of about one hundred years until around 400 BC when a catastrophic interlude occurred, in which the gates were burned and bodies were disposed roughly in pits, and a succeeding period when the site remained gate-less, although still in use.

During this earlier stage of occupation a number of circular houses, roughly 7 m in diameter with walls built of vertical planks with a substantial porch set in the south-east/south-west arc, were built on the site. Small four-post 'granaries' or 'fodder stores' appeared in great numbers, to be closely succeeded by the digging of bell-shaped storage pits, both mainly in the northern sector of the hill-fort enclosure.

The later phases of Danebury's development commenced some time after the first burning of the gateway, when the rampart was remodelled on a larger scale. Repeated clearing out of the ditch led to the creation of a counterscarp providing the perfect 'killing zone' for projectile weapons – in particular the sling, an immensely powerful weapon, easy to maintain and munition. A long dual carriageway gate-passage was then made, the gates set well back with, in all likelihood, a tower set above to provide command. This gate was, in turn, remodelled by narrowing to a single track, with a barbican earthwork being carried forward beyond the limits of the rampart to lengthen the flanked approach. The vulnerability of this 'barbican' was then recognized, and a great 'lobster claw' bulwark was built out from the ramparts on either side to surround and protect it – a scheme which experienced at least one break in its execution. With

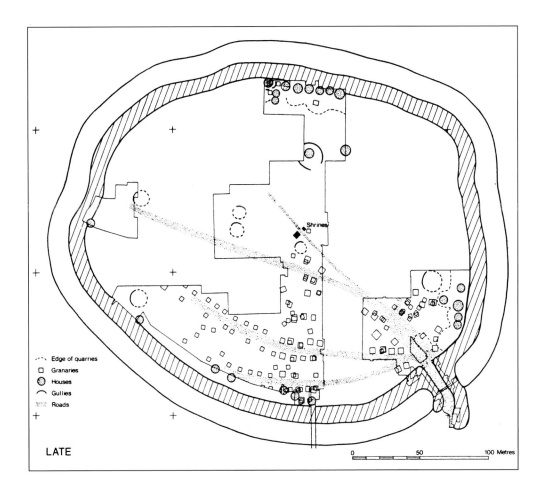

Edge of quarries
□ Granaries
◉ Houses
⌢ Gullies
 Roads
+

LATE

0   50   100 Metres

this phase the gateway was once again widened to dual carriageway status. At some time during this phase of development a major annexe was built along the south side of the fort for the containment and protection of animals.

During this long phase (lasting probably three hundred years) numerous circular houses of more variable size (some reaching 10 m in diameter), and now built of hurdling coated with clay, were constructed on the site. Massive four-, five-, six-post granaries were also built, with a huge increase in numbers in the southern sector of the fort.

While the population of Danebury may have decreased slightly during its later phases of occupation, its status seems to have increased. By 350 BC it was the only hill-fort occupied in the block of land between the Rivers Test and Bourne, and growing power may have been concentrated in the hands of its population. If this was the case, it may eventually have provoked a trial of strength. It is clear that around 100 BC an episode occurred when the main gate was burned again and groups of bodies were roughly interred in pits. The remainder of the population then deserted the site, and there followed a period of, essentially, 'squatter' occupation, when the former intensive use of the site broke down; gates were not replaced and the site gradually sank into disuse. This pattern of hill-fort desertion around 100 BC is widely reflected through Britain as a whole.

Throughout the period of occupation barley and wheat were the principal staples of food production. Pork was eaten quite regularly – the ability of pig-herds to regenerate swiftly being the key factor here (see also above, p. 25) – while milk and its products were undoubtedly popular. Beef would be culled as economically appropriate from the dairy herds, sheep were husbanded for their wool, and mutton was eaten a great deal.

HEREFORDSHIRE BEACON (Hereford and Worcester) (NT) The enclosure at the centre of the view was a multivallate Iron Age hill-fort of similar character to that at Danebury discussed in the text. The outer fortifications have the unusual feature of placing the ditch inside the rampart. It is difficult to say much about the history of the site because it has never been excavated

Chickens were also kept, probably for their eggs. Extensive use was made of local woodland for the collection of honey and doubtless of fruits and nuts. This dietary economy, established by 500 BC, remained virtually unchanged throughout the life of the site.

Danebury sat at the centre of an extensive communications system. From the earliest stages of defensive enclosure development on the site (about 500 BC) sophisticated pottery manufacture, taking place in close proximity to Danebury, was supplying the hill-fort itself as well as a range of sites at up to 40 km distance to the north-east and west, and regional pottery distributions of a similar extent, to which Danebury is linked, persisted throughout the period of the site's use.

Less easily detectable archaeologically, but almost certainly more important, must have been the necessary importation of iron and the likely export, in exchange, of the substantial overproduction of wool strongly indicated by sheep remains on the site. A hoard of twenty-one ingots or 'currency bars' of iron were found in a house of the later phases of the fort's occupation. Iron-working certainly took place on the site although its precise location is not known. Bronze-working also took place on the site, as did sheet metalworking, using a source of metal that originated probably in Devon or Cornwall.

A vital component in maintaining large herds of stock, as well as in the curing of meat for its preservation, was salt. This commodity again had to be imported, often in

CRICKLEY HILL (Gloucestershire) (NT) (opposite) The defences of the Iron Age hillfort, viewed from across the ditch

coarse ceramic containers the debris of which (briquetage) was strewn about as the containers were broken to extract the salt for use. Stone was also necessary for millstones, whetstones and weights, and was again imported from a wide catchment to the south and west. The stone weights may indicate that a weight standard of general validity was in use – a small step on the route to the first face-value and then token value coinage that appears among southern British prehistoric societies in the last 160 years BC and the remaining period up to the Roman Conquest.

Finally there have been found the true exotica – rare and no doubt treasured items of personal adornment: amber from the Baltic and coral from the Mediterranean as well as 'jet' from nearer at home on the Dorset coast, and glass beads, some of which may be of relatively distant origin.

The likelihood is that the surpluses of grain and wool formed the economic basis for all this imported wealth. The storage facilities carefully built within the fort tell of vast resources, far beyond those that could ever have been produced or used by the likely population of the site. In all probability the surrounding population deposited a share of its produce with the fort's population (in tribute?) in order to prime the entrepreneurial pump that would suck the imports into the region.

GUSSAGE ALL SAINTS

Gussage All Saints (Dorset) is the site of long-lived farmsteading which operated from about 500 BC until well into the Roman period. Hierarchically subordinate to sites like Danebury, the site is situated on the chalk downland of southern England and, like so many others there, has been badly damaged by ploughing over successive generations of farming activity. As a consequence the traces of less substantially founded structures almost certainly do not survive on the site and thus, while pits and the substantial four-post 'granary' foundations are well known, the houses are less clear. Nevertheless the picture of consistent and growing prosperity afforded by the evidence is a clear one, reflecting many aspects of late prehistoric life at a level set apart from that in the great fortified centres like Danebury.

At some point around 500 BC a 1.5 hectare enclosure was established, enclosed by an irregular ditch with an external bank. The entrance on the eastern side had 'antennae' ditches running away from it, like a gigantic funnel, to allow the easy herding of animals into the enclosure precinct. During the earliest phase of activity, which lasted two centuries, the centre of the site, as it remains to us, was dominated by a large number of four-post 'granary' foundations 2 m x 2.5 m. As well as these structures 128 cylindrical pits were dug to enable grain storage which, as they became contaminated, were abandoned to rubbish disposal (and occasionally human burial). The lack of domestic structures is belied by the vast quantities of pottery located in the pits – 592 restorable vessels relating to this period. Saddle querns for grinding of corn were found in numbers as well as a hint at luxury in the form of a fine bronze brooch dating to about 400 BC.

From around 300 BC the settlement pattern changed somewhat, although there is a clear continuity with the preceding phase. The gateway was strengthened and the enclosing ditch recut and widened. From this phase one round house foundation has survived (with a possible trace of a second). This structure is 9 m in diameter with a central roof-supporting post and a simple entrance. Fewer storage pits were dug (only sixty-nine) but their combined volume of 207 m³ is very consistent with the preceding period. This continuity is further exemplified by a total of 569 restorable pots found broken and discarded on the site.

With the advent of Period 3 (around 100 BC) a lesser element of continuity is present. The site occupied more or less the same area as before, but it changed to become a non-nucleated settlement comprising three separate enclosures. Chief among these was a ring-ditch 35 m in diameter with a single, strongly constructed gateway which must have afforded protection for a house. The two other enclosures were probably for stock. From the filling of the ring-ditch came a number of luxury items including metalwork and luxury imported pottery from the Roman provinces of Gaul. Also significant was the discovery of fragments of amphorae, which suggests that the inhabitants had a taste for wine imported from the Mediterranean. Evidently the farm lay at the centre of a system of communications and exchange that reached a thousand miles into the heart of the Roman world. Indeed, after the final confrontation came with Roman civilization in AD 43, it continued to function for another fifty years before eventually being deserted.

Throughout the long life of this farm, cattle would appear to have been worked for milk, with selective slaughter to foster the well-being of such a herd. Sheep would appear to have been husbanded for wool and perhaps milk with again only secondary use for meat. Pig meat was the principal source of meat consumption with older horses also used. There would appear to have been a sharp increase in the scale of meat consumption during Period 3. By contrast the pattern of crop husbandry on the site changed significantly over time. The evidence of seed remains might suggest that barley production fell with the passage of time from Period 1–3 and that of wheat increased. Interestingly, the decline of barley, which was probably grown in more marginal locations, is matched by a possible consequent increase in grass production (which, in turn, might reflect on the high meat consumption in Period 3).

During Period 2 the farmstead played host to the prolonged activity of a bronzesmith who left the debris of mould manufacture and casting in a number of pits. He was a craftsman of the highest accomplishment working probably at an early point in the first century BC. The deposits comprised iron slag, bronze and iron scrap, hammer-scale, a small ingot of tin bronze, approximately six hundred fragments of crucibles and over seven thousand fragments of clay investment moulds. The whole mass is in absolutely fresh condition and must have been shovelled into the pits immediately firing was completed. The working area was located close to the entrance of the settlement (probably away from houses and flammable structures) and there are signs that metalworking took place in this vicinity over a long period of the site occupation.

A wide range of specialized items were manufactured, all related to the ornamentation and function of chariots and the twin pony teams that pulled them. There were bridle-bits (in matching pairs), fasteners, terrets (rein-gathering rings) and the decorative bronze terminals for linchpins that clamped the chariot-wheel to the axle terminal. In all, a reasonable estimate (on the basis of the thousands of fragments) is that a total of fifty sets of horse and chariot harness is represented by the debris. There is a distinct range of 'quality' with rich and more mundane fittings.

The smith who made these items was no mere itinerant craftsman. He was an armourer of the highest order who must presumably have worked on this site over an extended period of time. His consumption of fuel, raw materials and other necessary and scarce commodities like beeswax (for lost-wax casting) denotes a complex standing

A Gilded Youth

One of the difficulties of studying prehistory is that in the absence of written evidence it is all but impossible to identify by name any of the proprietors who lived on estates like that at Gussage. The earliest account we have of the Britons is Caesar's, written after his encounters with them in 55 and 54 BC. This has its value in giving a vivid picture of Cassivellaunus and the other British chieftains with whom Caesar came into contact. But its weakness is that it is a view of British society through Roman eyes. Its insights, therefore, are both partial and incomplete.

The most revealing insight into the character of aristocratic life in Britain in the first century BC is provided not by Caesar's account or any other literary source but by a princely grave discovered at Welwyn Garden City (Hertfordshire) in 1965. It contained the remains of a young adult, probably male and probably over twenty-five years of age, who was cremated and buried in about 10 BC. His passing was marked by the presentation in the grave of an extraordinary array of objects. Firstly to one side were five amphorae of a type known to have been imported through Hengistbury in Dorset but in this instance with the same manufacturer's markings as vessels imported into Colchester (Essex). These would have held a total of something like 50 gallons (350 bottles of wine). To assist with the serving of the wine he was accompanied by a fine silver cup with a strainer, and to amuse him he was furnished with a gaming board and pieces (a suite of twenty-four glass pieces divided into four different sets of six). He was given a bronze dish and a small triangular iron knife, perhaps for eating the provisions contained within the thirty-odd pots that filled the grave. Beads and bracelets were ready to impress whomever he was to meet – as no doubt were the items of clothing that could not survive in the archaeological record. For his personal care a bronze toilet set was probably buried with him (only one item, a nail cleaner, survived the exigencies of the discovery of the site). Two wooden vessels with bronze fittings as well as other wooden objects had hardly survived and were only recognized by virtue of their metal attachments.

Significantly no weapons of any kind were found in the grave. This would appear to be the grave of a highly civilized, somewhat hedonistic young man. It was men like him that Claudius was to encounter thirty years later in a conquest that completed but in no way commenced the changes that brought Britons from prehistoric to historical times.

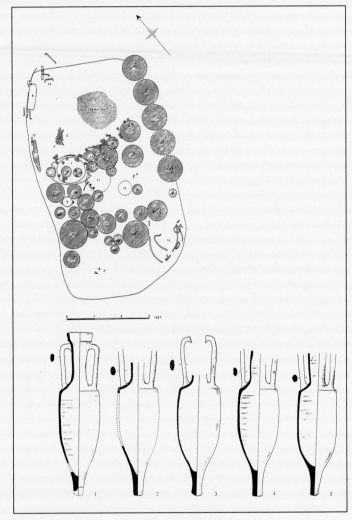

WELWYN GARDEN CITY (Hertfordshire)
above: A plan showing the disposition of wine amphorae and other food-containing vessels within the princely grave; below: cross-sections of wine vessels of Roman origin deposited in the princely grave

system of exchange and supply. He was presumably serving a master of considerable wealth and power who was willing and able to mobilize very considerable resources in the pursuit of the panoply of war. The '4000 charioteers' that Caesar says met him in 55 BC, often thought to be a grotesque, politically motivated, exaggeration, may not be so gross an act of hyperbole.

In all, Gussage All Saints gives an extraordinarily detailed picture of farm-life in the later metal-using period. Always a prosperous farm and a seat of prosperity, by the early part of the first century AD it was receiving imports directly from the Roman world, commanding access to exotic and luxury goods just as it had served as the focus for prestige weapon production in the first century BC.

CONCLUSION

Through the detailed examination of sites such as Hambledon and Stonehenge, Gussage and Danebury, a clear outline can be gained of the main developments in British society in the prehistoric period. Of particular significance is the long process of settlement and colonization, which by the first century BC had gone on for some five thousand years. The landscape of Britain by the late Iron Age was both densely peopled and intensely cultivated. Settlement extended out of the areas where soils were lighter into the richer but heavier claylands, and even into the high moorlands and mountains where complex pastoralism and transhumance practices became widespread. All over Britain there is evidence of growing intensity of cultivation and increasing specialization of agriculture.

In view of the clear evidence of increasing population it is all the more frustrating to be unable to say with any certainty just how large that population was on the eve of the Roman Conquest. Estimates made by demographers have varied greatly over the years. The latest suggests a figure for the late Roman period – the fourth century AD – of somewhere between 1.8 and 4.6 million. But when allowance is made for the margin of error (and some such allowance *has* to be made) the figure could be as low as a few hundred thousand or as high as six million. Earlier guesses by scholars were based on the idea of working back from what was supposed to be our one firm piece of data – Domesday Book of 1086. But as awareness has grown of the limitations of Domesday, that method has come to be viewed with disfavour. The modern trend has been to tackle the problem by guessing the average number of houses in settlements and the average number of identified settlements per kilometre. Whether that method brings us any nearer to the truth is to be doubted, however, because it rests on assumptions about contemporaneous occupation which detailed fieldwork is now calling into question. It seems almost certain that settlements shifted regularly, moving short distances amid their fields, thus giving the impression of two or three settlements when in fact there was but one. When the evidence is so restricted and so difficult to interpret, any estimate of population is bound to be one that is fairly limited in value.

Another area of British life of which we know little relates to the ownership and inheritance of land. The Romans assumed that the various kings enjoyed land 'ownership' in a rather Mediterranean sense, and may even have thought that a king had private possession of his kingdom. But it would be altogether more plausible to suppose that the lands were vested in the kindred, and that the king had only a life interest in

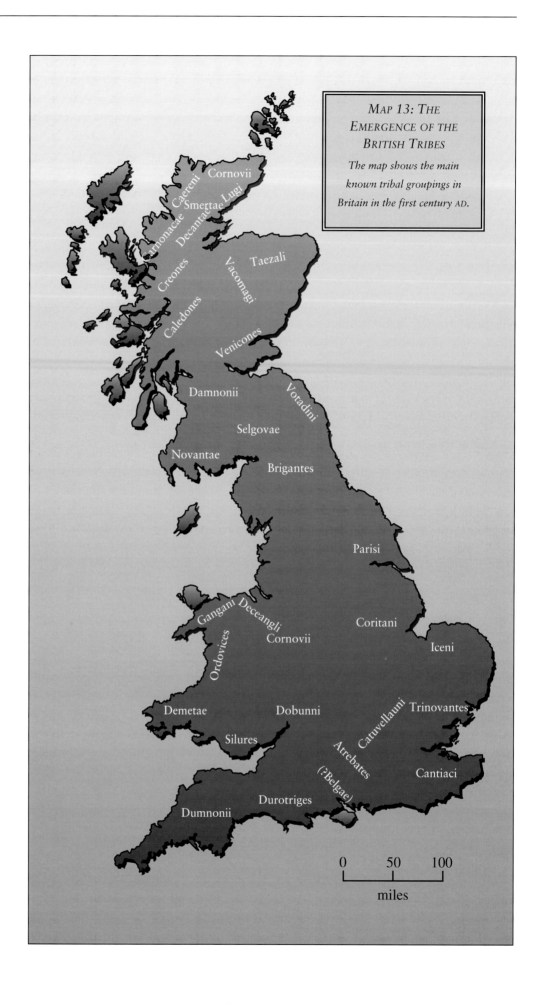

MAP 13: THE
EMERGENCE OF THE
BRITISH TRIBES

The map shows the main
known tribal groupings in
Britain in the first century AD.

Cornovii

Caereni

Smertae

Lugi

Carnonacae

Decantae

Creones

Vacomagi

Taezali

Caledones

Venicones

Damnonii

Votadini

Selgovae

Novantae

Brigantes

Parisi

Gangani

Deceangli

Coritani

Ordovices

Cornovii

Iceni

Demetae

Dobunni

Trinovantes

Catuvellauni

Silures

Atrebates
(?Belgae)

Cantiaci

Durotriges

Dumnonii

0   50   100

miles

them. If that were so, it would at least be easier to understand the anger and incomprehension aroused by the imposition on the Britons of a Roman view of possession in the generation after Claudius' conquest – evidence of which is afforded by the revolt of Boudica.

British society, though clearly very different from that which the Romans knew in the Mediterranean, was not without similarities to that nearer to them on the other side of the Channel. Affinities existed between British and Gallic society in such areas as law, coinage and the role and structure of kinship. Social and familial ties developed between the tribal hierarchies of the two groups of peoples, and immigration into Britain eroded whatever tendencies there may have been to insularity. Britain – or at least southern Britain – was in many ways a quite cosmopolitan society in the last centuries BC and first century AD. Are we to suppose, then, that it was inevitable that Britain would one day be absorbed into the Roman *imperium*? Almost certainly not. The Romans had for some time been happy to halt their conquests at the Channel; and after Caesar's expeditions in 55 and 54 BC they showed no interest in moving back into Britain. Why they suddenly changed policy in the first century AD is, in fact, more than a little puzzling. One suggestion is that they did so in anticipation of profit: mention has been made of Cornish tin in this connection. But the problem here is that the cost of conquering and occupying the country would have been such as to render any profit margin slight if not negligible. Another suggestion is that Britain was seen as a source of rebellion – this is what Caesar said in defence of his expedition in 55 BC. But fear of rebellion, if it was a factor in the last century BC, was surely not so later, once Gaul became integrated into the Roman power structures. Recent discussions have tended to focus on Claudius' own difficulties – his uncertain election to the throne, his lack of military experience, and the volatile politics of the Roman aristocracy. When the background in Rome was so very unstable, a swift expansion of the empire might have seemed to offer a relatively easy pathway to success.

PREHISTORIC SITES IN THE CARE OF THE NATIONAL TRUST

PALEOLITHIC ROCK SHELTER

Oldbury Hill (Kent)

NEOLITHIC FLINT MINING SITE

Cissbury Ring (West Sussex)

NEOLITHIC AXE FACTORIES

Pike of Stickle (Cumbria)
Mynydd Rhiw (Gwynedd)

NEOLITHIC CHAMBERED TOMBS

Coldrum (Kent)

Lanyon Quoit (Cornwall)
Long Stone (Isle of Wight)
Plas Newydd (Anglesey)
Carn Llidi (Dyfed)

NEOLITHIC CAUSEWAYED ENCLOSURES

Crickley Hill (Gloucestershire): a defended causewayed enclosure lying beneath a later
    prehistoric hill-fort
Barkhale (West Sussex)
White Sheet Hill (Wiltshire)
Windmill Hill (Wiltshire)

NEOLITHIC LONG CAIRNS AND BARROWS

Randwick (Gloucestershire)
Sampson's Bratfull (Cumbria)
White Barrow (Wiltshire)
Winterbourne Stoke (Wiltshire)
Afton Down (Isle of Wight)

NEOLITHIC STONE CIRCLES, HENGE MONUMENTS AND OTHER CEREMONIAL SITES

Avebury (Wiltshire): this complex site comprises avenues, stone circles and other
    monuments like Silbury Hill (English Heritage) in the immediate vicinity
Castlerigg (Cumbria): stone circle
Stonehenge (Wiltshire): (the monument is in the guardianship of English Heritage but
    much of the surrounding area including the Avenue and the Stonehenge Cursus is
    owned by the National Trust)
Stackpole Warren (Dyfed): standing stone
Trowlesworthy Warren (Devon)

BRONZE AGE BARROW CEMETERIES

Afton Down (Isle of Wight): linear cemetery
Stonehenge Cursus Barrow Group (Wiltshire): linear cemetery
Five Barrows (Isle of Wight): linear cemetery of eight barrows
Frensham Common (Surrey)
Stanton Moor (Derbyshire): complex of ring-cairns, cairns and standing stones
Stockbridge Down (Hampshire): cluster cemetery
Windmill Hill (Wiltshire): a cemetery of barrows

BRONZE AGE SETTLEMENT AND FIELD PATTERNS

Brean Down (Somerset)
Trowlesworthy Warren (Devon)

LATER PREHISTORIC HILL-FORTS

Badbury Rings (Dorset)
Brent Knoll (Somerset)
Cadbury Camp (Avon)

AVEBURY (Wiltshire) (NT)
An aerial view of the site, showing
the village in the centre and the great
stone circle at the top

Cadsonbury (Cornwall)

Castle Crag (Cumbria)

Church Hill (Buckinghamshire)

Cissbury Ring (West Sussex) (see also Flint Mining above)

Cley Hill (Wiltshire)

Coney's Castle (Dorset)

Crickley Hill (Gloucestershire) (see also Causewayed Enclosures above)

Croft Ambrey (Hereford and Worcester)

Dumpdon Hill (Devon)

Eggardon (Dorset)

Figsbury Ring (Wiltshire)

Haresfield Beacon (Gloucestershire)

Hembury (Devon)

Highdown Hill (West Sussex)

Ivinghoe Beacon (Buckinghamshire): bronze hoard

Kinver (Staffordshire)

Lambert's Castle (Dorset)

Little Solsbury (Avon)

Mam Tor (Derbyshire): Bronze Age occupation

Midsummer Hill (Hereford and Worcester)

Oldbury Castle, Cherhill Down (Wiltshire)

Oldbury (Kent)

Pilsdon Pen (Dorset)

Stokeleigh Camp (Avon)

Trencrom (Cornwall)

Uffington Castle (Oxfordshire): famous chalk-cut figure of conventionalized horse

White Sheet Hill (Wiltshire) (see also Causewayed Enclosures above)

Woolbury (Hampshire)

PREHISTORIC SITES IN THE OWNERSHIP OF THE NATIONAL TRUST FOR SCOTLAND

Clava Cairns (Highland)

Kintail and Morvich (Highland)

ROMAN
AND EARLY
MEDIEVAL
BRITAIN

PHILIP DIXON

Time Chart from the Roman Invasion until the Twelfth Century

	100–200 Roman Occupation	400 Sub Roman	500 Pagan Saxon	800 Middle Saxon	1000 Late Anglo-Saxon
INVASIONS	Claudius	Hengist and Horsa	Formation of the Anglo-Saxon Kingdoms	Vikings	Unification of Southern Britain; Knut; Normans
SITES	Hadrian's Wall; Villas; Town Walls	Pagan Cemeteries	Yeavering Palaces; Sutton Hoo	Anglo-Saxon Churches; Bewcastle Cross; Northampton Palace	Late Saxon Towns; Castles
ARTS		Anglo-Saxon Brooches		Lindisfarne Gospels	Winchester and Canterbury Schools of Manuscripts; Domesday Book
ARCHITECTURAL PERIODS	Roman	Late Roman	Merovingian	Carolingian	Ottonian; Romanesque
EUROPEAN EVENTS		Huns; Barbarian Invasions	End of the Western Empire; Byzantine Reconquest	Arabs; Charlemagne Emperor	Collapse of Carolingian Empire; Vikings and Hungarians; Expansion of Normans

V

INVASION AND CONQUEST

In the early summer of the year AD 43 a Roman army of four legions and an unknown number of auxiliary regiments, perhaps some forty thousand men in all, sailed from Boulogne to invade Britain. Where they disembarked is not recorded, but Dover is a possible site, as is Reculver, on the northern side of the peninsula. Some landed at Richborough, now silted up but once a great harbour where excavations have uncovered a huge enclosure of this period, defended by shallow banks and ditches, suitable for an invasion bridgehead.

Aulus Plautius, the Roman commander, brought his army west towards a river which was almost certainly the Medway in Kent. Here, perhaps between Rochester and Maidstone, the first of the battles of the invasion was fought. It is clear from surviving accounts that fighting was hard: the British were drawn up on the further bank, and the Roman light-armed troops had to swim across to hold up the enemy while the regular troops crossed. After two days the British were forced to retreat to the Thames, and Plautius and his army followed them into Essex, where the Emperor Claudius joined the troops to lead them into the enemy centre, Camulodunum (Colchester). One of the British leaders, Togodumnus, was killed, and the other, Caratacus, retreated into western Britain, where he carried out guerrilla attacks on the Romans for nearly a decade.

The British tribes were not all hostile to the invasion, and opposition had come largely from the Trinovantes of Essex (map 13). The Roman takeover was accomplished partly by conquest and partly by judicious diplomacy. Even before the battle at the Medway some of the Dobunni of Gloucestershire had submitted to Plautius, and in the months after the capture of Camulodunum other tribes surrendered without a struggle. We do not have a complete account, but they seem to have included the Iceni of Norfolk, the remaining Dobunni, the Corieltauvi of the East Midlands, the Cantiaci of Kent, and some of the Brigantes of the Pennines. For these tribes there were rewards. For example, the Iceni retained their possessions under their existing rulers. Other peoples may similarly have maintained some independence during a long period of transition: from Chichester, Sussex, we have a good Roman inscription set up with the approval of Titus Claudius Cogidubnus, who is called *rex magnus*, great king, and who seems to have ruled within the Roman province as a native prince, allied to the new overlords, for a generation after the conquest.

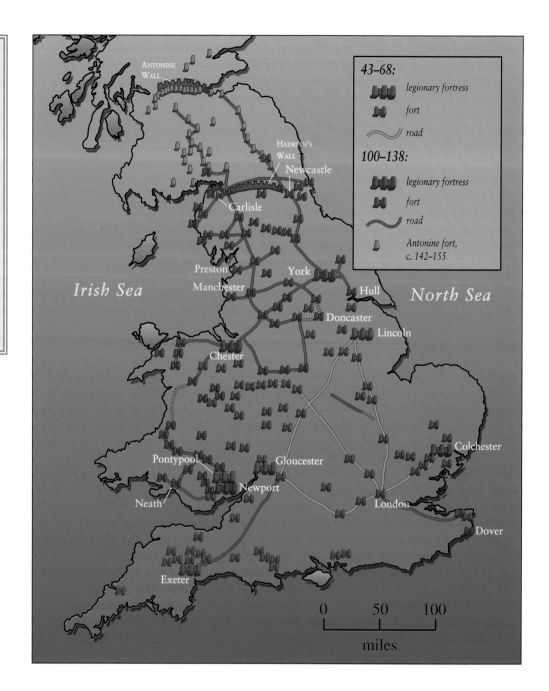

MAP 14: THE ROMAN
CONQUEST, AD 43–155

*The map shows the expansion
of the province in three stages:
in the first the area dominated
lay within the Lincoln—Exeter
line, with forts extending into
the West Midlands and Wales.
In the second, the completion
of the subjugation of Wales
and northern England was
marked by the building of
Hadrian's Wall. In the third
phase forts were established
along the east and west routes
to the Antonine Wall.*

Aulus Plautius remained as governor of the new province for some four years. During this period his troops established control of the conquered lands in the east, and expanded westwards. We lack detailed historical information about their progress, a gap not properly filled by the excavation of military works in southern England, since dating evidence from archaeology can only give us a general pattern measured in decades, rather than in successive annual campaigns. At Colchester a legionary fortress was built to the north of the huge enclosure of the Trinovantian capital, with a small fort about 2 miles to the south, close to the Camulodunum dykes at Gosbecks. The purpose of these works must have been to oversee life in the tribal centre, but neither fort can be shown to have been built in the immediate aftermath of the invasion. During the years 44 and 45 some of the army may have moved northwards and north-westwards, among the Iceni and the Coritani. One regiment, the Second Augustan Legion, led by the future Emperor Vespasian, attacked westwards through Hampshire and Wiltshire, and took the Isle of Wight. In the course of this march Vespasian is credited with the capture of twenty 'towns', or *oppida*: a word often used to refer to native hill-forts. Excavations at two large Dorset forts have produced evidence of Roman attack. At Hod Hill (NT) Roman projectiles were found around the houses of the settlement. At Maiden Castle, Sir Mortimer Wheeler's excavations in the 1930s identified a massively strong hill-fort whose defences, constantly expanding from the third century BC onwards, were assaulted by Vespasian and Legio II Augusta in AD 44: a small cemetery within the gateway contained a corpse shot through the spine by a Roman ballista bolt. Further excavation and fieldwork in the Dorchester area now suggest that the growth of the fort was matched by a diminution of homesteads and farms in the immediate vicinity. This is roughly what one might expect: the people concentrated within the hill-fort must have come from the neighbouring area. Late in the Iron Age, however, farmsteads were once again found around Maiden Castle, and the defences began to collapse and silt. Perhaps Vespasian's triumph may now be viewed a little differently, as the overcoming of hasty resistance within the rotting and sagging palisades of an obsolete fortress.

Some hill-forts were taken over by the army. At Hod Hill itself the northern part of the Iron Age hill-fort was rebuilt as a small Roman fort, and Roman military buildings have been excavated at the hill-forts of Hembury in Devon and Brandon in Herefordshire. Other sites, for example Badbury Rings in Dorset, have shown signs of destruction which may belong to this initial push, but we cannot confidently write a history of the campaign: at South Cadbury in Somerset the destruction of the hill-fort seems now to have been the result of a completely unrecorded skirmish or rebellion twenty years or more after the Roman invasion. The situation was clearly much more complex than the simple account of landing and conquest suggests.

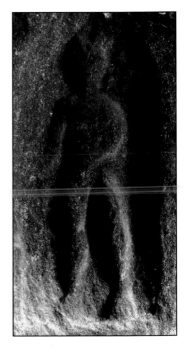

LEDSHAM (Yorkshire)
In the small Anglo-Saxon church is this roughly carved slab, thought to represent the pagan horned god of the British tribe of the Brigantes, who lived in the north of England

THE REBELLION OF BOUDICA

The principal danger to the new rulers lay in the west, in unconquered Wales, and to the north, where the Brigantes were clearly disunited, and included elements hostile to the new regime. During the AD 50s a series of governors pressed into the Welsh valleys, finding the terrain and the fragmentation of the tribes increasingly awkward for their armies, and necessitating a network of strong forts and military roads to control the land won by campaigns. In AD 60, in the last stages of the conquest, when the Roman governor, Suetonius Paulinus, had just invaded and seized the island stronghold of Anglesey, a massive revolt broke out in the centre of the Roman province. The immediate cause was the death of Prasutagus, King of the Iceni, and the violent seizure of the royal possessions by the Emperor Nero's agents. The tribe united behind the king's widow, Boudica, and were joined by the Trinovantes, angered by the foundation of the new town of Camulodunum (Colchester), a colony of veteran soldiers whose territory must have included much of the former tribal land. Other once-loyal provincials joined the rebellion. The Roman historian Tacitus explains the reason: British leaders had been lent large sums of money by private Romans who were now recalling their debts, and official subsidies which Claudius had paid out were being reclaimed by the provincial procurator. For many the outcome must have been ruin.

The scale of the rebellion caught the province by surprise. Boudica's forces attacked and destroyed Camulodunum, and burnt the new towns of Verulamium (St Albans, Hertfordshire), and London. No fewer than seventy thousand civilians were said to have been killed. Paulinus, with his army scattered around the province, could assemble no more than a quarter of his troops, but in a pitched battle somewhere in Hertfordshire he scattered the rebels, killing, according to the Roman account, eighty thousand of them.

THE CREATION OF THE PROVINCE

Signs of a change of policy are visible after the revolt. Paulinus' treatment of the defeated tribes was harsh enough to lead to his recall. He was replaced by a series of successors who made the province secure, and who seem to have treated the provincials with greater consideration. In the next generation the historian Tacitus contrasted this inactivity with the renewed burst of conquest in the 70s and 80s; but he was concerned to show the energy of his own father-in-law, Agricola, governor from 77 to 84, and the gentler governors before Agricola seem to have begun a process of devolution and organization of authority designed to pacify and civilize the citizens of the new province. The province was divided into regions, *civitates*, which bore the names of at least the latest of the pre-Roman tribal units, and presumably fossilized some at least of the national boundaries which the Romans found in the AD 40s. In some areas there must have been dislocations – for example, in those parts where the army had considerable territory allocated to them, such as around Camulodunum. In most of the south, however, there is little sign of an army presence, and the new local administrators of government are most likely to have been the native aristocracy, given a new legal status as the town council of the *civitas*, under the watchful eye of the governor and his staff. The *oppida* continued to develop; the normal pattern is of continuity of the site into a form which archaeology distinguishes as 'Roman' rather than native because of regular street planning, complex rectangular buildings, and public buildings such as town hall, market square and theatre which owe their concept to continental rather than native traditions. The details of the buildings, however, are a little different from those to be found in Italy or even Gaul, and the conclusion of the most recent research on Romanization in Britain and Gaul suggests that the towns and buildings of the new provinces were built by local workers, interpreting and redefining foreign ideas of what was appropriate to the new status of the old site. In some cases we can see a shift of location – for example, from Bagendon southwards some three miles to Cirencester in Gloucestershire. Originally this was thought to be Roman policy – to separate the natives from their independent past. It seems now most likely that it was simply the position of the old site in relation to the new road network that determined the probability of its survival into the new age, as at Silchester (Hampshire) or Verulamium/St Albans, or its replacement by a new town beside the Roman road.

THE SETTLEMENT OF HADRIAN

When the Emperor Hadrian arrived in Britain in 122, he probably found a province still recovering from recent attack – heavy losses are recorded, probably in the period 117–19. His response was the creation of the most remarkable frontier in the whole empire: a stone wall, 80 miles in length, running from the Tyne estuary to the Solway coast, with associated forts, roads and watch-towers, which eventually extended nearly 50 miles southwards along the Cumberland coast; and a colossal earthwork, which we call the Vallum, which may have been intended to mark and to give some protection to the immediate military zone of the wall. Work began in 122, or a little before, and was still going on, after several changes to the plan, after 136. The cost in labour – all three legions were involved – and materials must have been extraordinary. Later Romans described the purpose as being to divide the Romans from the barbarians, but there were many cheaper ways of doing this, and 'barbarians' were numerous within the province. More than fifty forts, in which garrisons were necessary during Hadrian's reign, stretched from this frontier through the Lake District and the Pennines to Lancaster, Ribchester and Manchester, and across Wales. The great work is of a piece with Hadrian's other projects – massive, logical and brutal. Symbolically it served less to mark off the Roman army from the northern tribes – since forts were built well in advance of the wall itself – than to place a massively strong military boundary at the northern end of the early Hadrianic province, beyond which Hadrian did not intend the empire to expand.

If that was the aim it was soon thwarted. Hadrian died in 138, when the turf rampart in the western section of his great wall was probably still being rebuilt in stone. Within two years his successor, Antoninus Pius, was preparing to reconquer southern Scotland, and to build a new wall between the Forth and the Clyde – a shorter line of turf rather than stone, but more densely packed with forts. It is unlikely that this abandonment of Hadrian's Wall, which involved the demolition of the milecastle gates and filling in of parts of the Vallum, was due to military need; more plausibly, Antoninus Pius was seeking some military reputation and was providing a safety valve for men and commanders frustrated by a long period of quiet. The move was clearly premature, since the new frontier lasted little more than a decade; the forts on the Antonine Wall were dismantled and burnt, and patchy rebuilding is visible on Hadrian's Wall. An attempt about 160 to re-occupy the Antonine frontier was swiftly abandoned, and from about the middle of the 160s until the end of the Roman province the northern end of Britannia was the line of Hadrian, supplemented by outpost forts on the northern roads into Scotland.

HOUSESTEADS (Northumberland) (NT)
An elaborate latrine block, flushed by running water, was a feature of this important fort on the Wall

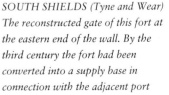

SOUTH SHIELDS (Tyne and Wear)
The reconstructed gate of this fort at the eastern end of the wall. By the third century the fort had been converted into a supply base in connection with the adjacent port

Expansion and Withdrawal

Wales and the north still proved troublesome, and further expansion of the province was undertaken by three successive governors, Petillius Cerialis, Julius Frontinus and Gnaius Julius Agricola, who in the space of fifteen years conquered all the remaining territory of Roman Britain. Cerialis' campaigns are little known, but included campaigns in Wales, and a major onslaught on the loose federation of the Brigantes of the Pennines, one of whose centres, the oppidum of Stanwick (where the Great North Road and the Stainmore Road divide in North Yorkshire) used to be thought of as a fortress hastily contrived in the face of the Roman advance; the site seems from recent excavations to have been a tribal centre which grew and prospered as the northern neighbour of the Roman province, but which was swallowed up and abandoned as the district fell under Roman military control. Cerialis or his successor Julius Frontinus may have been responsible for the transfer of the Ninth Legion from its base at Lincoln, by now far south of the military zone, to a new station at York, commanding the eastern fringes of Brigantia. Otherwise, Frontinus' activity was directed at the Welsh, with the building of two new legionary fortresses at Chester, under the modern city, and Caerleon on the River Usk in South Wales, together controlling access into the Welsh coastal plain, and the stationing of units in small forts along roads which penetrated almost all the Welsh valleys and ringed Snowdonia.

Frontinus' successor, Agricola, completed the conquest of North Wales, and turned his attention to the Brigantes and their northern neighbours. In AD 78 he crossed the land of the Brigantes to the Tyne-Solway gap, and in the next year pressed northwards into southern Scotland. At the narrow isthmus between the Forth and the Clyde, forts were built, but the army continued beyond into Aberdeenshire. Agricola's progress has been graphically illustrated by aerial photography, which reveals regular rows of large marching camps, the temporary halting-points of an expeditionary force, set about 10 miles apart along the eastern side of the Scottish Highlands south of the Moray Firth. In 83, in his final campaign, Agricola's army met and defeated the massed warriors of the Caledonian tribes at Mons Graupius, an unknown spot somewhere between the Tay and the Spey, and the other peoples of the north, including the Orcadians, surrendered. In his settlement of the newly-won territory, Agricola began a new legionary fortress in Perthshire, at Inchtuthil, linked to a chain of forts along the Highland foothills back to the Clyde, and so across the Southern Uplands to Brigantia. Inchtuthil, excavated almost in its entirety by Sir Ian Richmond, is a remarkable testimonial to the thoroughness and power of the Roman army, so far from its bases. The fortress is over 50 acres in extent, a square whose sides are more than 1,500 feet long, and contained sixty-four barrack blocks, storehouses, headquarters, officers' houses, workshops and a hospital. This was all built in two or three years because the fortress was still not fully operational when it was abandoned soon after AD 86, leaving the pottery in the storerooms and over three-quarters of a million iron nails, bent and twisted from the demolition, hidden in a pit in the workshop, presumably to keep them out of the hands of the natives.

The rapid Roman withdrawal from the new conquests may have been a realization of the difficulties involved in holding on to the eastern coast of Scotland without a full conquest of the Highlands, but the change of policy seems too quick for this to be plausible, and some of the Agricolean defence works in north-eastern Scotland remained in use a few years longer. Events outside Britain are a more likely cause: in or after 87 Legio II Adiutrix was transferred from its new base in Chester to the Danube frontier, where the Emperor Domitian was facing the collapse of the province of Dacia, and its place was taken by Legio XX, which was probably the force intended as garrison at Inchtuthil. After the reduction of the army in Britannia to less than three-quarters of its original strength, maintenance of the new lands must have seemed impossible, at least for the time. Withdrawal from the north did not mean the abandonment of all the recent gains, however, since

HARDKNOTT *(Cumbria) (NT)*
A view of the second- to fourth-century fort built by the Romans as part of the system of defences of northern Britannia

forts in the southern uplands of Scotland were restored and strengthened to produce a defence in depth from the Clyde to the Solway and the Tyne. During these years the remaining three legions of the army in Britain were established at Chester, York and Caerleon, and two new colonies of former soldiers were founded on military land at Lincoln and at Gloucester. It seems that consolidation was to follow retrenchment.

Excavation in half a dozen of the new forts, most notably at Newstead on Tweed and Corbridge in Northumberland, has shown a phase of extensive burning about AD 100. An unrecorded war is likely, and the response seems to have been a further withdrawal to the line of the Tyne–Solway gap, where the military road, known to the Middle Ages as the Stanegate, joined the army bases of Corbridge and Carlisle. The exact sequence of building during these years is still in dispute, but it seems that some at least of the forts along the line of the Stanegate, and some of the signal stations and watch-towers in the area, belong to this period of withdrawal, and others were added during the generation which followed, before the arrival of the Emperor Hadrian in Britain during the summer of 122.

VI
CONSOLIDATION
AND DECLINE

During the first half-century of Roman control the new towns on or beside most of the pre-Roman regional capitals began to flourish. Excavations at Verulamium/St Albans, Silchester and Chichester, for example, have shown regular networks of streets and public buildings; squares, laid out on a large scale, and high-quality public buildings, built even before the Boudican rebellion of AD 60 or 61, have been found in the colony at Camulodunum. Rapid town-building may not have been confined to this site, since digging beneath the stone market-place at Silchester has shown that that structure was preceded by an extensive but quickly built timber phase. Similar work is suspected at Lincoln and Exeter, and more may well be discovered in the future.

The works continued into the next generation: Tacitus, speaking of the 70s and early 80s, says that the governor, Agricola, privately encouraged and officially aided the building of temples, squares and houses. Examination of the structures in these early towns shows no sign, in either their plan or details of their stone-carving, of similarities with military works; thus it cannot be supposed that the army was directly involved in building. Civilian craftsmen, perhaps from Gaul, are therefore most likely. Other Romanizing influences are to be found: Martial claimed at the end of the century that his poems were being recited in Britain, and in our very fragmentary written records we have casual references to Roman, Gaulish and Greek lawyers and teachers in Britain.

The tempo of building continued into the second century, and the 120s and 130s saw the rebuilding and completion of market-places at Wroxeter (Shropshire) and Silchester, and perhaps at Leicester and Caistor-by-Norwich. During these years, of course, Hadrian's Wall was being built, and the massive investment it implies often draws attention from other changes to the province which belong to this period, and which, like the wall itself, may have been due to the emperor's own ideas. We can see, for example, some attention to the organization of the land. Reclamation is visible in the Fens of Lincolnshire and East Anglia; the hand of Hadrian himself has been claimed here, and the project is one which might indeed have appealed to him, but we have no direct evidence of its original author. Within this region, however, at Stonea Grange, near March to the east of Peterborough, excavations have revealed a large planned settlement of streets and some houses around a massive tower-like building which has been identified as an administrative centre. In the Iron Age a small contour fort and perhaps a temple stood nearby, and these were lands probably once of the Iceni but were now perhaps imperial; at Stonea it is possible that Hadrian was attempting to set up a new town to manage the lands of the southern Fens, beside an Iron Age tribal or royal centre.

How much land in Britannia was in the direct control of the emperor – that is, part of the privy purse, the *res privata* – is disputed. Inscriptions show that some, if not all, mining was imperial and was carried out by the military or by others under the eye of an imperial official. Royal estates, like those of King Prasutagus of the Iceni, or indeed King Cogidubnus of the Regni, presumably passed eventually into the emperor's control, as did lands bequeathed to the emperor by testament, but without official inscriptions we cannot know their location or quantity. A good case has been made for imperial ownership of the Fenlands; others have pointed out that the irregularity of crop-marks of settlements and field boundaries here suggests a more haphazard colonization than one would expect of developers of imperial estates. We know too little about the pattern of management of these estates in Britain to be sure on these matters.

Some of the province land remained in the hands of the military. Without inscriptions once again we lack detailed knowledge, but a recent estimate of the farmland attached to each of the three legionary bases in Britannia has suggested that as much as 3,000 to 7,000 square kilometres of territory – larger than the average size of a modern English county – might be expected to be available for fodder and foodstuffs for each of the legions. Archaeologically we might expect little trace of this, since the army could and did encourage tenants and lessees to provide the manpower for food production, and their houses and farms need have looked little different from those on civilian estates. From the point of view of the economy, however, the problem of ownership is crucial, and it has an archaeological aspect: the building of sometimes large country houses.

VILLAS

The country houses of the Roman world are obvious in aerial photography, and have for centuries been found by ploughmen striking walls and uncovering mosaics and tiled floors in their fields. Their complex rectangular plans, their stone and brick construction, and, frequently, their possession of bath-houses, distinguish them from the wooden round houses of the Iron Age. They form a clear group, and are normally called by a Latin word, 'villa'; but it is a classification which covers a wide range of types and functions, from the elaborate double or treble courtyard houses extending over several acres, to small farmhouses of three or four rooms whose floor area was little different from that of the largest of the Iron Age round houses.

Excavations on villas have been underway for more than two hundred years, and something at least is known of more than eight hundred sites; many more are identified from aerial photography. The earliest were built during the first couple of generations after the invasion, in the south-eastern part of the province, in Essex, Sussex and Kent. The sites on which villas were built were not necessarily new: where good information is available, usually from more recent excavations, these new-style houses seem normally to have had some pre-Roman predecessor. We might, therefore, expect them to be the houses of the traditional British landowner, who was thus updating his 'native'

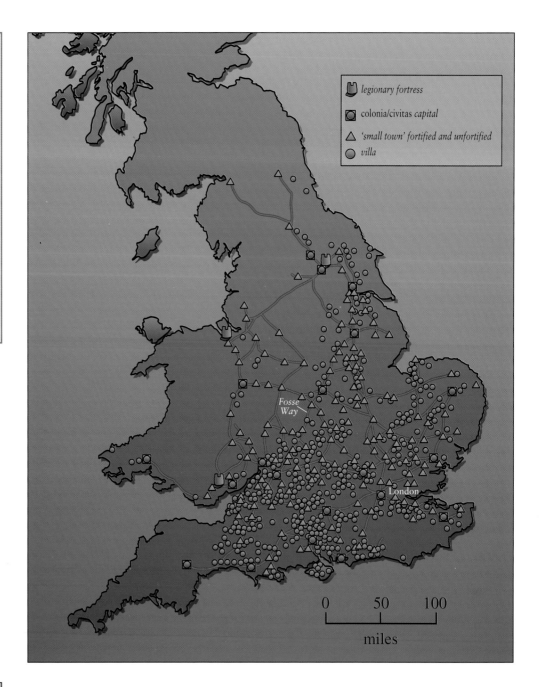

MAP 15: THE
SETTLEMENT OF THE
ROMAN PROVINCE

The map shows the 'large' and the 'small' towns, and the distribution of villas, most of which belong to the second century and later, with a flourishing in the early fourth century. It demonstrates the dominance of the zone to the south and east of the Fosse Way, at least as far as the distribution of 'country-house' estates is concerned.

legionary fortress

colonia/civitas *capital*

'small town' fortified and unfortified

villa

Fosse
Way

London

0   50   100

miles

ROMAN ROAD *(North Yorkshire) Roads were important in linking together the towns of the Roman province. The best surviving example is this stretch, nearly a mile long, on the North Yorkshire Moors near Whitby*

house in keeping with continental fashions. Such a proprietor would be living on his old lands in the new province as before, but now under Roman control. Like the Kings Cogidubnus and Prasutagus, but at a lower social level, he would be a bridge between the old kingdoms and the new province. The idea is attractive, and increasingly popular among archaeologists, but is quite unsupported by evidence. In particular, continuity of the usage of a site, which may well be true, tells us nothing about the continuity of the ownership of that site, and a reasonable case has been made to suggest that some at least of this rapid initial growth of villas was due to immigrants from the empire, probably largely from Gaul, business men settling on newly acquired lands. The weight placed on interpretations of the evidence oscillates in accordance with archaeological fashion. The villa at Fishbourne (West Sussex) is a case in point. Initially this great house was dated to the first generation of the conquest, and, indeed, attributed to King

Landed Society in Roman Britain

*T*ucked among woodland on the slopes of a combe above the River Coln, about six miles north-east of Cirencester, the ruins of Chedworth Villa (NT) are among the most extensively exposed remains of a Roman country house in England. The site was discovered in 1864, and partially excavated; little record, unfortunately, was kept of this work. More recent clearance in the 1950s and 1960s has greatly increased our understanding of a long and complex history. The first house, of stone and timber, consisted of three separate buildings of the early second century AD, arranged around three sides of a square, perhaps enclosed by a courtyard wall. During the third century and early in the fourth century the house was rebuilt on a much grander scale, with corridors to link the ranges, and extensive bath-house suites. After reconstruction the villa seems to have been arranged in three parts. To the south lay a series of rooms with neither mosaics nor underfloor heating; here a mass of coins suggests a steward's office. Linked to this to the west lay a succession of decorated dining and living rooms, ending in a bath-house. To the north a still grander range of dining and living rooms formed a completely separate suite of apartments ending in a second bath-house. The arrangements suggest the housing of two completely separate establishments within a single courtyard. Whether this represents two families, or an extended kindred, or, indeed, the housing of an owner (perhaps in the northern range) and a farming family, in the fashion of a medieval and modern French *proprieteur* and *rentier*, is one of the unsolved disputes of Romano–British archaeology.

The quality of the new accommodation in both the north and the west ranges was very high: at least fifteen of the rooms and most of the corridors were floored with coloured mosaics, and six rooms (in addition to the bath-houses) were heated by underfloor hypocausts. Fragments of painted plaster showed that the interior walls were extensively decorated, and broken pieces of sculpture and bases remained from statues which had once adorned the living rooms. Among the rubble was window glass and a wealth of bronze, glass and metal objects. Several other Roman buildings, including a pagan temple, have been found in the immediate neighbourhood of the villa, and the collection of buildings gives us a clear picture of a complex and extremely prosperous country estate.

The coin evidence suggests that the villa continued in use until at least c. 380. In its final phase the house was damaged by fire. Whether this marked the end of occupation is not yet known: the earlier house, too, had been burnt during the second century, perhaps by accident. The latest object found here, a belt buckle of Roman official type, need not be later than c. 400, and the excavations showed that after its abandonment the villa was quarried for its stone, which was burnt in a lime kiln beside the house.

CHEDWORTH (Gloucestershire) (NT)
Chedworth is the best surviving Roman villa in Britain. This general view of the west wing shows the mosaic floor of the warm room, the hypocaust pillars of the hot room and the semi-circular bath

CHEDWORTH (Gloucestershire) (NT)
The Mediterranean life-style transported to the Cotswolds: a close-up of the western panel of the southern mosaic of the dining room

Cogidubnus himself; further work on the site has suggested a date a little after the invasion, and the owner has been identified as a Roman official or perhaps an Italian merchant, since the construction of the building seems very close to Italian models. In the last few years, however, the attribution once again to Cogidubnus, perhaps in the last years of his reign, seems to have become more acceptable.

Individual interpretations will always be disputed, but trends in villa building are now becoming apparent. In the first century of the province the numbers of villas remained comparatively low, but the buildings themselves included some of the largest houses built in Britannia. During the later second and the third century new large houses became rare, but the overall number of villas swelled threefold. Numbers reached a peak during the fourth century, a high proportion of them of only modest size. Whoever occupied the few large villas of the early province, by this date the proprietors are most likely to have been British natives. What this pattern seems to be showing is an expansion of Romanization, and a fashion for Roman building which descended the social scale to the level of farmers of only local importance. For many years it has been clear that the archaeological distribution of villas across the country is not even, and that the larger towns have normally more villas in their territories than do the smaller towns. Easy access to markets in the towns is the conventional explanation. To estimate the correctness of this, it is necessary to turn to a survey of town development.

TOWNS IN THE ROMAN PROVINCE

During the first century of the conquest, as we have seen, there was an expansion in the size of Roman towns, many of them on the old tribal centres of pre-Roman Britain. The rectangular layout of streets, and public buildings including the market-place (forum), and in a few cases temples to divinities from outside the island – the divine emperor in particular – shows the foreignness of the imposition. Excavations at the three towns burnt during the revolt of Boudica have shown numbers of small houses and shops, much as one would expect of a new and apparently thriving urban development, and though Tacitus' figure of seventy thousand victims of the revolt may well be exaggerated, he certainly envisaged a high population in these new trading posts of Camulodunum, Verulamium and London. If prosperity can be measured in terms of the laying out of public buildings, those towns located in the centre of the regions, which today archaeologists tend to call the 'civitas capitals', reached a peak of prosperity in the course of the second century.

During the next two centuries several linked trends are apparent. Throughout the empire, apart from the occasional gift from an interested emperor, the entire cost of public buildings fell as a public duty upon the decuriones, the town councils (made up of wealthy residents). In a British context these will presumably have consisted, to a large extent, of the old landowners and perhaps in some cases of others who had bought their passage into the landowning class. Enthusiasm for building in these circumstances could not always be assumed, especially, of course, enthusiasm for completing the works begun by others. Public building, begun so hopefully (and often on a very large scale) during the late first and early second centuries, eventually languished. In Wroxeter, for example, the city bath-house, still incomplete, was replaced by a huge forum, completed in AD 130, and burnt down about fifty years later. This was partially rebuilt, and was abandoned about AD 330, at about the same time as a nearby bath-house. In Exeter the baths seem to have fallen out of use as early as the second century, and even in London, a town apparently solely functioning as an administrative and trading centre (since it was a new foundation and had no predecessor as a tribal capital), the recent excavations have shown that the Cheapside and Huggin Hill bath-houses were demolished during the third century. At Silchester the current excavations have suggested that the great hall of the market-place was never even completed, and that metalworkers set up their workshops inside its shell.

All this points to a considerable decline in the '*civitas* capitals'. But it is during this same period that these towns were surrounded by walls. Considerable ingenuity has been spent in identifying the crisis which led to these urban fortifications. The walls themselves, however, seem to have been constructed over a long period, and include a strong feeling of simple show: at both London and York mural towers covered not the direction of likely threat but dominated the visitor's view on the river front. The towns, then, still contained structures which the town councils wished to enclose, and these seem to have been large town houses. Since most of these towns are the sites of modern cities excavations can only be partial, but the picture is emerging of large and widely spaced courtyard houses inside the third- and fourth-century walls. Of all these centres only Caerwent in South Wales presents us with rows of small, densely packed houses – the sort of thing which one would expect to find in a mercantile centre; and Caerwent, with its army base and iron mines nearby, was not a typical centre. Other evidence points to the continued importance of the '*civitas* capitals': cemeteries in Roman Britain are still surprisingly hard to find, considering the huge numbers who in the normal way of things must have died during the four centuries of occupation – perhaps as many as 50 or 60 million. The most obvious of these cemeteries lie around the '*civitas* capitals', at Winchester (Hampshire), Dorchester, or Cirencester. At the very least, this suggests that these towns remained religious foci for their regions. '*Civitas* capitals' do not, in short, appear to have had a strong marketing function, and their houses seem most likely to have been those of the rural landowners rather than of the poorer classes. Studies of the regional pottery industries confirm the pattern: in the beginning local potteries are common, but from the first to the fourth century the overall number of kiln sites declined; those in the countryside farthest from towns survived best, and in consequence became of increasing importance to the whole ceramic trade. The towns, particularly the '*civitas* capitals', played little or no part in this activity.

These '*civitas* capitals' were not the only towns in Britannia, and for the past twenty years increasing attention has been paid to the 'small towns' of the province. Some of these, especially in the south-east, replaced Iron Age settlements, but most seem linked to the road network, and prospered through good communications. In the main they lacked the elaborate public buildings found in the '*civitas* capitals', and the impression given by most of those excavated is that they were somewhat haphazardly laid out. Their buildings, however, included the small houses and workshops so conspicuously absent from the '*civitas* capitals', and the period during which they reached their greatest extent (when some were walled, and presumably achieved official recognition as towns) was in the third and fourth centuries, when the tribal centres had changed most from their early form. They thus seem to be settlements for marketing and production in a network – still presumably under the control of local magnates – separate from that of the '*civitas* capitals'.

The result of recent research, therefore, is beginning to give us a clearer picture of change and development in Roman Britain. The tribal centres which had formed in the

WROXETER (Shropshire)
A general view of the remains of the town, showing part of the public baths

initial years before the conquest, and which were then selected as the central points in the new provincial organization, at first included some of the elements – marketing and manufacture – common in long-established Mediterranean towns: the importation into Britain of a foreign mental blueprint of what a town should be. The country houses of this first period were large, and confined to the south-east, and may have been the residences of incomers. These early towns reached a peak in the second century, but changed gradually to become solely social and administrative centres for a landowning class whose country residences clustered around them. The marketing and production of the province developed separately in the rural industries and in the network of road-side settlements, some of which grew as large in area as the smaller '*civitas* capitals', but which lacked the numbers of the upper classes whose wealth provided the *civitates* with public buildings for communal display.

THE END OF THE PROVINCE

This discussion of the development of the Roman province of Britain has been almost entirely based on interpretations from the evidence of archaeology. The historical record, so helpful in tracing the course of the invasion and the early second century, is extremely scanty thereafter. After the withdrawal from the Antonine Wall we hear of barbarian incursions in 180; and the brief civil war fought in Gaul in 195–6 involved some of the army from Britain, under the Governor Albinus. Between 209 and 211 the Emperor Severus himself led a major invasion northwards, and was probably intending to extend Roman control at least into the lowlands of north-eastern Scotland, but he died in York in 211, with his conquest incomplete. The empire-wide crisis of the 250s

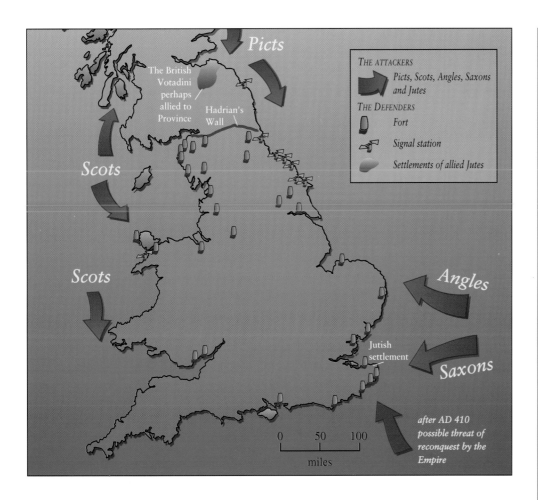

MAP 16: THE ENEMIES
OF ROMAN BRITAIN,
c. AD 350–450

The map shows in green those forts which are known to have been occupied at the end of the Roman control of Britannia, and the fortlets which are believed to have been built to form a signalling network against sea-borne raiding parties. In addition there are two areas in orange: the zone to the south of the Forth, the land of the Votadini, which is believed to have been in alliance as a buffer state between the province and the Picts; and the settlement of Hengest in Kent, which (whatever its outcome) was intended to support the provincial defences. In red are shown the apparent aggressors; in the case of Kent, it is hard not to see the threat as coming less from the Picts and Scots, as suggested by Gildas, than from continental Europe.

and 260s may have affected Britain, but there is little sign here of the dislocation of society and economy which is all too evident in Gaul, and the province was perhaps a mere spectator of the turbulent events abroad. The provincials may have favoured some withdrawal from the empire and its troubles: between 286 and 296 Britannia was controlled by two successive usurpers, Carausius and Allectus, who seceded from the empire, apparently with local support. It took a reconquest of the province by the Emperor Constantius in 296 to bring Britain firmly back into the western empire. Constantius himself returned in 306, to campaign in Scotland, allegedly with complete success, but (like his predecessor Severus) he died at York while returning southwards.

Excavation has revealed piecemeal repair and alterations to forts throughout these years, but few of these need be anything other than the normal maintenance of ageing buildings. In the later part of the third century and extending into the fourth, however, we can see signs of a new military policy. From East Anglia to Portchester in Hampshire a series of strong coastal forts shows us defence against an attack from the sea (a good example is Brancaster, Norfolk (NT)). Dates for their foundation are difficult to establish, but the earliest forts were probably being built in the 270s, and the latest, Pevensey in Sussex, perhaps about 330–50. Poorly sited for land communications, and thus inadequate as strongpoints to defend the interior of the province, they were probably intended as protected bases for the fleet which policed the Channel and the southern side of the North Sea. The name by which this region was known during the fourth century was the Saxon Shore, and the cause of this new building may have been the onset of raiders from the north German coastal plain.

It is evident that there was some trouble in the province in 342, when the Emperor Constans paid a hasty visit, and continuing discontent is obvious during and after the usurpation of Magnentius in 350. The provincials may again have been showing signs of secession, for the reprisals against them were heavy, and led to the suicide of the governor of Britain. Landowners and town councillors are likely to have been involved, and disturbances in villas, notably the abandonment of a large and recently rebuilt house at Gadebridge Park (Hertfordshire) have been attributed to this period.

During the 360s barbarian attacks increased, and in 367 a concerted assault from Picts, Scots, and Atecotti on Britain, and Franks and Saxons on Gaul, led (according to the somewhat biased account of Ammianus) to the collapse of the province into a 'chaos of barbarians and deserters'. In the next two years Britain was pacified and restored by a strong army under Count Theodosius, most of whose work seems to have been in the reorganization of military units and repair of the forts. A revolt during this period, however, suggests that independence and not restoration was favoured by some of the provincials.

From 383 until at least 388, and perhaps until the end of the century, Britain was once more in revolt, in support of a general, Magnus Maximus, who was successful in unseating the western Emperor Gratian. Maximus' eventual defeat by the emperor of the east, Theodosius, may not have led immediately to the restoration of Britain, for nothing is known of the province until 398 when campaigns were being fought against the northern tribes. This was the last effective imperial intervention in Britain; by 401 troops were being withdrawn to defend Italy against the Visigoths, and the collapse of the Rhine frontier under the onslaught of a wave of barbarians in 406 cut Britain off from the rest of the empire. The army in Britain elected a series of usurpers to the throne, the last of whom, Constantine III, crossed the Channel and managed to hold on to a ramshackle Gallic empire until 411. Though they lacked loyalty to the current emperor, both Maximus and Constantine III were clearly interested in the power and politics of Europe. What followed suggests that there were others whose interests were confined to Britain, for the British (according to the late fifth-century imperial official and historian Zosimus) drove out their governors and lived by themselves according to their own laws. Britannia was to all intents and purposes independent again.

VII
INDEPENDENT
BRITAIN

At the time the loss of Britannia may well have seemed simply another episode in that series of rebellions succeeded by reimposition of authority which formed the history of the Roman province since the second century. An army list, probably of the 420s, goes so far as to list the by-then-vanished regiments in their British forts, presumably as a temporary measure until such time as control could be re-established. Thanks to the deteriorating state of the western empire, and to increasing pressure from the barbarians in central Europe, the opportunity for a new invasion never arose, and Britain remained isolated. For nearly two centuries we have no reliable narrative of events in the island. Instead we have a handful of terse statements by continental writers (useful because they were contemporaries of the events, but provoking because their brevity makes it hard to see their meaning), and a farrago of native sources, many of which are full of detail, but incorporate so much mythology and legend that contradictions and errors abound. Scholars, in consequence of the inadequacies of the records, have adjusted some of the account to produce a narrative made more plausible by the inclusion of tales written down centuries after the event. Many parts of this traditional picture are quite reasonable, and very little is clearly impossible. Almost all of it, however, falls a long way short of certainty.

GILDAS AND THE *CHRONICLE*

At the root of our view of this period lie two principal narratives, those of Gildas and the *Anglo-Saxon Chronicle*. Gildas, by his own account, was born about AD 500, perhaps (as later legend tells us) in the British kingdom on the Clyde. He entered the Church, and is so particularly associated with South Wales that it is at least possible that he trained and worked there. He died, according to late sources, in 570. His most famous work, the *Ruin and Conquest of Britain*, belongs on internal evidence to the period about 540. His purpose, as he says, was to draw attention to the then current dangers facing his countrymen from the wickedness of their rulers and the corruption and indolence of their clergy, and this underlies his fifth-century 'history', a series of events picked out and dramatized to emphasize contemporary issues. The early fifth century was by then well outside living memory, and Gildas' account of it is garbled and obscure. It is a suggestive point: he had few documentary sources to help him, and the sort of events he describes, and the morals to be drawn from them, owe much to the Old Testament, in particular the Prophets, in whose footsteps Gildas was walking.

The *Anglo-Saxon Chronicle*, by contrast, is full of details, including dates, but how much its compilers really knew about the fifth and sixth centuries is doubtful, for the prototype of the various manuscripts which now survive was composed in the later ninth century, making use of earlier work such as Bede's *Ecclesiastical History*, Gildas himself, and other sources now lost – including foundation legends and battle myths. A traditional story, which itself might not be too far from the truth, is given a spurious precision by the expansion or contraction of its stages to fit the span of years available: the conquest of central southern England before the middle of the sixth century, for example, proceeded at strangely regular intervals – a recorded event about every five years.

This version of the conquest, the traditional Anglo-Saxon account, proceeds in three quite distinct phases, located in Kent, Sussex and Hampshire. We begin in the time of the Emperors Martian and Valentinian (that is, 449–56) when three boatloads of English, led by Hengest and Horsa, who had been invited over by Vortigern, king of the Britons, landed in Kent 'to fight against the Picts'. The strategic inappropriateness of Kent in this context has worried several commentators. Horsa was killed in 455, in a revolt against Vortigern, and between 456 and 473 Hengest and his son Oisc won three battles against the Britons. The accession of Oisc to the kingdom of Kent is noted under 488, but thereafter we hear no more of Kent for nearly a century. In 477 the account of Sussex begins, and from then until 491 Aelle and his son defeated the Britons of the south coast at regular intervals. In 495 the scene shifts to Hampshire, and from then until 547 the *Chronicle* ignores all episodes in the invasions other than the piecemeal conquest of Hampshire and Wiltshire. We hear of two sets of heroes, Cerdic and his son Cynric and their 'kinsmen' Stuf and Wihtgar, who appear at intervals of about six years from 495 to 544, and of Port and his sons Bieda and Maegla, who appear at Portsmouth in 501, and are never heard of again. At some point in this series of assaults, the invaders were defeated. Gildas gives us a date which might be close to AD 500 for a battle at a still unlocated 'Mons Badonicus', and implies that for forty-four years since then the British kings have been at peace. He warns that the Saxons still provide a threat. It is no surprise that English sources make no mention of the reversal, or of the enforced armistice, but their silence emphasizes the incompleteness of our records.

ARCHAEOLOGICAL PATTERNS

For over a century the results of excavation have been used to supplement this meagre historical record. In the 1840s and 1850s it was noticed that the pottery from crema-tion cemeteries in the Midlands so closely resembled that from similar sites in Germany (notably the Perlberg cemetery near Hamburg) that 'one single people was responsible: if it is German in Hamburg, then it is German in England'. The link was an important one, since the pottery in England had been attributed both to prehistory and to the Roman period, and now was set firmly in the period between the 'Roman withdrawal'

Rheged

Craven
Elmet
Peak

area of late
English control

- place-name including element 'walh' (e.g. Walworth, Walcot)
- place-name derived from Wicham and Wictun (e.g. Wickham, Wycombe)
- named kingdom of British origin

0   50   100

miles

MAP 17: THE ANGLO-SAXON SETTLEMENT: THE EVIDENCE OF PLACE-NAMES

Place-name evidence as well as archaeology can shed light on the process of settlement in the fifth and sixth centuries – as the map shows. Shown in green are place-names incorporating 'walh', signifying a foreigner, in this context a Welshman (i.e. a Briton), and in red those place-names where the English '-tun' and '-ham' are prefixed by the Old English 'Wic-', which is believed to be derived from the Latin 'vicus'. What emerges is that all over central and eastern England communities of British and Anglo-Saxon origin were living in close proximity to one another.

and the seventh century, when the arrival of Christianity was followed by the abandonment of pagan burial practices. Excavations and chance discoveries of the succeeding century-and-a-half broadened the picture, since pottery and associated metalwork of similar types were found in hundreds of cemeteries and on dozens of settlement sites. The material has been used to provide the answers to a series of questions: when and where is the earliest Anglo-Saxon occupation? From which part or parts of the continent did the people come? And how did the process of conquest spread across England? The conclusions gradually reached during the course of the last two generations often bore out the traditional historical account. The earliest pottery was identified in East Anglia and eastern Yorkshire; the closest parallels lay not in the nearest parts of the continent, but in the coastal plain to the west of the Elbe, and in the southern Jutland peninsula (that is, Saxony and Angeln); the changes of style in brooches, and to a lesser extent in pottery, suggested a spread across England to a line between the Pennines and the Wash by the end of the sixth century. Maps showing these largely cemetery-based distributions and the location of place-names of apparently early English origin indicated a broadly similar pattern.

To judge from the cemeteries, the earliest settlements of the Anglo-Saxons were not concentrated in any one area. Pottery and brooches of the first half of the fifth century have been reported from East Anglia, Yorkshire, Bedfordshire, and the Thames. These communities were widely scattered and mostly quite small. Material from Kent in this early phase is slight, and is perhaps not earlier than the middle of the fifth century, when the *Anglo-Saxon Chronicle* follows Bede in describing the arrival of Hengest and Horsa in the Isle of Thanet, and a little later the conquest of the county by the new-comers.

THE LAST BRITISH RULERS

To an observer across the Channel in Gaul the early triumph of the invaders would have seemed natural and inevitable. Imperial authority in the Gallic provinces had been effectively destroyed in the space of forty years or less – between the 450s and 480s. In Britain, however, despite the impression given by the rapid conquest of the south-east, native resistance turned out to be both stiffer and more prolonged. The rulers of the still-flourishing British states in the centre and south of the country were, for some time to come, to prove more than a match for their adversaries.

Gildas provides us with the names of some of these rulers. First in his list is Constantine, 'the tyrant offspring of the foul lioness', a man with a Roman name, recently deposed from power in Dumnonia, an area (Devon and Cornwall) then still known by its Roman name. Gildas' attention then turned northwards towards the Severn, to the Latin-sounding Aurelius Caninus ('immersed in the . . . morass of parricide, fornication and adultery'), perhaps in Gloucestershire or Gwent. To the west, in Dyfed, ruled Voteporix, 'tyrant of the Demetae besmirched with wickedness'. Between Dyfed and North Wales, and so presumably in the neighbourhood of Powys, Gildas places another king with a Celtic name, Cuneglasus, 'the opponent of men and God'. Finally he turns to Gwynedd in North Wales, whose king, Maelgwn (Maglocunus), the dragon of the island of Anglesey, was 'greater than almost all the commanders of Britain', but was 'more extravagant in sin', not least because he had taken and then renounced monastic vows. In Sir Frank Stenton's words 'a king who sinned in moderation had no interest for Gildas', and these five are the only named British kings of Gildas' time, though he clearly knew of more. He refers obliquely to commanders who will soon rise up against the sinful quintet and, unless they repent, bring vengeance on them. No further details identify the latter's kingdoms. One may have been Elmet, the upland and rolling region of West Yorkshire, which stretched from the Pennines near Leeds to the limestone ridge by the Great North Road. Another may have been Rheged, a northern kingdom which some have located in the vicinity of the Roman town of Carlisle, but which may have extended over the Pennines into the county of Durham. Further north lay Gododdin on the Forth, and the British-speaking kingdom of Strathclyde ('Valley of the Clyde') and its chief stronghold, Dumbarton ('fort of the Britons'), which remained independent until the eleventh century. All these were western and northern kingdoms, mostly in the uplands, and all survived at least into the seventh century. There must have been others further to the east, kingdoms whose very names are now lost, in the districts which passed into Anglo-Saxon hands in the late sixth century, in the generations after Gildas finished his *Ruin of Britain*. These eastern British regions may have included Wiltshire and a zone in the middle Thames, including Buckinghamshire and Bedford, which (according to the *Anglo-Saxon Chronicle*) was captured by the English in 571.

CHANGE AND DECAY IN THE ECONOMY

Despite much excavation in the past two generations remarkably little in these lowland kingdoms can be shown to belong to the fifth or sixth centuries beyond the pottery and metalwork which is conventionally attributed to the Anglo-Saxon immigrants themselves. Part of the problem lies in the abrupt ending of the importation of coins early in the fifth century, and part in the absence of dated inscriptions, which in any case had never been common in Britain. The end of the Roman pottery industry is normally placed in the generation around 420; but without the dating framework which coins and inscriptions provide we cannot be confident about either the date or the manner of the end of the Roman factories. The discovery of late Romano–British sherds in the same layers as imported Mediterranean pottery of a century or more later suggests that some continued longer than we now suppose.

The fate of the towns is crucial here. Trade and economic activity seem increasingly to have focused on the small towns that straggled along the network of Roman roads. The public towns, the 'civitas capitals', continued in use into the fifth century. At Wroxeter, near Shrewsbury, excavations have revealed a rebuilding in the area of the baths, perhaps of a mansion which continued in occupation until the sixth century. At Cirencester unpublished reports imply the use of the amphitheatre to the west of the town as a fortress while the town itself lay empty. At Verulanium/St Albans a water-pipe was laid, implying the survival during the fifth century of a community cooperating over municipal works.

But what sort of communities were these? The evidence from the last centuries of Roman Britain suggests that the walls of the *civitates* sheltered houses of high quality as well as public buildings and monuments of the kind that adorned every major Roman town. The houses were the dwelling-places of the upper-classes, the people whose presence in the *civitates* was essential to their functioning as administrative and social centres of their districts. As long as the upper-classes' security was assured, so too was that of the *civitates* they lived in; but in the fifth and sixth centuries it began to come under threat. The danger came from a number of quarters – partly from invaders, partly from lower-class uprisings, but most of all from the usurpation of power by individual members of the class itself. Large and well-ordered oligarchies gave way to smaller groups of despots, and these in turn to individual monarchs. As a by-product of this process the towns themselves changed in character. Where there were once rows of stately town houses, there were now single palaces with gardens providing accommodation for the new rulers. At York such a palace was formed from the great headquarters building of the legionary fortress; here and at London, Canterbury and Winchester the palaces were eventually joined by the cathedral churches built to serve the needs of the new Christian religion. The fate of the towns, therefore, is indicative of much more than a shift from one type of economy to another; it is evidence of the transition from the upper-class oligarchy of the Roman world to the dominance of monarchs that characterized the Middle Ages.

The Settlement Period: Archaeology Versus History

Research during the 1950s and 1960s changed the traditional account of the Anglo-Saxon invasions, and suggested that the first recorded Anglo-Saxon settlements of Hengest and Horsa in Kent were in fact late in the sequence of incursions. The argument turns on three elements, Romano–Saxon pottery, Germanic-style belt fittings, and fourth-century German pottery. In the first place, some Roman pottery of the fourth century was decorated with motifs that can be found in the pottery of the north German coastal plain. The distribution of this 'Romano–Saxon' ware is predominantly on the eastern side of England. In broadly the same districts bronze buckles and belt fastenings have been found in a series of graves and have been identified as Roman products ornamented in Germanic taste, suitable for the garments of Germanic soldiers, forerunners of Hengest and Horsa, perhaps installed to guard the Saxon Shore. Some cremation urns, notably from the cemetery of Caistor-by-Norwich in Norfolk, may be paralleled with Anglian pottery sometimes dated as early as the third century. The English cemeteries in which this early-looking pottery has been found lie close to Roman roads or outside the walls of Roman towns, implying that these features of the countryside were still the focal points of settlement at the time the burials were made. Altogether, then, we may suppose a period of controlled settlement of Germans on the eastern coast of England, perhaps during the fourth century, under the supervision of the Roman military authorities; this reconstruction of events is already beginning to appear (with the authority of 'the consensus of archaeological opinion') in recent general accounts of the period.

The case for early migrants, however, is less firm than it seems. The 'Romano–Saxon' pottery was a Roman product, and is found largely on purely Roman sites. Who used it we do not know, but parallels for the decorative motifs can be found in the pottery of Roman and even pre-Roman eastern England. The bronze belt fittings are entirely of Roman manufacture, and have no obvious connection with Germans. The early date for some urns is a complex matter, for the dating of the continental pottery, on which it depends, is not firm. There is, indeed, general agreement on the order in which fashions changed in the design of the pottery, but there are few chronological pegs on which this sequence can be fixed. In the last resort dates for metalwork or for pottery derive solely from documentary references or from coins, and the discovery of a coin in a buried pot demonstrates only that the pot was buried after the coin was minted.

A dating framework has been constructed from associations of this sort. The more associations there are, the more precise is the chronology. But this form of calculation can fix only the earliest possible time for a deposit, and can never prove a terminal date before which the objects must have been interred. When, as is normally the case, the principal dating is by means of Roman coins, the further from the area in which these coins passed as regular currency the more likely it is that the stray coins found in burials were already old when they were deposited. Errors are thus likely to lie on the side of too early date for objects far from the frontiers. In consequence, continental scholars have long worked on the basis that, since a contemporary Gallic chronicler attests that it was possible to believe that Britain fell into the hands of the Saxons in 441, the pottery and metalwork which is found on the continent but not in Britain must belong to the period before 420 or 430. Objects which are precisely the same in both Britain and on the continent must belong to the years of greatest contact, say the second half of the fifth century, and those which are judged to be of later types, and occur rarely on the *continent, must belong to a period of growing isolation and insularity in the sixth and seventh centuries.*

Fresh excavations since the setting up of this framework have revealed new objects, some of them of earlier types than previously found. These have been used to show that the arrival of the Saxons should be placed in the fourth century. The conclusion is probably incorrect: the identification of new early material shows simply that the dates given previously were too early, and that the pottery and metalwork attributed to the beginning of the period must be made a little later to accommodate the new material into the 420s and 430s. A measure of agreement has now been reached over the dating of important fourth-century German metalwork: all but a handful of these continental objects found in Britain belong to the early fifth century or later, and none is so firmly early that it must have been buried before the end of Roman administration in the province in the first decade of the century.

VIII
THE NEW KINGDOMS

Precisely where the mid sixth-century frontier lay between the new Anglo-Saxon territories and the British Kingdoms is unknown. A frontier of some sort there certainly was, for Gildas is able to speak of 'divortium', partition, with the barbarians. For two generations it must have seemed that the English land-taking had reached its limit, and few in Gildas' time can have suspected how swiftly their world was to change. The first hints come from the *Anglo-Saxon Chronicle* – which, of course, nowhere acknowledges the check to English progress. Under 552 the *Chronicle* records the start of a series of victories. These later chroniclers saw the foundation of the kingdom of Wessex as a single process, entirely the work of the ancestors of the then ruling house of Wessex. More recent historians have noted the excessive prolongation of the campaigns and the discrepancies in the early family tree of Cerdic's descendants. In the English victories in Wessex during the 550s and 560s we may see not the culmination of an English invasion, but the seizure of power, from the previous authorities, by a commander of the local troops, who may himself have been partly or wholly of British or Irish origin, but whose role was finally taken over by the English-speakers who founded the dynasty of King Alfred. It is an anachronistic view that British and Anglo-Saxons must needs be opposed. Gildas' civil wars were between British princes, supported by foreign troops; and among the first victories of Ceawlin, King of Wessex, was a war between English, the routing of Aethelberht of Kent. At this period we must envisage the formation of new kingdoms in the hands of men whom their descendants might consider kings, but whom their contemporaries might have called warlords or even brigands.

In the north we have a few brief historical notices to underline our ignorance of the formation of the great kingdom of Northumbria. Bede noted the beginning of the reign of Ida in 547, and derived the royal house of the Northumbrians from him; the version of the *Chronicle* copied at Peterborough adds that he built the fortress of Bamburgh, first enclosed with a hedge and later with a wall. Small-scale excavations within the medieval castle of Bamburgh are reported to have revealed that this great rock beside the Northumbrian coast was occupied from the Iron Age right through the period when the area was part of the Roman frontier zone, and that it was in use, perhaps as a military post beside a signal beacon, during the post-Roman period. Ida might then have fortified a coastal defence station, for which he, or some similar warrior, had been responsible, in the way suggested for Cynric and his associates in Wessex. The virtual absence, in the lands to the north of Hadrian's Wall, of pottery, metalwork, burials, or indeed of any trace of Anglo-Saxons at all, until the middle of the seventh century suggests that Ida's northern kingdom of Bernicia was a separate British territory.

The victor of the battle of Degsastan, and perhaps of Catraeth too (see p. 80), was Aethelfrith, grandson of Ida, a heathen king much admired by Bede for his strength and success. Soon after defeating Aedan, Aethelfrith supplanted his brother-in-law, Edwin son of Aelle, and took over the kingdom of Deira (roughly Yorkshire). The British territory of Elmet in western Yorkshire remained independent until soon after Edwin's restoration in 617, but with this exception Aethelfrith united in one kingdom all the lands to the north of the Humber and to the east of the Pennines, and towards the end of his reign he is found taking decisive action in the west, where, at the battle of Chester in 616, he defeated the princes of North Wales, and massacred 1,200 monks who had come from the monastery of Bangor-on-Dee with the army to pray for victory.

ST AUGUSTINE AND THE KINGDOM OF KENT

Bede's account of this deplorable incident reveals much about the relationship between the English and the British churches: the monks of Bangor, he says, were heretics who learnt through death the evil of their ways. Bede belonged to the English church, by then firmly Roman, and he was bitterly critical of the Celtic churchmen for their long neglect of their pagan neighbours. Nowhere do we hear of any attempt by British clerics to convert the English, and even when the latter became Christian the British clergy maintained their distance: we hear of them refusing to worship beside Angles, and of their insistence that an Englishman who joined them should previously undergo a purification fast of forty days.

It is, therefore, no surprise that those who converted the English came from abroad. The charming story of the encounter of the future Pope Gregory with English slaves in the market at Rome and his whimsical remark ('not Angles, but Angels' – an equal pun in Latin) is perhaps fanciful, though it has its modern supporters. Gregory planned at first to buy Anglian slave boys, train them and send them back as missionaries. In 596 he decided on a more direct scheme, and sent a legation under the leadership of St Augustine to Kent, the most continental of the English kingdoms. The Frankish kings, whose ancestors had been Christian for nearly a century, had just reached a concord with the Papacy after a series of squabbles, and supported the plan; and Bertha, the daughter of King Charibert of Paris, had for ten years or more been the wife of Aethelberht, King of Kent. Bede reports that Queen Bertha was accompanied to Kent by a Frankish bishop, that she practised her religion, and did this in an ancient church repaired for her in Canterbury, perhaps the church of St Martin on the hill to the east of the city. The Pope presumably knew something about southern England from Bertha's religious attendants, and there is clear evidence in the Kentish cemeteries of contact with the other side of the Channel. Brooches of the later sixth century, identical to those of the Franks of the Rhineland and eastern Gaul, have turned up in graves from the Isle of Thanet to the Sussex Downs.

ST MARTIN'S, CANTERBURY (Kent)
This was almost certainly the church used by Bertha, the wife of King Ethelbert. The core of the existing chancel (foreground) is Roman, and it is possible that worship has been continuously practised in the building since Roman times

The Bernicians and the *Gododdin*

*I*t was against the Bernicians – recently arrived Angles or British separatists under new leadership – that the forces of the north marched towards the end of the sixth century. In a particularly jumbled passage the ninth-century history of Nennius names four British opponents, the kings of Rheged, of Strathclyde, and two others, one who probably ruled Elmet in West Yorkshire and a king perhaps of Galloway. We do not know that the attack was concerted, though this is normally assumed; we know of three campaigns, only one of which is dated. First perhaps was a series of battles ending in the blockade of the island of Lindisfarne (NT) beside Bamburgh, which ended with the assassination of King Urien of Rheged, perhaps in the 570s. In 603 a combined army, led by King Aedan of Dal Riata (Argyll), and including a prince of the Irish Ui Neill, and the son of a former king of Bernicia, was decisively defeated at an unidentified place called Degsastan. Around 600, perhaps before the battle of Degsastan, a campaign took place about which we know more details than any other in the Dark Ages. Our source for this war is ostensibly contemporary, an epic poem attributed to Aneirin, the Gododdin, which survives in a Welsh manuscript copy of about 1250, in two versions, the longer of some eighty-eight verses. The treatment is lyrical: a series of heroes is honoured each with his own verse, praising his generosity and his prowess in battle, and lamenting his death – for all the army of the north except for the poet were killed by the Bernicians. It seems that Mynyddog, King of Din Eidyn (Edinburgh) assembled an army, mostly of his people, the British tribe from the lower Forth, whose ancient name (Votadini) had been transmuted into Gododdin. The army of three hundred warriors spent a year in truly heroic feasting, before riding to Catraeth:

> and there was slaughter. Though they were slain they slew, and they shall be honoured till the end of the world; and of all us kinsmen who went, alas, but for one man none escaped.

If the Catraeth of the poem is Cataracta ('Waterfalls'), the Roman name for the town of Catterick in North Yorkshire, as is widely believed, the tactics are clear. The men of Gododdin rode through Rheged, the British lands to the west of the Pennines, along the Roman road from Brough over Stainmore, and appeared in the plains of North Yorkshire. Had they been successful, we might have found out why they thus avoided the nearest enemy in Bernicia and went so far around. But, as it is, they were defeated, and the reasons for their offensive remain obscure. To speak, as some have done, of an attack to drive a wedge between the new English kingdoms of Bernicia (Northumberland) and Deira (Yorkshire) is to fit modern notions into the wrong age, for three hundred or even three thousand men cannot long provide a barrier between kingdoms. We may, of course, have in the poem no more than a celebration of a spectacularly unsuccessful cattle raid, an attempt to win booty and honour directed so far afield because Bernicia was too formidable to attack; hardly in that case the great war visualized by some commentators, even though the size of the disaster would justify the epic poem. Catterick was at a later period a royal centre for Deira, and those who wish to bring back some of the grandeur to the campaign may postulate an intended ambush of English nobles and kings. That Catraeth is Catterick is, of course, only a conjecture, and if Aneirin were calling by this place-name some other waterfall on some other river all we could know *is that the men of* Gododdin *were decisively defeated. The significance of the* Gododdin *in the history of the Dark Ages is thus two-fold: it emphasizes our profound ignorance of the real motives of the characters whose names are provided by our sources; and it shows us something of the courtly ideals which underlay the behaviour of the upper-classes, behaviour which scarcely differed among the British, the Irish, and the English, and which could hardly be further removed from the aspirations of the citizens of the* civitates *at the time of Tacitus. One may well doubt whether these aspirations had penetrated far into the notions of the Romano–British of the countryside, especially of the western uplands and the northern frontiers.*

King Aethelberht himself remains a shadowy figure, seen in a few chronicle entries, and through the eyes of the religious communities who were under his protection. An Aethelberht, who may have been this man, is recorded in 560; if so his reign spanned the period of the consolidation of the English kingdoms. What part he played in this is hard to see, since the only record of his prowess occurs in 568 when the new leaders of the West Saxons drove him back into Kent and killed two generals. Much must be omitted, for Bede, probably relying on his Kentish sources, describes the limits of Aethelberht's power as the Humber estuary, and includes him among the series of overlords, who in the old English speech were described as Brytenwealda, or Bretwalda – 'lord of Britain'. In his old age, when Pope Gregory's mission arrived in Kent, Aethelberht emerges as a lawgiver and statesman, who received the missionaries, housed them, and permitted them to preach, and who himself later accepted baptism, presumably when the success of the conversion of his people was assured.

Pope Gregory entrusted the conversion to Augustine, the abbot of the monastery in Rome which Gregory himself had founded. Augustine accepted the duty with reluctance, and his correspondence shows him to have been no enthusiast, but a serious man full of doubts, anxious to adhere strictly to the form of Christian obligations and practice. This severity of manner perhaps caused Augustine's principal failure: in a meeting arranged by Aethelberht, held somewhere in Gloucestershire, Augustine discussed with the leaders of the Britons the union of the British and Roman Church. The Pope had tactlessly placed the British under Augustine as archbishop, and the support which he was receiving from the leading king of the southern English and his own abruptness were sufficient to bring the discussion to an end, and to separate the two churches for centuries.

With kings of the English, however, Augustine and his successors had greater success. The King of Essex, Aethelberht's nephew, and Raedwald, King of the East Angles, and at that time an underking, both accepted baptism, but in neither case did their kingdoms pay much heed. Raedwald himself (much to Bede's distress) chose, through imperfect understanding, or a conservative wariness, to place the altar of Christ beside the old sacrificial table in his temple, and worshipped at each in turn. If, as many believe, it was Raedwald whose magnificent tomb was discovered in the boat-mound at Sutton Hoo (Suffolk), it seems that in death too the East Angles were cautious, for the pagan-seeming burial included apparent baptismal spoons, esteemed perhaps because of their assumed magic virtue.

KINGSHIP AND CHRISTIANITY

When Aethelberht died in 616, Raedwald had as his guest Edwin, formerly King of Deira (Yorkshire), but now exiled by Aethelfrith. In 617 Raedwald defeated and killed Aethelfrith in a battle to the south of Doncaster, and installed his protégé Edwin as king of a united Northumbria. By 625 Edwin extended his rule across the Pennines. In the process he annexed the kingdom of Elmet, whose last ruler had poisoned Edwin's nephew. On Edwin's accession Aethelfrith's own sons had more cautiously fled far to the north, among the Picts and the Dal Riata, where they awaited their opportunity. Edwin's overlordship was soon acknowledged by all the English kingdoms, and Bede is quite clear that his authority extended even over the islands of Anglesey (and so presumably over Gwynedd) and Man. For Bede, Edwin was the beneficent ruler, in whose realm 'a woman and a new-born child could walk from sea to sea without harm'. His second wife was a Christian, Aethelburh, daughter of King Aethelberht, and in the same way that the Roman mission had followed Bertha into Kent, so now Augustine's companion, Paulinus, followed the Kentish princess to convert Edwin and baptize thousands of his people.

The Roman mission had suffered reverses, and had even seen a temporary paganism in Kent, under Aethelberht's son and successor Eadbald, but now seemed to have won a breathing space. A cynical pagan of the seventh century, however, might well have noticed that conversion to the new religion was no sure way to victory in battle. Aethelberht was the last great king of Kent, and his Christian successors sank into increasing dependence on others. At the same time the other kingdoms touched by Christianity fell into decline, and the 630s, 640s and 650s saw the deaths of a series of Christian kings at the hands of heretics and pagans. Edwin, of course, had enemies among his underkings long before his conversion, quite apart from the dispossessed Bernician princes of the house of Bamburgh. We hear in 626 of a West Saxon plot of assassination which ended in the ravaging of Wessex and the killing of five West Saxon kings in retaliation, and there may have been other less dramatic incidents before the final rebellion. In 633 Edwin was opposed by a formidable combination of the old and the new – Cadwallon, King of Gwynedd, and Penda, who may already have been recognized as King of the Midlanders. At Haethfeld (probably in Hatfield Chase, near Doncaster) these remarkable allies, a Christian Briton and a pagan Angle, killed Edwin and swept away his brief empire.

Paulinus, Queen Aethelburh, and Edwin's children retired to the safety of Kent, and the conversion of Northumbria was abandoned. But after an extended campaign across the north in one of the sudden changes of fortune so common to the royal houses of the Dark Ages, Cadwallon was defeated and killed near Hexham, south of Hadrian's Wall, by Oswald, a son of Aethelfrith newly returned from exile in Dal Riata. As a result of his exile Oswald's Christianity was the teaching of the Celtic church, and with an enthusiasm that pervades Bede's account of his doings he obtained Irish missionaries from the Dal Riadic monastery of Iona, and settled them on another island, Lindisfarne, a short distance from his family seat at Bamburgh. By 635 Oswald had reestablished control over the southern kingdoms, but Penda and the Mercians remained unsubdued. Six years later at Maserfeld, Oswald met Penda in battle and was defeated and killed. The common identification of the site with Oswestry in Shropshire suggests that Oswald was the aggressor; but we know nothing with certainty, and Bede tells us little more than a series of edifying stories about the miracles achieved by the dismembered portions of the Northumbrian king's body.

BEWCASTLE (Cumbria)
Two views of the imposing 14 ft high cross, the lower one showing the panel of St John the Evangelist. The cross was once thought to be a memorial to Alchfrith, the son of King Oswiu, but historians are no longer so sure of its significance

In the wake of this defeat Oswiu, Oswald's brother, rallied what he could of the Northumbrian forces and established himself as their leader. Penda, in the meantime, consolidated his control of central and southern England. He interfered with impunity in the internal affairs of Lindsey (North Lincolnshire), Middle Anglia and East Anglia, and deposed a king of Wessex who gave him offence. Finally he collected an army, which contained the forces of no fewer than thirty underkings, and invaded Northumbria. Oswiu, considerably outnumbered, offered submission, but this was refused. In the battle which followed, however, at Elmet near Leeds, the tables were once more turned: Penda was killed, and his army routed. Oswiu as a result became supreme throughout England, and was counted as the seventh (and to Bede the last) overlord of Britain. His territory extended sufficiently far north to include even the once-powerful kingdoms of *Gododdin* and Rheged in what is today Scotland.

In Mercia, however, Oswiu's control proved transitory. Two years after Elmet there was a rebellion, and Wulfhere, a son of Penda, was proclaimed king. Oswiu's activities in southern England seem as a result to have become largely confined to developing contacts with the Church of Rome. In 664 at the Synod of Whitby he abandoned Celtic Christianity and adopted Roman forms, bringing his kingdom

The Anglo-Saxon Church

*A*lmost the only relics of the Anglo-Saxon period which still stand above ground are the churches. More than four hundred are known, and discoveries of unexpected Anglo-Saxon masonry within parish churches are still being made from time to time. Few of these, however, are in anything like their original condition, since almost all have been rebuilt – in some cases several times – in accordance with the fashions of later ages. They show us an interesting pattern of contacts with the continent of Europe, and indeed on occasion even with the East, and of foreign ideas interpreted and changed by often very insular and odd English tastes.

The early Roman Church of the fourth century, the period during which Christianity was set up as the official religion of the empire, was essentially urban, catering for often large congregations in the Mediterranean cities. In Britain, with its smaller populations, small Roman churches have been found, such as the apparent fourth-century church excavated within the Roman town of Silchester, and the very early, and perhaps Roman, shell of the tiny parish church of St Martin, just outside the walls of Canterbury. The organization of this officially recognized Church, so different from that of the early Christians, mimicked that of the empire itself, with a hierarchy of ranks ordered under bishops, whose territories took their name, the diocese, from the name used for the region of a Roman provincial governor. At this period Church and state were not merely in harmony, they were both aspects of the same process of governing.

A quieter and more contemplative life was found by hermits in the deserts of the Middle East. The disasters which befell the empire in the fifth century made withdrawal from the world an increasingly popular option, and the hermits were so numerous that organization of them into communities became essential: in this way monasteries came into being. No Roman monasteries have yet been found in fourth-century Britain; 'pagans' signifies country dwellers in Latin, and one may suspect that the new religion had not yet spread far beyond the towns. In the west, in Wales and in Ireland, however, Christianity survived the fifth century, and developed in comparative isolation from the Roman world. The west was a land without urban centres, with a terrain suitable for hermits, and the Celtic Christianity, which was eventually brought by missionaries from the west into Scotland and into parts of Anglo-Saxon England, was one whose bishops and abbots were based in monasteries and which included such archaic-seeming habits as an odd shaven hairstyle for a tonsure, Easter celebrated in accordance with an obsolete timetable, and priests who married – an early practice largely eliminated from the Roman world during the sixth century.

The Roman missionaries under St Augustine who converted Aethelberht's Kent after 596, and attempted the conversion of the rest of England, introduced the new styles of their world – Roman Easter, bishops' seats in towns, and a diocesan administration. Monasteries were founded, normally at first (even in Kent) under Irish monks, within old Roman walled areas, such as the forts of Reculver and Bradwell (Essex), perhaps because these former imperial defences by now belonged to the English kings, and could be given away. After the Synod of Whitby in 664 the Churches of the English kingdoms joined the Roman communion, but incorporated some insular practices. For example, whereas generally the male saints of the Roman Church were sanctified by their actions and the female saints

MONKWEARMOUTH (Tyne and Wear)
The west front and the doorway, both dating from the late seventh century, are the sole survivors above ground of the double monastery of Monkwearmouth and Jarrow, the home of Bede

by their virgin martyrdoms, in the English Church, until the onslaught of the Vikings and the consequent slaughter and beatification of priests, the saints were frequently royal females – princesses who were the leaders of monastic communities, in an age in which power and royal lineage were inseparable, and in which appointment as abbess was an alternative to dynastic marriage. Women could not become priests, and needed some male assistance with their work; in consequence of this arose double monasteries, in which communities of men and women lived under the control of an abbess.

The small shrines and open-air altars of pagan religions were unsuitable for the services of official Christianity, and, for their new churches, Roman architects imitated the public halls (basilicas) – law courts, market and bath halls – which they knew in the towns. The rectangular plan, with transepts and an eastern sanctuary ending in an apse, was well established by the time of the conversion of the English kingdoms; the basilical plan was brought into Kent, and is later found across the country. The best surviving example is the monastic church at Brixworth (Northamptonshire), perhaps of the eighth or ninth century. In the north a tall, narrow style of church is found: nearly complete examples can be seen at Escomb and Jarrow, in County Durham. They have been considered 'Celtic' because of the influence of the Celtic Church in the north, but Celtic parallels are hard to find, and it may be that they borrowed their design from the royal great halls of the period, such as have been excavated at Yeavering or Northampton. Even the largest of these buildings seem modest and primitive beside the basilical churches of Italy, but excavations in the small churches of the Rhineland and France have shown that this is not an insular phenomenon: the new churches were appropriate for landscapes in which population density was low, and worshippers few in number.

During the two centuries after 750 great changes in design are to be seen in the new churches of Europe. Some of these were ideas brought from the East, particularly from the great imperial capital of Constantinople, now Istanbul, the largest city in the world, where circular or square churches had become a fashion. These 'centre-plan' churches have been excavated in England, and may lie behind the odd English churches in which the 'nave' is a tower, such as at Barton-on-Humber. In Germany during the ninth century massive towers were constructed at the western end of churches. These too found their way into England, to be incorporated into the major churches at Winchester and Sherborne (Dorset). Later continental developments, which introduced twin western towers and the style which we call 'Romanesque', are poorly represented in England: it may be that the huge taxes collected to pay the Danegeld impoverished the patrons of church-building at the very moment when these new designs were becoming common. In consequence, when the Normans surveyed the churches of their new realm, they found them small and very old-fashioned. Within a generation all the Anglo-Saxon cathedrals and most of the abbeys had been demolished and were being rebuilt in Romanesque style.

BRIXWORTH (Northamptonshire)
One of the greatest surviving Anglo-Saxon churches; even without its former aisles Brixworth encloses a space as large as a medieval church

85

closer in spirit to Kent and to the Papacy, and making possible the Romanization of the whole Church in England. In 670 he was, perhaps in consequence of this concentration on religion, the first of the northern kings for nearly a century to die peacefully. Thereafter the authority of the Northumbrian kings continued to decay in a series of assassinations and secessions which do little to illuminate the confused history of the decline of the once great northern kingdom in the eighth and ninth centuries.

IX
THE RISE OF MERCIA

Penda was not the first king to rule over a state in the midlands, but he was the first to gain notoriety. His family, the Icelingas, took their name from Icel, a tribal leader who probably lived at the beginning of the sixth century, a period when pagan cemeteries and Anglo-Saxon objects become common in the midlands. The unity of Mercia survived Penda's death, and after two generations of disturbances, Aethelbald, descended from Penda's brother, assumed power. During a reign of more than forty years he re-established Mercian supremacy over southern England. In a charter of 736 gifting land in Worcestershire, Aethelbald described himself as 'King not only of the Mercians but of all provinces which are called by the general name Sutangli [South English]'. As if this were not enough, at the foot of the document, which still survives in the British Museum, Aethelbald had himself written down as 'Aethelbald, King of Britain'. Some confirmation of the extent of his influence comes from other land charters, for in them the king appears as the donor of land in other kingdoms, as the conqueror of part of the West Saxons in Somerset, and as the remitter of tolls on ships coming into the Port of London. Far off in his monastery of Jarrow on Tyne, Bede noted in 731 that the English provinces as far as the Humber were at that time subject to the Mercian king. After Bede's death the historical record, especially in the north, is poor for nearly a century, but it is clear that Aethelbald was a king in a true barbarian mould, tyrannical and violent, and in consequence of some unknown feud in 757 he was murdered in his palace near Tamworth (Staffordshire) by his own bodyguard.

On Aethelbald's death the Mercian hegemony at once collapsed, but the throne was seized by another distant relative of the Icelingas, the last of the great Mercian kings, Offa. In his case for almost the first time in the post-Roman centuries sufficient contemporary records survive to allow us to form an impression of a ruler more detailed than the bare record of his accession, family, victories and death. A renaissance of learning led, in both England and the Frankish kingdom, to the writing of many more charters, letters and literary works than before, and from these a picture can be built up of the career and achievements of the great king.

Offa's first years were spent in a steady expansion of his authority beyond the boundaries of Mercia. Some of the stages can still be recognized: early in the 760s he

Early Mercia

Something of the early development of the area may be glimpsed in a brief, fascinating and controversial document, now preserved in manuscripts of the eleventh century and later, and generally known as 'The Tribal Hidage'. The text consists of a series of names of peoples, followed by a number of land units:

Of the dwellers in the Wrekin, 7000 hides; of the dwellers in the Peak, 1200 hides; of the dwellers in Elmet, 600 hides; Lindsey 7000 hides with Haeth feld land [Hatfield] . . .

and so on through central and southern England, until the text closes with more summary mention of the southern kingdoms:

East Anglia, 30,000 hides; Essex, 7000 hides; Sussex, 7000 hides, and Wessex, 100,000 hides.

The document is undated, but is clearly Mercian in its interests, and belongs to a period of Mercian dominance not only over the south, but also over the extremity of Northumbria itself – Elmet and the Lindsey and Hatfield Chase: debatable lands (map 18). The eighth century, a period of complete Mercian supremacy, is the normally assumed date for the compilation. There is much to be said, however, for the proposal that the Tribal Hidage reflects the situation of the later seventh century, perhaps during the last years of Wulfhere, after the renewal of war with Northumbria.

Whatever the date of the list, there is no doubt about its purpose. Like the familiar (but probably slightly earlier) Senchus fer nAlban of the kingdom of Dal Riata, the Tribal Hidage is a survey of tributary lands, in the English example measured for tax purposes in terms of the hide – once the land needed to support a household, but here a notional and perhaps quite transitory assessment of the value of lands and a calculation of the extent of the obligations laid upon its occupants. The names of peoples fall into three different classes: kingdoms, provinces and small tribes. In the first category are well-known names of independent kingdoms: Wessex, Sussex and the rest. The large single assessments for these must represent the comparative indifference of the Mercians to the details of tax collection in these areas: this must have been left to local officials to organize. In those midland districts which formed part of Mercia itself, or of the adjacent regions, however, the treatment is different, and we can see in detail what elsewhere is only hinted at – that a kingdom might consist of many tribal groups, distinguished by a district name (the Peak-dwellers) or by the name of a kindred (the Hurstingas or Faerpingas – the people of Hursta or Faeppa). Because of the manner of tax assessment we cannot be sure to what extent the groups varied in real size, but a genuine difference can be seen between, for example, the round figure of 7000 hides attributed equally to tributary kingdoms and to provinces of Mercia, and the 300 or 600 hides which are the assessment for many of the smaller units, some of which are never heard of again, in the marshy lowlands of middle Anglia. When we look more closely at these internal subdivisions of the Mercian kingdom we can see a major block, which is 'what was first called Mercia', in the middle Trent around Lichfield and Derby. Whatever its origins, by the date of the Tribal Hidage this region was a unity. To the north and to the west, however, lay other large provinces of Mercia, two of which (the people of Elmet and of the territory of Wroxeter (Wocensaetna)) were the former lands of independent British kingdoms. The Western Men may represent the once independent British kingdom of the Hwicce (Hereford and Worcestershire). Mercia was thus divided into small eastern and large western districts, which remained distinctively separate enough to provide the basis for tax collection, and presumably for other local administration too. The *eastern and the western divisions correspond remarkably with archaeological findings: 'Germanic' pots and brooches are confined to the east of Mercia. Where this material is common, the Mercian districts were small; where it is rare or non-existent the provinces were large. If the pottery really does represent the presence of Anglo-Saxons, then their coming led to a fragmentation of power. In other areas local administration was in large blocks of territory which seem to correspond to earlier* civitates *or* tribes, *which had survived the end of Roman Britain, only to be swallowed up by the new ruling classes.*

Some of these tribal groups must have had their own rulers, including men who even in the eighth century might be allowed the name 'king', if only in the form subregulus, *'underking'. Among such men must be counted the four* subreguli, *including the king of the Hwicce, who witnessed the confirmation of a grant by Firthuwold, yet another* subregulus, *of an estate to Chertsey Abbey (Surrey). Other names for such rulers are found: prince (princeps), duke (dux), count (comes), and more generally, in English, ealdorman. By the eighth century most of these men were the officials of the greater kings, but their position was normally hereditary, and among their ancestors they could count independent monarchs of the lands of which they were now the administrators. In the Tribal Hidage we see an intermediate stage between the disunity of initial conquest and the fully developed kingdoms of the ninth century. But the extent to which the independent outlook of the component parts of a kingdom had by then been eradicated is exaggerated by our sources, which concentrate on the leading families of a province: the consequent emphasis on the history of single royal dynasties conceals the fragility of the bonds between the various parts of their realms.*

made grants of land in Kent, and in 765, as overlord, he confirmed a charter of a sub-king of Kent. In 771 he is recorded as conquering the people of the Kent–Sussex border, the Haestingas. A victory in 779 led to the absorption into Mercia of the Wessex lands north of the Thames, and perhaps to formal submission: in his earliest charters he called himself merely 'king of the Mercians'; during his last twenty years, however, he appears as 'king of the Angles', and once (though in a copied charter whose accuracy is disputed) even as 'king of the whole land of the Angles'. The reality behind these words is made clear by Offa's own charters, and by the charters of others in Kent and Sussex which, after compilation, were taken to Offa for confirmation; indeed, when King Ecgberht of Kent gave land to Christ Church, Canterbury, without prior approval, the lands were confiscated on the grounds that it was wrong that a minister should give away without licence property that his lord had given him. It is as part of the same pattern that King Osmund of Sussex appears in another of Offa's charters merely as 'Duke Osmund'. Despite occasional opposition the south-east remained in the hands of the Mercians, and the principal port of the Thames, London, became a Mercian town, from time to time the residence of Mercian kings and the meeting place of the Mercian council. Other areas felt Offa's hand: in Wessex the king placed a protégé on the throne, and maintained him against rivals; in East Anglia, for an unknown cause, he ordered the execution of King Aethelberht.

The clearest sign of the growing power of Mercia is not to be found in the written record at all, but in the surviving banks that marked the western frontier. From the mouth of the River Wye, near the boundary between Gwent and Gloucestershire, to the River Dee at Basingwerk in Clwyd is a distance of more than 120 miles. Along this line

REPTON (Derbyshire)
The crypt under the church, built in
the early ninth century as part of the
mausoleum of the kings of Mercia.
Aethelbald, Offa's predecessor, was
buried here

a massive earthwork, with a ditch originally about 24 ft broad on its western side, winds through the high foothills of the Welsh mountains. It generally maintains a position which commands approach routes to it from Wales, and effectively controls the driving of animals back into Wales after cattle-rustling. Recent studies have shown that this massive barrier was built in several stages, and included two or more earlier earthworks to the north near Flint. An eighth-century date seems reasonable for most of this, and the statement made at the end of the ninth century by King Alfred's biographer is credible, that this great earthwork, generally known as Offa's Dyke, was the work of Offa of Mercia. Border incidents between Gwynedd and Mercia are occasionally recorded in the 760s and 770s, and provide a context in which the colossal works were undertaken (after 787, according to the uncertain witness of much later Welsh account) and the scale of the building, and the consequent complexity of its organization, reveal very clearly both the ruthless vision and the manpower to carry it out, which a great king of Mercia could deploy.

All this raises the achievement of Offa high above that of earlier kings, but the picture is still one-sided, for in the final decade and a half of his forty-year reign Offa developed an influence which spread further than that of almost any other English monarch until the Angevin kings of the twelfth century. We see this most clearly in the surviving copies of letters which were sent to Offa from the Frankish kingdom, some from the simple and elegant pen of the Englishman Alcuin, once master of the archbishop's school at York, and later abbot of the ancient monastery of St Martin at Tours. One of Alcuin's letters shows Offa's concern for education at his court. Alcuin is sending one of his pupils to teach in Mercia, as Offa had requested, and he asks the king to look after him: 'Do not let him wander in idleness or take to drink, but provide him with pupils, and strictly charge him to teach diligently.' A letter from Charlemagne himself, to his 'Dearest brother, Offa, king of the Mercians', tells us something of the delicate negotiations underlying international trade and the extent to which even great kings might involve themselves, not merely in the promising of protection to each other's nationals, but even in the dimensions of grinding stones or the length of imported cloaks.

During the same period some traces appear of what should be called a religious policy. When St Augustine came to England he had intended to base the new Roman Church on the old provincial capital of London, but trouble with the Londoners and the then supreme position of the king of Kent made Canterbury the only suitable seat for an archbishop. Later, the growing power of the Northumbrians made a second province, based on York, desirable. Now in the changed circumstances of the eighth century, with a Mercian king dominating southern England, some shift was sought, and in 787 the province of Canterbury was split to create a third archbishopric, with its seat at Lichfield, close to the old Mercian royal centre of Tamworth. The attempted reform was unpopular with the established clergy, but was carefully managed: papal legates (whose report to the Pope still survives) attended synods in Mercia and Northumbria, and wrote favourably. Offa (who received the Pope's 'sacred letters with immense joy', as the legates noted) promised to pay an annual gift to the Pope of a gold coin every day, and was allowed his Mercian archbishop.

The respect for the Holy See, the desire to bring the Church more closely into harmony with the kingdom, the development of a secretariat capable of bureaucracy, and the growth of a centralized autocracy at the expense of regional separatism and of the ambitions of less powerful men – all these trends in the work of Offa paralleled that of Charlemagne; and Offa's new midland archdiocese is perhaps a reflection of the new centre which the Frankish king was at that time creating around his palace at Aachen, for the kingdom of Mercia still lacked a proper focus for Church and state in its own heartlands. But, to an extent even greater than the Frankish empire, the new Mercia was dependent on a single man, and Offa's attempts to ensure the succession of his son Ecgfrith proved disastrous. In 787 Ecgfrith was consecrated king in his father's lifetime, the first time we hear of the consecration and not the simple election and acclamation, of an English king. This was in accord with the recent continental practice of the Carolingians, and gave the chosen successor something of a head start over his rivals. But Offa was more ruthless, and by the time of his death in 796 he had killed all other claimants to his throne. When Ecgfrith died without heirs after a reign of less than four months there was no obvious successor from the immediate family, and the choice fell upon a distant relative, a remote descendant of Penda's youngest brother, who seems to have had neither the claim to loyalty, nor (despite a thorough ravaging of Kent) the energy of the old king. By the beginning of the ninth century the decline of Mercia was clear, but the pattern had been observed as early as 797 by Alcuin, who wrote to a Mercian ealdorman:

MAP 18: THE GROWTH OF MERCIA

The map shows the regions which were tax units in the Mercian kingdom at some point between c. 670 and c. 830. It is based on the 'The Tribal Hidage', a manuscript of the eleventh century, the date of whose archetype is still uncertain, but may be c. 670. What emerges clearly from the map is how the local administrative units then in vogue fossilized the quite separate origins of the various parts of the kingdom.

territory probably once Romano-British tribal area

'Ancient Mercia': the heartland of the kingdom

approximate area of 'foreign', i.e. non-Mercian, tributary kingdoms

area of most frequent Anglo-Saxon finds

( ) location conjectural

Elmedsoetna

Heath feld land

PECSAETNA

LINDES FARONA

(Bilmiga)

MYRCENES LANDES

WOCEN SAETNA

(Wigesta)

?Widerigga North gyrwa
Sweordora South gyrwa

EAST ENGLE

Arosaetna

West Wixna *East Wixna*
(Spalda)

?WESTERNA

HEREFINNA

(West East)
(Willa)

HWINCA

Gifla Hicca

?Faerpinga

CILTERN SAETNA

EAST SEXENA

(UNECUNG-GA)

(NOXGAGA)

?HENDRICA

(OHTGAGA)

CANTWARENA

WEST SEXENA

SUTH SEXENA

Wihtgara

0   50   100

miles

The vengeance for the blood shed by the father has come upon the son . . . [the killing] was not a strengthening of his kingdom but its ruin.

Mercia was pre-eminent among the English kingdoms in the eighth century. The next century was to see the rise of Wessex as the new great power in the south. But the emergence of Wessex was coupled with much more striking changes than a mere transference of hegemony, for in the last years of King Offa a new and, it seems, unexpected threat had arisen, as shiploads of Scandinavian pirates began to ravage the coasts of Britain.

X
WESSEX AND THE CHALLENGE OF THE NORTHMEN

It is nearly three hundred and fifty years that we and our fathers have inhabited this most lovely land, and never before has such terror appeared in Britain from a pagan race, nor was it thought that such an attack from the sea could be made.

Letter of Alcuin to King Aethelred of Northumbria and his counsellors, summer 793

On 8 June 793 the monastery of Lindisfarne was pillaged and some of its inmates killed: a carved stone from the site, depicting a row of men holding weapons, may even be a crude memorial to the dead. Alcuin promptly wrote a series of horrified letters about the attack, advising defence by prayer, modest dress and canonical behaviour. At about the same time – the event is not precisely dated – three shiploads of Northmen landed on the Dorset coast at Portland. The royal reeve of King Beorhtric of Wessex came up to them, believing them to be merchants. According to the chronicle written in the tenth century by ealdorman Aethelweard:

He addressed them in commanding tones, and ordered them to be brought to the king's vill. But he was killed at once, together with his companions.

The middle of a raid was no time to enquire the place of origin of the pirates, and there is understandable confusion about the nationality of these and other groups of Scandinavian Vikings. Some versions of the *Chronicle* state that the Portland raiders came from Hordaland, the hinterland of Bergen between Hardangerfjord and Sognefjord in Norway, and it is possible that the raiders on Lindisfarne were Norwegians. To English chroniclers of the eighth and the ninth centuries the pirates were *pagani* or heathens, or very often simply 'Danes' – even in one entry which attributes their origin to Norway. At most periods the chroniclers of the Franks called all of them simply 'the Northmen'. A similar uncertainty surrounds their earliest activity outside Scandinavia. Alcuin found the Lindisfarne attack unexpected, but he was far off. A few Kentish charters of this period (one even before the Lindisfarne raid) include references to defences against seaborne raiders. Piracy was on the increase, and in the space of five years we hear of a spate of attacks, which might even have been the work of a single freebooting fleet. Iona was plundered, and part of the Dal Riadic kingdom of Kintyre; then followed raids on the Irish coast, Man, and Morganwg in South Wales. In 799 raiding spread to islands off the coast of Aquitaine in France. Thereafter through most of this area the raids ceased as suddenly as they had begun, and nearly two generations were to pass before they were resumed. Only in Ireland and the Western Isles is it clear that Scandinavians were still active: 'The sea', proclaimed the Annals of Ulster under the year 820, 'spewed forth floods of foreigners over Erin', and in 807, after three devastations of Iona, the survivors built a new monastery in the greater safety of the Irish mainland at Kells.

THE RISE OF WESSEX

At about the time that the spate of raids was drawing to a close a major shift was occurring in the balance of power in England. Mercia under Offa's successors was going rapidly into decline. Wessex under King Egbert was at the same time moving equally rapidly into a position of ascendancy. A series of campaigns in the 820s gave Wessex control of the former kingdom of Kent – an achievement significant because it provided access to the trading wealth of London and the south-east. In 825 the revolution was completed by Egbert's defeat of Beornwulf of Mercia at Wroughton near Swindon in Wiltshire. There were to be revolts in Mercia against Wessex rule in the 830s, but never again was Wessex supremacy to be successfully challenged by a native English dynasty.

This same quarter of the ninth century also saw the beginnings of a shift in the balance of economic power in England. In 838 Egbert defeated the Cornish, and brought their independence to an end. Henceforth it was the wealth of the south-west rather than of the south-east which was to underpin dynastic imperialism. By the end of the 800s Alfred and his sons were tapping the profits of tin-mining in Devon and Cornwall and, still more significantly, of silver-mining on the Mendips in Somerset to bolster their military endeavours. Possession of that wealth was to be crucial to them in the long struggle that lay ahead with the Vikings.

THE COMING OF THE GREAT HEATHEN ARMY

From the 830s for more than half a century there are few years in the Irish annals in which Viking outrages are not recorded. The entries generally lack detail, and little emerges from the simple lists of battles, burned monasteries and deaths. In England at this time the *Chronicle* records the start of the second wave in Egbert's last years, when 'heathen men' ravaged the Isle of Sheppey in the Thames estuary. For nearly twenty years thereafter the victories and defeats of the ealdormen and kings of Wessex are reported. The enemy are normally 'heathens' or 'the Danish here (force or band)', and are counted, if at all, in shiploads. In 836, for example, thirty-five (or in some manuscripts, twenty-five) ships' crews were defeated by King Egbert at Carhampton in Somerset; in 840 thirty-three ships' crews were defeated at Southampton. In 851 an ominous development was noted: the Vikings did not return home in the autumn, but built a camp in the Isle of Thanet, and remained through the winter. In the same year a huge army, believed by the chronicler to be 350 shiploads, captured Canterbury and London, and defeated the opposing Mercian army.

The numbers involved in these raids need not have been very large: a force which filled thirty-five ships perhaps numbered under a thousand in all – sufficient to terrorize a region, but few enough to be defeated by the levies of a province under its ealdorman. Historians have been inclined to accept these modest figures as genuine. The huge totals of 851 and subsequent campaigns, however, have proved harder to believe, and serious objections have been raised to the estimates of ten thousand or more men which the figures imply. One may well accept that the English chroniclers exaggerated the numbers to excuse the English defeats, and inflate their victories, without necessarily agreeing to the likelihood of one figure over another. The army of 851, at all events, was small enough to be defeated, probably somewhere in Surrey, by Egbert's son Aethelwulf and his Saxon levies. From time to time in the next few years fresh devastations are recorded. But these could not have been too serious because in 853 the kings of Wessex and Mercia made a joint expedition, not against the Vikings, but against the Welsh, whose submission they received. The chronicler, writing later in the century with the gift of hindsight, chose to highlight the Viking raids because they were to be a problem in his own day. But this does not mean that they were a problem half or three-quarters of a century earlier. The people of Frankish Europe and, in the British Isles, of Scotland and Ireland probably suffered a good deal worse than the English did.

In the year 865, however, the Vikings shifted their focus of activity significantly. Around that time a host, called by the *Chronicle* the 'micel here' (great army), arrived in East Anglia and so intimidated the people there that they supplied them with horses to go away. The *Chronicle* does not say who the leaders of the forces were, but later sources name Ivarr Ragnarrsson and his brothers, the former leaders of Viking Dublin, and it may be that the whole enterprise was managed from there. In 867 the army moved north and took York. Two Northumbrian kings, a usurper and his predecessor, were killed, and the survivors made a hasty peace. In 868 the army moved south into Mercia, and was inconclusively blockaded at Nottingham by the combined forces of Wessex and Mercia. The army then withdrew northwards under truce, and ravaged Northumbria. In York a puppet king was set up to rule in the Danish interest, and the army crossed again to East Anglia where they fortified a base at Thetford. It may have been their plan to take booty and to set up another friendly king. In the event King Edmund of the East Angles refused their demands and was executed by the Vikings, who took over his kingdom. His cult laid the basis of the prosperity of the future abbey of Bury St Edmunds.

Ivarr himself then went back to his base at Dunbarton, in Scotland. In the following year he returned to Dublin with his booty, and died there in 873. Meanwhile the great army, under the command of his brother Halfdan, advanced to Reading, where King Aethelred of Wessex and his brother Alfred were defeated outside the gate of the Viking camp, but saved the situation four days later by a second battle to the south, on the Berkshire Downs, when Halfdan's ally and five of their jarls (earls) were killed. A series

MAP 19: THE ANGLO-
SAXONS AND THE
VIKINGS

*The first phase of the
invasions is shown by the
Burghal Hidage forts, which
defended Alfred's Wessex
before c. 920, and the
comparable fortresses of the
Danish Boroughs. The second
phase is shown by the place-
names of Danish and
Norwegian origin, which mark
the Scandinavian settlement.
The final stage is shown by the
forts of Edward and
Aethelflaeda, which lie on the
boundaries of an expanding
kingdom of Wessex.*

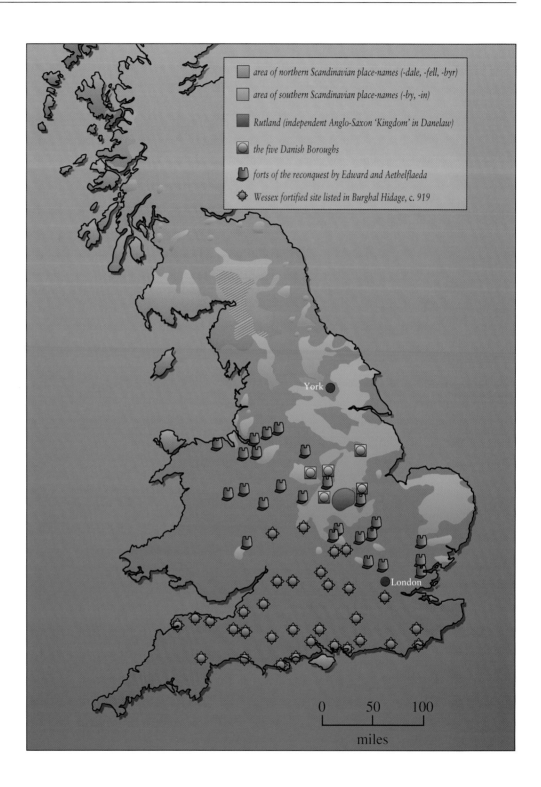

area of northern Scandinavian place-names (-dale, -fell, -byr)

area of southern Scandinavian place-names (-by, -in)

Rutland (independent Anglo-Saxon 'Kingdom' in Danelaw)

the five Danish Boroughs

forts of the reconquest by Edward and Aethelflaeda

Wessex fortified site listed in Burghal Hidage, c. 919

York

London

0   50   100

miles

of indecisive battles followed, until at Easter 871 Aethelred died, and was succeeded by
his brother as King of Wessex. A month later, at Wilton near Salisbury, Alfred was
defeated in battle by a Viking army much stronger than before, since another host, led
by three kings, the most important of whom was the Danish Guthrum, had just arrived.
The peace which Alfred now made was conditional upon tribute, and the Danes moved
down to London, where the Mercians too made peace. A remarkable charter of 872
records the sort of peace made, whereby the Bishop of Worcester leased two hides of

land to raise money 'chiefly because of the now pressing affliction and immense tribute paid to the barbarians, when the pagans stayed in London'.

After the submission of the Mercians the Viking army split by arrangement into two parts. Halfdan took his host, who had come with him and his brother Ivarr into England ten years before, and went into Northumbria, to the Tyne, whence they pillaged the Picts and the Britons of Strathclyde. Finally in 876 the bulk of the army divided up the land of the Northumbrians – almost certainly meaning the Vale of York, where the Scandinavian place-names include a greater proportion of archaic personal names than elsewhere in England – and turned themselves, perhaps with relief, into landed gentry.

In 875 the second part of the great army, under Guthrum (who may have been allotted the kingdoms to the south of the Trent), transferred operations from Repton in Mercia to Cambridge, and then advanced southwards to subdue Wessex. His attempts in 876 and 877 were notably unsuccessful, and disagreement in the Danish army is clear, for some of the warriors decided to abandon the war and settled down on the land. The eastern part of Mercia was divided up and taken over for farming, principally in the shires of Lincoln, Nottingham, Derby and Leicester, where the place-names show dense Scandinavian settlement. In January 878 Guthrum, whose army was by now comparatively small, attempted a sudden attack on Wessex, and occupied Chippenham, a royal manor. Though the *Chronicle* does not say so, his purpose was probably to catch King Alfred while he was celebrating Christmas with a few followers, and thus to put an end to Wessex's independence with a single blow. Alfred, however, eluded capture and escaped to the Somerset marshes where he fortified a small island. At about this time another of Ragnarr's sons attacked the north Devon coast, presumably in a concerted attempt to trap Alfred, but was killed by the local Saxon levies. Guthrum, who had been settling his men around Chippenham, was subjected to guerrilla attacks, and was provoked into a battle at Edington, in which Alfred was victorious. After negotiations the Danish army came to terms; Guthrum accepted baptism, and, in due course, led the remainder of his men into East Anglia where he settled down and even issued coins under the Saxon name Athelstan, which Alfred had given him at his baptism.

While these agreements were being made, another Viking fleet, the third in this series of great armies, arrived in the Thames, where it fortified a camp at Fulham. The settling of the war with Wessex presumably persuaded the newcomer that at that time there were no advantages to be gained in England, and so they moved their operations across the Channel to Ghent. For the next five years the *Chronicle* observed their ominous progress across the tottering Frankish empire. By 885 they were ready to try their fortune again in England, but a siege of Rochester proved fruitless, and, on the approach of Alfred and his levies, most of the Vikings withdrew to Paris, where for another seven years they pillaged the lands of the Franks. The siege of Rochester had shown the vulnerability of the Thames, and in 886 Alfred therefore took London and repaired its fortifications, entrusting it to Aethelred, a Mercian ealdorman. Aethelred married Alfred's daughter, the formidable Aethelflaed, and remained, until his death in 911, the principal defender of the northern borderland of Wessex. Shortly after the seizure of London, Guthrum and Alfred agreed a frontier from the Thames through Bedfordshire and along the line of the old Roman Watling Street from London to the West Midlands, a frontier which formed the division between the English and Danish kingdoms; the latter area was afterwards called the Danelaw.

THE ALFRED JEWEL
This famous 'Jewel', now in the Ashmolean Museum, Oxford, was possibly the pendant of a bookmark. Its association with King Alfred rests on the inscription around the edge, 'AELFRED MEC HEHT GEWYRCAN' ('Alfred had me made')

In 892 the third army returned from its continental exploits, and the larger part entrenched itself on the Sussex coast, while a smaller force encamped in northern Kent. The subsequent campaign, traced in detail in the *Chronicle*, was more rapid and wider-ranging than the previous onslaughts, and the Vikings, from their allied bases in East Anglia, were able to launch successive raids as far as the middle Severn near Welshpool, Chester, and Bridgnorth in Shropshire. English levies followed the invaders and sometimes blockaded them, but were unable to force a decisive engagement. Equally, the Vikings were unable to do more than forage: they were unable to establish a secure foothold in English territory, and the kingdom of Wessex remained united. In 896, therefore, the army broke up, some Vikings joining in the settlement of East Anglia and Northumbria, while others, who had not yet made enough capital to settle down, returned to the rewards of pillaging the Carolingian empire. 'By the grace of God', the *Chronicle* records, 'the army had not on the whole affected the English people very greatly'.

XI
THE RECONQUEST OF ENGLAND

Alfred died in 899 with a still largely hostile Danish people in occupation of his frontiers. The reconstruction which he had begun was continued by his son, Edward the Elder (899–924), and daughter Aethelflaed and son-in-law Ethelred, ealdorman of the Mercians. The main area of conflict lay to the north of London, and Edward and his allies built fortifications to check the Danish incursions. The first of these lay in a belt from Hertford to Bridgnorth. Subsequently the Anglo-Saxon territory was extended northwards by new defences at Tamworth and Stafford, and eastwards by fortifications at Bedford and Buckingham. By the end of the 910s the Saxons had established control of the lands up to the Trent, and when Aethelflaed died, perhaps in 918 or a little later, Edward annexed Mercia to his kingdom of Wessex.

The momentum was maintained by Athelstan, who succeeded to the throne in 924 and brought all the northern peoples to acknowledge his overlordship. That this was no mere pretence is shown by their frequent visits to his court – visits which can be traced in charter witness lists, which include the names of kings of Dyfed, Gwynedd and Brycheiniog.

In reality, however, the reconquest of the midlands and north was a slower and more complex process than the simple record of battles and enforced submissions would suggest. Southern kings could overrun and annex lands to the north of the Trent, but their control did not long outlast their return south, and few new territories were secure. More thorough-going was the kings' absorption of the former Vikings of the Trent valley and east midlands. On the evidence of place-names it is possible to suggest one reason why this was so. Many names in the area preserve Scandinavian personal names compounded with -thorp (outlying farm) or with -by (farm or village) – such as Scunthorpe (the farm of Skuma), Grimsby (the settlement of Grima), or Danthorp (the farm of the Danes). Some such settlements lie on good land, but many more are isolated farms on the edge of marginal areas settled after the initial partition of the 870s. The implication is that the Vikings had become farmers; they needed security and were happy to look to the Wessex kings for protection.

Evidence of the changing character of society in this period is afforded too by the growth of the towns. The Vikings, for all the fear that they induced, were not only raiders; they were traders, and under their influence urban life flourished. Norwich, Lincoln, Leicester, Derby, Nottingham and Stamford are all towns that grew rapidly in this period. Excavations at Thetford (Norfolk) have uncovered densely packed buildings arranged in regular rows. In one of the streets the ground was found to be 4 ft deep in iron-working residues. From this it is clear that the towns were not only residential in character; they were industrial as well. In the workshops that they harboured, a variety of goods were produced, of which the most important were pots. Thetford, and similar late Saxon wares, were the first to have been made in really large quantities since the Romans left. They penetrated into the countryside, and in the more settled conditions of the tenth century found a ready market among the peasantry. It would be wrong to portray England in this period as an incipient consumer society, but undoubtedly economic development was rapid; and by the 970s, in the reign of King Edgar, there was enough surplus wealth to support a vigorous revival of learning and religion. Monasteries, such as those of Glastonbury and New Minster, Winchester, were founded or re-founded, and scriptoria and painting workshops re-established. Manuscript illumination in England reached a new peak.

At the very end of the century, however, these achievements were put in jeopardy by a revival of the Viking raids.

THE COLLAPSE OF THE ANGLO-SAXON KINGDOM

The renewed Viking interest in England can be attributed to a number of factors. Trade with the East, which had brought Arab silver up the rivers of Russia to the Baltic, to Britain and to Ireland, was shrinking fast, and by the 970s had almost disappeared; traders and pirates needed fresh markets. Iceland, newly colonized, was becoming heavily populated, and settlers needed to look elsewhere; and in Denmark itself King Harald Gormsson, nicknamed 'Bluetooth', was establishing a strong monarchy, which entailed the suppression and expulsion of his opponents.

The initial raids were sporadic, and are most notable because of a single incident in the campaign of 991, which became the subject of a noble Old English poem, the Battle of Maldon, which commemorates the death in battle of Brihtnoth, ealdorman of Essex, and of his household (thought to have been fought at or by Mersea Island, Essex [NT]). As the dead ealdorman's retainers gathered to make their final stand, the poet makes one follower encourage his companions: 'Thoughts must be the braver, heart more valiant, courage the greater as our strength grows less . . . I am old in years; I will not leave the field, but think to lie by my lord's side.' In the next generation such heroic sacrifice becomes much harder to find.

These successes encouraged the raiders, and in 994 a great fleet of ninety-four ships, commanded by Svein, King of Denmark, and Olaf Tryggvason who was soon to become King of Norway, ravaged southern England, and was finally persuaded to leave by the payment of tribute in the form of 16,000 pounds of silver. The burdens which this and the subsequent tributes laid upon the English are well shown by a remarkable charter of 994 or 995, a copy of which survives in the archives of Canterbury Cathedral. The document records the transference of an estate in Buckinghamshire which had belonged to the archbishop, and details the reasons for the exchange, for the

NEW MINSTER CHARTER
(opposite)
One of the most beautiful illuminations to have come down from the reign of Edgar is the frontispiece to the foundation charter of New Minster, Winchester. It is dated 966, but may have been produced a little later. King Edgar, standing between the Virgin Mary and St Peter, is shown offering his charter to Christ. Surrounding the whole is a rich acanthus leaf border which is the leitmotif of the English illuminators of the day (British Library, MS Cotton Vespasian A. viii, fol. 2v)

archbishop 'when the pagan race, raging in its slaughters, was devastating Kent' had bought peace from the Vikings for his city, and was now forced to sell one of his estates to the Bishop of Dorchester in order to raise the cash. Another charter of King Aethelred himself records the sale of two estates to provide the gold necessary to pay the tribute. The purchaser of the king's lands, ironically, was himself a Dane. The will of a later archbishop adds further details to our picture of these times, for in 1005 Aelfric gave a ship to the 'people of Kent' and the 'people of Wiltshire', to help them meet their obligations for military service, and forgave the monies owed him (probably for the same purpose) by the counties of Kent, Surrey and Middlesex.

These terrible events came in the reign of Aethelred II (979–1016) – known to posterity as 'Aethelred the Unready'. Aethelred's weakness was actually not so much that he was ill-prepared as that he was ill-advised ('unraed' = ill-counselled). He was prone to take decisions which he would later regret. Easily his worst miscalculation occurred in 1002 when he ordered a massacre of all the Danes in England. Among the victims, according to later writers, was a sister of King Svein of Denmark. As a result of this for more than a decade England was never to be free of her brother's fleets. Campaigns followed the familiar pattern of pillage: in 1009, for example, Svein sent a force which burnt its way from Oxford to East Anglia, and which captured Canterbury and murdered the archbishop. In the next year Svein himself landed in the Humber estuary apparently intent on complete conquest. He received the submission of the north, and after a few weeks that of London too; Aethelred fled to safety with his brother-in-law, the Duke of Normandy. Shortly afterwards, in February 1014, Svein died at Gainsborough in Lincolnshire, and Aethelred was recalled. His re-election was not without qualms: his nobles got an assurance that he would in future attend to their complaints, and that he would forgive their past treasons – which gives us a strong hint to explain the rapidity of Svein's victory. Two blows followed: in 1015, for motives that are somewhat obscure, Aethelred's son Edmund (nicknamed 'Ironside') rebelled and formed an independent and short-lived principality in the Midlands, an area which was still smarting from the ravages of both the Danes and of Aethelred. At this moment, Knut (Canute), younger son of King Svein, arrived with a fleet off the coast of Wessex, and with the help of discontented English nobles seized both Wessex and Mercia. Once Ironside died at the end of the year Knut took control of the whole kingdom.

A settlement made at Oxford in 1018 provided the outlines of a new Anglo-Danish realm, which was to be governed under the same laws and customs as in the time of King Edgar in the mid-tenth century. By this time Knut had disbanded his army: the taxes needed to pay off his crews amounted to over 80,000 pounds of silver. Henceforth he relied on his concordat with the English and on the loyalty of a small army of retainers, his huscarls or household knights. The word 'huscarls' is Danish, and at this time, too, the Danish jarl (earl) supplanted the old English ealdorman as the title of the principal nobility. The change was not just in the word – for although men of Anglo-Saxon origin continued in authority, the crown's chief agents were new men. Of the great nobles only Leofwine, ealdorman of the Hwicce in Worcestershire, survived the first years of the new reign, and handed down his position to his son, the Leofric who until 1057 was Earl of Mercia. These new earldoms matched only generally the old ealdormanries, for the latter corresponded to one of the old English kingdoms, or to some part of it, while the earl was often in control of an artificial and temporary unit, established to serve immediate needs, as a royal official.

Knut's reign in England was comparatively tranquil: his troubles lay abroad, principally in Norway. England recovered some of its prosperity, although one of the main indicators of surplus weath, benefactions to the church, shows a still weakened country: new church building falls off sharply for two generations. In consequence, those rapid changes of architectural styles, which are so obvious a feature of the years after 950 on the continent, are little represented in England. Late Saxon architecture seems insular and primitive by comparison with European fashion (see over).

When Knut died in 1035 his son and most obvious successor Harthacnut was in Denmark. The latter's half-brother Harald was, however, on hand and was elected regent. Harthacnut remained abroad, pre-occupied with Scandinavian troubles, and Harald was chosen king by the English in 1037. He died in 1040, at the moment when Harthacnut was poised in Flanders with an invasion fleet. Harthacnut's reign, too, was short, and he did little worthy of note, except perhaps to invite to England from Normandy his remaining half-brother Edward, sole survivor of Aethelred's children, who succeeded to the throne in 1042, when Harthacnut, at the early age of twenty-five, collapsed and died while at his drink.

THE CONFESSOR AND THE CONQUEST

The politics of King Edward the Confessor's long reign (1042–66) were dominated by his relations with his principal magnate, Earl Godwin. One of Knut's leading English supporters, Godwin was a man of relatively modest origins whom Knut had raised to an earldom in 1018. By 1042 Godwin had become the greatest landowner in the south; but he was believed to have been involved in the murder of Edward's brother Alfred, and the new king, unfamiliar with England and with the Anglo-Danish aristocracy, remained aloof. Edward, furthermore, was married to Godwin's daughter, whom he seems to have disliked. Godwin's sons, however, continued to prosper, and received earldoms which included Mercia, Wessex and East Anglia. Tension rose high in 1051, after a riot in Dover; with the support of Godwin's chief rivals (Leofric of Mercia and Siward of Northumbria) Edward succeeded in exiling the whole of the Godwin family. The next year the exiles launched a sudden invasion, and compelled the king to accept them back into their former positions, and to repudiate the main cause of discontent, the favour (natural enough after an exile of nearly thirty years) which Edward showed to Frenchmen, especially Normans. Godwin himself died shortly after his reinstatement, but his sons Harold, Earl of Wessex, and Tostig, from 1055 Earl of Northumbria, maintained their power against a king less and less capable of controlling the activity of his magnates.

During the 1040s and 1050s Edward's earls became involved in adventures which were significant for the futures of Scotland and Wales. In 1040 Duncan I, King of the Scots, had been killed, perhaps as part of a feud or as an attempt at secession, by a northern lord, Macbeth, mormaer ('high steward') of Moray, who took his place on the throne of Scotland. Earl Siward of Northumbria supported Duncan's son Malcolm and invaded Scotland in 1046 and in 1054, without success. Macbeth was finally defeated and killed in 1057, and, thanks to his Anglo-Danish support, Malcolm was crowned king. He remained linked to his benefactors, and his court proved a refuge for English

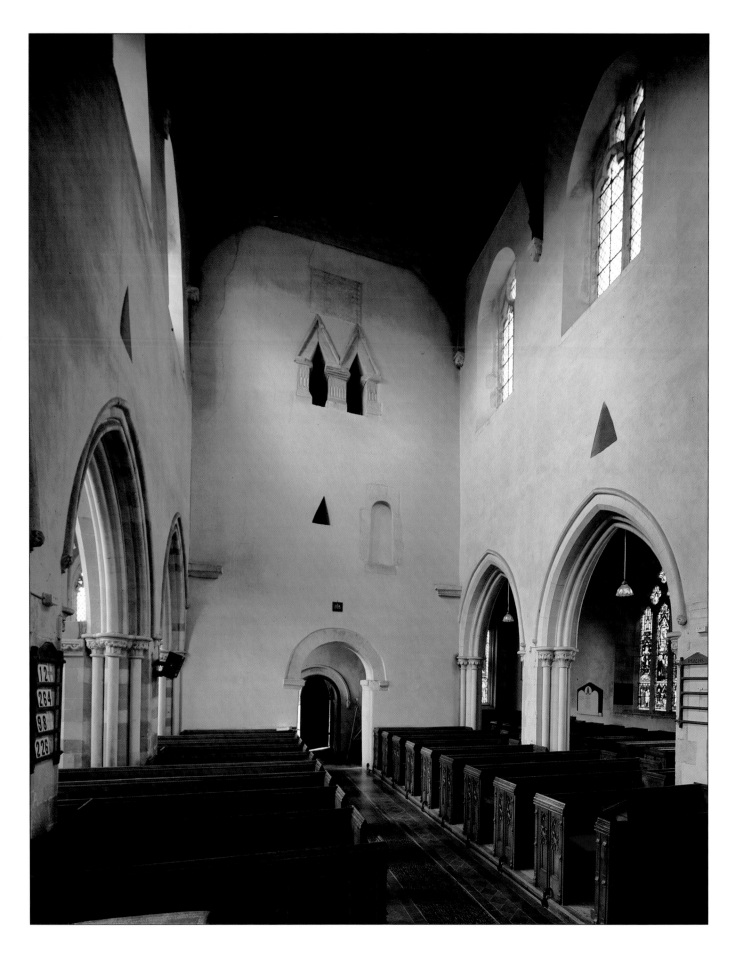

*BRADFORD-ON-AVON
(Wiltshire) (above)
This exquisite little church, only
25 ft by 13 ft, probably dates from
the last century of Anglo-Saxon
England. However, it almost
certainly rests on earlier foundations*

exiles during the turbulent years of the Norman Conquest of England: he himself was a thorn in the side of the new overlords of the north until his death on the Aln in 1093, while once more ravaging Northumberland.

On the Welsh frontier the long peace which followed the supremacy of Wessex was broken by the rise of an ambitious leader, Gruffydd ap Llywelyn, who was King of both Powys and Gwynedd, and who devoted himself to the crushing of the princes of South Wales. By 1055 he had made himself overlord of the whole of Wales, and in alliance with Aelfgar, son of the Mercian Earl Leofric, he ravaged Herefordshire. When Earl Aelfgar died in 1062, however, Harold and Tostig Godwinsson seized their chance, burnt the Welsh palace at Rhuddlan and then, with a fleet from Bristol, Harold moved up the western side of Wales. Tostig marched along the north Welsh coast, and together they closed in on the centre of Welsh resistance. Gwynedd collapsed, and in the confusion the Welsh king was killed by his own retainers. His kingdom at once broke up into its separate parts, and never again was united under native rulers.

The successful reduction of Wales left Harold Godwinson without rivals in England,

*DEERHURST (Gloucestershire)
(opposite)
Deerhurst flourished as an
independent monastery in the pre-
Conquest period before being
assigned to Westminster Abbey. The
church, as it survives, is largely ninth
to eleventh century, with later
additions. Note the great height of
the building in relation to the width*

at a time when the succession to an ageing, childless king was a matter of urgency. Edward's natural heir, his great-nephew Edgar, was too young; the King of Norway, Harald Hardrada, cherished his dynasty's claim to rule in England, and William, Duke of Normandy, regarded himself as nominated by Edward as his successor – an event which, if it occurred at all, probably did so in the interval between the exile and the return of the house of Godwin. In the event, when Edward died in January 1066, even he seems to have agreed to the naming of Harold as his heir, leaving a man (by now well accustomed to war and politics) poised between the Norwegian hammer and the Norman anvil.

XII
THE NORMAN CONQUEST AND SETTLEMENT

In September 1066 King Harald Hardrada of Norway, accompanied by King Harold Godwinsson's brother Tostig, landed in England, defeated the northern earls, and threatened York. Harold, who had been watching the south coast against William, Duke of Normandy's threatened invasion, hurried north, and on 25 September met and defeated the Viking army at Stamford Bridge, to the east of York. Harald Hardrada and Tostig were killed, and the Scandinavians dispersed. Three days later William landed at Pevensey and began ravaging the south coast. Harold came southwards with great speed, and on 14 October met William's troops on a low hill at Senlac to the north of Hastings, now the site of Battle Abbey. The death of Harold and his brothers left William the principal claimant to the throne. London remained threatening, and for several weeks the duke led his troops around the Home Counties, until the end of the year when he was accepted into the city; he was crowned King of England on Christmas Day 1066.

William's position was strong, but his enemies remained: Scandinavian claims to the throne continued to be a threat during the 1070s, and the north of England, which had always provided trouble for the rulers of Wessex, was as unruly for the new Norman lord as for his predecessors. In addition, his Duchy of Normandy, which he had fought to retain for more than two decades, was regularly pressed by its neighbours, the King of France and the Count of Anjou, and needed regular attention. His immediate need was to secure the south and reward his followers; he had the resources to hand in the royal estates and the earldom of Wessex, both now his, as well as in the lands of the Anglo-Danish noblemen and their followers: a writ to Bury Abbey orders the surrender to the king of the lands of all 'who stood against me in battle and were killed there'.

FEUDALISM IN ENGLAND

Normandy before 1066, in common with much of the continent, contained a mixture of lands – Church lands, royal and ducal estates, and hereditable lands – which passed

Domesday Book

At the end of 1085 William 'held very deep speech with his council about this land – how it was peopled, and with what sort of men'. During the next year teams of commissioners travelled around the whole of England south of the Tees and the Ribble, to compile an account which, in the words of the contemporary Bishop of Hereford, Robert de Losinga, covered the lands of every shire, and the property of every lord in fields, manors and men, slaves or free men, cottagers or farmers, plough-teams, horses and stock, in service and rents. The task, says Bishop Robert, was done twice – the second team to check the results of the first and to sort out the problems of illegal landholding and disputes. The great parchment volumes of the Domesday Book which resulted are the most detailed and revealing survey documents of the medieval world. They have their antecedents in the tax lists and census surveys of ancient Rome, and in the individual estate surveys of Charlemagne's kingdom, but none of these seems to have been at the same moment so detailed and so vast as those of King William's surveyors.

Behind Domesday lay a mass of documents, tax lists and estate accounts, a few of which survive, some probably compiled as a first stage in the survey. It seems that the lords' clerks too prepared listings of their masters' landholdings. Since some of the fiefs are listed in Hundred order within their counties, the courts of the Hundreds (administrative subdivisions of the shires) clearly had some part to play, perhaps as oath-takers to the detail of the individual estates. All these documents were gathered together into drafts which arranged individual feudal estates in sequence. One of these survives, in the library of Exeter Cathedral, the Exon Domesday, a volume of 532 parchment sheets covering most of the area from Dorset to Cornwall, arranged by lordships. As a further stage the drafts were copied into an arrangement of lordships within counties. In the Public Record Office in London is a volume of this sort, the Little Domesday Book, 451 pages covering the counties of Essex, Norfolk and Suffolk. Finally the individual counties were re-ordered into belts, doubtless relating to the circuit journeys of the commissioners, and copied (from the handwriting probably by a single scribe) into the final somewhat abbreviated form of the Great Domesday Book. This volume is also now in the Public Record Office and contains 383 large parchment sheets listing the fiefs, the manors within each fief, and the agricultural land and occupants within each manor. Though thus ostensibly feudal, the ordering of fiefs into counties emphasizes the older shire organization, since one lord might well hold lands within several counties. The identification of a feudal territory therefore requires considerable searching, and it is clear from variations in the layout of our manuscripts that the information was at first stored in separate booklets of a few sheets each through most of the early Middle Ages.

Throughout the entries in Domesday runs the phrase 'in the time of King Edward', since the individual estates which made up the fief were identified by their pre-Conquest owners; the value before the Conquest, too, is given, which allows some estimate of the result of the first twenty years of Norman rule on the prosperity of England – on the whole fairly neutral for the south, and a massive decline for parts of the north of England. We can see that some Norman lordships were simply transfers from Saxon landowners; in these cases the Conquest meant little more than a change of owner for the villagers. More commonly, the lands of many Saxons were gathered into a single Norman's hands, such as the estates of more than eighty Saxon landlords brought together in the Honour of Tickhill in South Yorkshire. Here one may suspect greater change as the new owners imposed uniformity of service and dues. On the whole, however, recent studies have emphasized the continuity of England's life and landholding under its new masters.

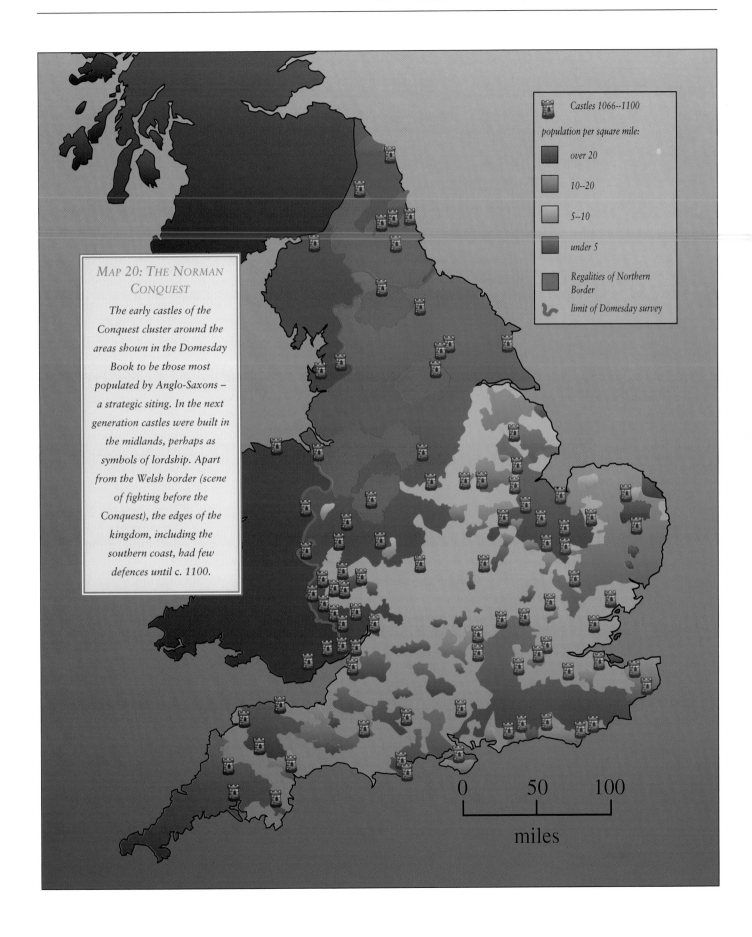

MAP 20: THE NORMAN CONQUEST

The early castles of the Conquest cluster around the areas shown in the Domesday Book to be those most populated by Anglo-Saxons – a strategic siting. In the next generation castles were built in the midlands, perhaps as symbols of lordship. Apart from the Welsh border (scene of fighting before the Conquest), the edges of the kingdom, including the southern coast, had few defences until c. 1100.

Castles 1066--1100

population per square mile:

over 20

10--20

5--10

under 5

Regalities of Northern Border

limit of Domesday survey

0   50   100

miles

from owner to heir. During the break-up of the Carolingian empire, however, the practice had grown among the greater lords of entrusting estates to followers in return not for rent, but for specific services, usually military; these lands they regained on the death of the follower, who was known as the tenant or 'vassal'. This system allowed the maintenance of (expensive) knights, and encouraged the building of private fortifications, but was at bottom an expression of the relationship between lords and lands, and took its name – the feudal system – from the estate, the fief or *feu*.

Old English military obligation had developed on different lines in the same period. Landowners were required to perform service here as on the continent: but it was service to the king via his royal officers, and not to any other sworn lord: there was emphatically no feudal tenure. The land itself seems to have been divided between a series of royal and noble estates, each of which sat in the centre of a cluster of dependent settlements, which paid their tribute and their taxes to the centre. These 'multiple estates' may have been ancient in some areas, notably in Wales. In England, however, there are signs that they formed part of a new re-organization of the land, perhaps after the reconquest of England during the tenth century, when the old English kingdoms were divided into the shires which survived until our own time. It was a new order for a newly united realm, and it bore little resemblance to the new structures of authority emerging on the continent.

The introduction of these structures to England was carried out by the Normans in the years after 1066. Coming as they did from a society already feudal, the Normans naturally thought in feudal terms when ordering the affairs of their new realm. William, therefore, when distributing land to his immediate followers – the tenants-in-chief, as they were called – granted it not unconditionally but in return for future military service; the tenants-in-chief did likewise when granting it to their vassals; as did those vassals in turn to their men . . . and so on down the line. From the king to the humblest knight landholders were linked by an intricate network of relationships which, when fitted together, made up the new feudal structure of authority.

The weakness of the system was that it was highly decentralized. A tenant owed his service to his immediate lord and never, unless he was a tenant-in-chief, directly to the king. Without some mechanism for the preservation of royal authority the kingdom would run the risk of disintegrating into a congeries of competing lordships – a fate that nearly overtook Normandy in the 1030s. To overcome this problem William in 1086 summoned all his tenants-in-chief to Salisbury, and in the words of the chronicler Florence of Worcester, commanded their knights 'to swear allegiance to himself against all men'. Thus he was asserting the primacy of royal authority in the feudal framework. The knights were reminded that whoever they held their land from, it was ultimately to the king to whom they owed fealty. A measure of control was imposed on the potentially centrifugal tendencies of the new system.

CASTLES AND LORDSHIPS

The new Norman landholders were numerically insignificant by comparison with their Anglo-Saxon subjects – a few thousand perhaps in a population of 2–4 million. But what they lacked in numbers they made up for in wealth. Already richly endowed in Normandy, many of them were still more so in England. Particularly favoured were those in the Conqueror's immediate circle – men like his two half-brothers Odo, Bishop of Bayeux (who probably commissioned the Bayeux Tapestry) and Robert of Mortain; his close ally William FitzOsbern; and magnates of his generation like Roger of Montgomery, William of Warenne and Geoffrey, Bishop of Coutances. On the evidence of Domesday Book it seems that close on a quarter of the landed wealth in England – that is, about half of the wealth not held by the Church – was granted to only ten men, many of them related to the Conqueror himself. A few of these were younger sons who had very successfully sought fame and fortune in England. But many more were heads of families who found themselves in the fortunate position of holding inheritances on both sides of the Channel. Roger of Montgomery, for example, already Lord of Bellême in Normandy, now found himself lord of vast estates in England centred on Arundel in Sussex and Shrewsbury in the Welsh Marches. It was the creation of great cross-Channel inheritances like these that was to bind England and Normandy together for the next century and a half.

Because of their relatively few numbers the Normans resorted to castle-building to secure the land that they had conquered (map 20). Simple motte-and-bailey fortifications, of the kind shown on the Bayeux Tapestry, could be thrown up quickly in a matter of weeks; and from them their lords could hold sway over all the surrounding countryside. Very few such structures are thought to have existed in pre-Conquest England. Indeed, according to the chronicler Orderic Vitalis, it was the very lack of them that allowed the Normans to march as freely as they did round England on winning Hastings. The great age of castle-building came in the reigns of William the Conqueror and his son William Rufus, when some ninety to a hundred were built. The earliest were almost certainly palisaded structures of wood. Only the very grandest – those built by the king, like the Tower of London – would have been of stone. The great rebuilding which produced massive tower keeps, like the one at Corfe (NT) (Dorset), came later, in the early twelfth century.

To contemplate the dynamics of Norman imperialism in the late eleventh century is to be immediately conscious of the enormous drive and energy of the Normans. It was not just in England that they settled; they went on to colonize Ireland, Scotland and the lowlands of South Wales. Further afield they established a presence in Sicily and southern Italy, and put a Norman dynasty on the throne at Palermo. In a final burst of energy in the next generation, they provided one of the largest contingents on the First Crusade (1096–1099). Members of Norman families were to figure prominently among those that settled in the Latin Kingdom in the wake of the Crusade's triumph.

Everywhere they went the Normans left their mark – whether it was in the influence that they exerted on language and social structures, or in the sheer physical presence that they stamped on the landscape. Today it is that physical presence that affords the most forcible reminder of their achievement. From Sicily in the south to Durham, in England, in the north the castles and churches that they built still dominate the landscape. Many of them – such as the churches of Cerisy-la-Forêt and St Georges-de-Boscherville in Normandy or the cathedrals of Peterborough and Durham in England – stand virtually unaltered. At Durham the sight of the great pile of buildings is particularly dramatic – and particularly instructive. High on the narrow tongue of land cut by the loop of the River Wear stand side by side the twin symbols of medieval authority – the castle and the cathedral. The city at their feet is dwarfed by their presence. Here, better than anywhere else in Britain, we can understand what the coming of the Normans meant to people. It meant the imposition of an alien yoke. The English were no longer masters of their own destiny. They were reduced to being a subject race in a foreign empire – the empire of the Normans.

DURHAM CATHEDRAL AND CASTLE

The cathedral, seen here from the west, was begun in 1093, and the castle at probably about the same time. Churches and castles were the two most visible symbols of the authority of the new Norman rulers of England

ROMAN AND EARLY MEDIEVAL SITES IN THE CARE OF THE NATIONAL TRUST

Brancaster Fort (Norfolk)
Chedworth Roman Villa (Gloucestershire)
Hardknott Fort (Cumbria)
Hod Hill (Dorset)
Housesteads and Hadrian's Wall (Northumberland)

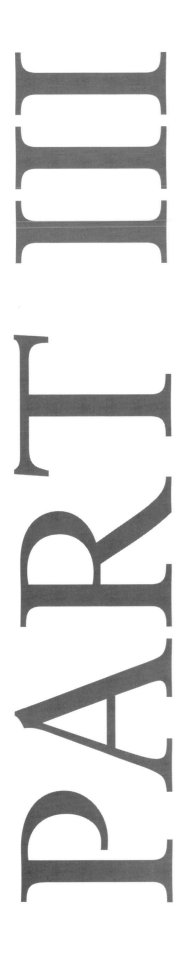

PART III

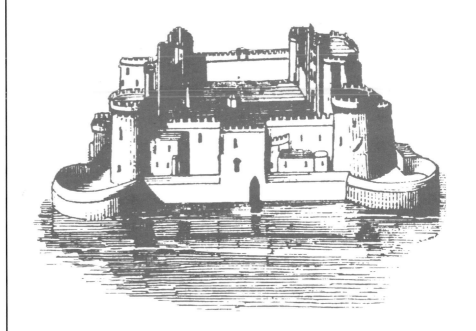

MEDIEVAL BRITAIN

NIGEL SAUL

Timeline chart (read left to right by period):

	1100	1150	1200	1250	1300	1350	1400
ENGLISH KINGS	Henry I 1100–35; Stephen 1135–54	Henry II 1154–89; Richard I 1189–99	John 1199–1216	Henry III 1216–72	Edward I 1272–1307; Edward II 1307–27	Edward III 1327–77	Richard II 1377–99
SCOTTISH KINGS	Edgar 1097–1107; Alexander I 1107–24	David I 1124–53; Malcolm IV 1153–65	William I 'the Lion' 1165–1214	Alexander II 1214–49; Alexander III 1249–88	John Balliol 1292–6; Robert I (Bruce) 1306–29	David II 1329–71	Robert II (Stewart) 1371–90; Robert III 1390–1406
WAR & POLITICS	Civil War 1138–53		Magna Carta 1215	Provisions of Oxford 1258; Conquest of N. Wales 1277, 1282	Bannockburn 1314; Scottish Wars 1296–1328	Peasants' Revolt; Hundred Years War 1337–1453	Glendower's Rebellion 1400–8
THE CHURCH	Archbishop Anselm 1093–1109	Cistercian expansion	Murder of Becket 1170	Arrival of the friars 1224		John Wyclif writing, 1370s	Suppression of Lollards
THE ARTS	Durham Cathedral 1093–1133; ROMANESQUE	Bury Bible c. 1135; Winchester Bible c. 1160–80; Canterbury Cathedral choir begun 1174	Jedburgh Abbey; Wells W. front 1230s on.	Salisbury Cathedral 1220–1266; Matthew Paris's chronicles; Westminster choir begun 1245; GOTHIC	Eleanor Crosses	Luttrell Psalter c. 1340; Ely octagon 1322–46; Gloucester choir 1337–50	Canterbury Tales, c. 1387–1400; Langland's Piers Plowman c. 1370–90; Wilton Diptych c. 1395
EUROPE	1st Crusade 1096–9; 2nd Crusade 1148		3rd Crusade 1189–92; 4th Lateran Council, Rome, 1215	Early Italian Renaissance	Crécy 1346	BLACK DEATH 1348; Poitiers 1356; Avignon Papacy 1305–78	Turkish advance into Europe; Schism in Church 1378–1417

XIII
ENGLAND, THE CELTIC LANDS AND EUROPE

Though England was to be part of a French-speaking empire for the next century and a half, the nature of that empire changed with the passage of time. The union of England and Normandy, forged by William the Conqueror, lasted until the mid-1140s, when it was shattered by the civil war of Stephen's reign – England being held by Stephen, and Normandy by his rival Matilda, Henry I's daughter. A decade later, in 1154, it was reconstituted under Matilda's son Henry II as part of a very different political structure – one that was both larger and more diverse than its predecessor. Henry II's 'Angevin empire' stretched from Hadrian's Wall to the Pyrenees. It comprised not only England and Normandy, which he had inherited from his mother, but also Anjou, which he had inherited from his father, and Aquitaine, which he acquired by marriage to Eleanor, the black-eyed heiress of that duchy. And in the course of a long reign he was also able to extend his dominion over territories to which he had inherited somewhat vaguer claims of overlordship. He advanced into Wales on several occasions in the 1150s and 1160s; he made a long-delayed descent on Ireland which enabled him to receive the submission of the native princes; and he took advantage of the King of Scots' capture in 1174 to secure recognition of his suzerainty over the northern kingdom. Very likely he saw himself at the apex of a hierarchy of rulers in which the Scottish king and the Celtic princes all had a place. It is small wonder that Henry was regarded as such a mighty king by his contemporaries.

Inevitably, given the sheer size of his dominions, decentralization had to guide his approach to their governance. Any alternative would have been unrealistic. But that is not to say that he allowed the exercise of personal kingship to go by default. Quite the contrary; he kept constantly on the move, tiring his courtiers out as they tried to keep up with him. Thus there was no such thing as a 'capital' in the modern sense. The 'capital' was wherever the king happened to be. It might be Chinon one month, Rouen the next and Westminster the month after that. But if there was a 'centre of gravity' – as surely there must have been – then it was Anjou. Henry was an Angevin by descent and upbringing. He was born at Le Mans; he died at Chinon; and he was buried at Fontevrault. It was the Loire Valley that he loved best.

The consequences for England of its absorption into the Angevin dominions were far-reaching. For the second time in a century England was exposed to a wave of influence from abroad. This time the impact was less cataclysmic than it had been in 1066. There was no revolution in the upper ranks of society, no replacement of one élite by another – only the invigorating effect of being brought back into the European mainstream after a break of fifteen years. For the people of England it was an opportunity rather than a challenge. They had never really been out of touch with European currents of thought, even before the Conquest. But because of their ethnic origin their links had been much more with Scandinavia and the Germanic world. What the Conquest did was encourage a re-orientation southwards. The Channel ceased to be a divide; it became a thoroughfare joining the two halfs of the empire. Backwards and forwards across it sailed traders plying their wares, pilgrims visiting shrines, churchmen pursuing claims in Rome, courtiers and officials carrying messages from the king, not to mention a host of other travellers. The peace which Henry II established within his dominions encouraged the free movement of people among them; and the wars which periodically erupted on their frontiers failed to discourage people from crossing them. Men went wherever opportunity and the prospects of employment beckoned. John of Salisbury, for example, one of the greatest scholars of his day, went to study in Paris, but then returned to England to join the household of Archbishop Theobald, Thomas à Becket's patron. When Becket himself became archbishop, John entered his service and shared his trials and tribulations. After Becket's murder in 1170 he remained at Canterbury for a while. But then he was elected Bishop of Chartres, and it was there that he ended his days in 1180. Thomas Brown's travels took him much further afield. Unlike John he was not a 'wandering scholar' but a civil servant of a more practical turn of mind. He was 'head-hunted' by the King of Sicily for whom he worked for many years; but later in life he returned to his native land, to work in Henry II's exchequer. Other Englishmen combined working abroad with the pursuit of knowledge. Most notable in this connection are two men who found their way to Spain. In the 1130s there was Adelard of Bath, who collected treatises on philosophy, mathematics and astronomy, which he translated into English, and in the next decade Robert of Chester, who visited Segovia and translated the algebraic system of the Arab mathematician Al-Khowarizmi.

That men from the British Isles should have been found living, working, training and observing in these various parts of the European mainland is a measure of the interest that they took in the wider world. But it is also in a sense a measure of the lack of opportunities that plagued them at home. Until roughly the 1190s, when Oxford became established, England had no 'studium generale' or university; and though it had some well-established schools attached to abbeys like Abingdon in Oxfordshire, it lacked teachers of renown. Thus any aspirant to learning had to go abroad for instruction, in particular to France – to the university at Paris made famous by Peter Abelard, or to one of the cathedral schools such as Chartres or Laon. There, if anywhere, were to be found the knowledge, the books and the masters. There too, as John of Salisbury said in 1164, were to be found 'wealth and abundance on all sides', 'light-heartedness in the people' and 'respect paid to seekers after truth'. Nowhere else were such amity and accord in evidence, as well as such bounty and exuberance.

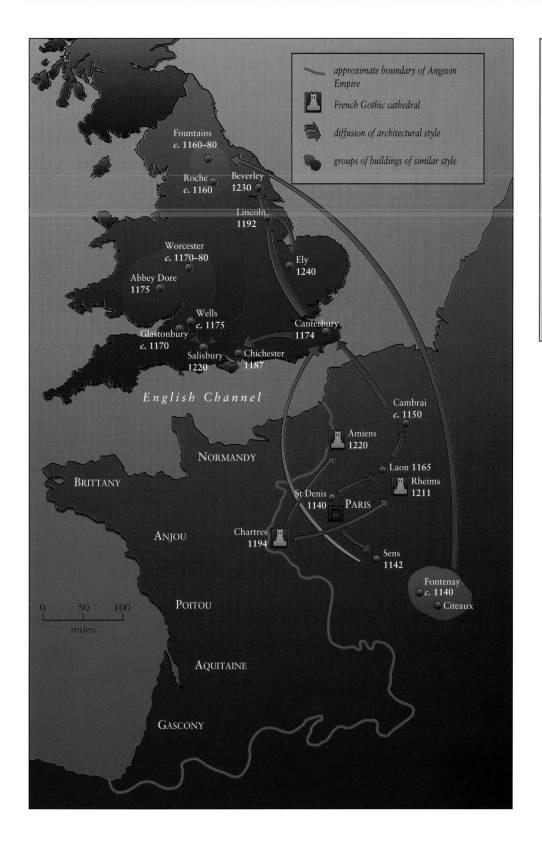

Fountains
c. 1160–80

Roche
c. 1160

Beverley
1230

Lincoln
1192

Worcester
c. 1170–80

Ely
1240

Abbey Dore
1175

Wells
c. 1175

Glastonbury
c. 1170

Canterbury
1174

Salisbury
1220

Chichester
1187

English Channel

Cambrai
c. 1150

NORMANDY

Amiens
1220

BRITTANY

Laon 1165

Rheims
1211

St Denis
1140

PARIS

ANJOU

Chartres
1194

Sens
1142

Fontenay
c. 1140

Citeaux

POITOU

0   50   100
miles

AQUITAINE

GASCONY

approximate boundary of Angevin Empire

French Gothic cathedral

diffusion of architectural style

groups of buildings of similar style

MAP 21: CULTURE AND POLITICS: THE ARRIVAL OF GOTHIC IN ENGLAND

The Gothic of the Île de France was first adopted in England at Canterbury in 1174. Burgundian Gothic was introduced by the Cistercians at their houses of Fountains (North Yorkshire) and Roche (South Yorkshire). Elements of both styles were incorporated in the distinct type of Gothic articulated in the west of England.

SENS CATHEDRAL (opposite)
Sens was one of the first cathedrals
in the Île de France to show the
influence of the new architectural
styles of Paris. It was begun in the
mid- to late 1140s, but finished only
much later

France under the Capetians was a kingdom at ease with itself. At home its rulers enjoyed a favourable public opinion; abroad their country was known as 'sweet France', '*la douce France*'. At the root of this cultural supremacy lay a spirit of optimism which was transforming the way that men looked at the world. They became more confident of their abilities; they took a naïve pleasure in self-expression; they even cultivated the art of letter-writing. The creative impulse for all this activity came from the literature of classical antiquity. In the writings of Aristotle and Plato, Cicero and Virgil men found not only a model of Latinity far purer than their own but also a recognition of the dignity of Man which was altogether novel to their experience. So preoccupied had they become with the problem of Man's sinfulness that they had been almost blind to the possibility of his redemption. The cosmic struggle between God and the devil, so graphically depicted in Romanesque art, was one which held them spellbound, but in which they did not see themselves as having any active role. In the early twelfth century, however, as the mood of pessimism weakened, the scales began to fall from their eyes. The figure on the Cross was seen with a new clarity to be that of a man. The remote and formidable God who had dominated Dark Age art gave way to the figure of the suffering Christ – His head still crowned, but His face resigned and pained, His eyes shut and His feet pierced. The constellation of heaven was likewise humanized. The

CANTERBURY CATHEDRAL,
the choir, begun 1174 (below).
This was a building of seminal
importance in the dissemination of
Gothic in England. Note its
similarity to Sens

120

*LINCOLN CATHEDRAL, the
choir, begun 1192.
This was one of the first major
buildings to show the influence of
Canterbury. The set of wooden stalls
is later*

Virgin Mary was portrayed as a mother with whom other mothers could identify (see p. 146). The saints were portrayed as mediators through whom the mercy of God could be brought down on the suppliant. We see them on the great portals of Chartres – idealized, detached, aristocratic and so serene that, as Lord Clark said, they make the gods of ancient Greece look soulless. Pessimism had given way to hope, darkness to light, Romanesque to Gothic.

The mood of the new age was summed up by one of its most persuasive advocates, Abbot Suger of St Denis, the friend of King Louis VII. Speaking of the new images in his abbey church, he said:

Admire not their gold nor their cost, but instead the work that they represent, and the art. Like gold, a noble achievement gleams; but it gleams nobly. May it enlighten men's minds, and may its true lights lead them to the true light of which Christ is the gateway.

Suger's world was above all a world of light; and the church which he built at St Denis just outside Paris in the 1140s was the first in which the admission of light was made the governing principle of the design. The walls were opened up and the windows greatly enlarged, bathing the altars in sunshine and creating an atmosphere of resplendent luminosity which made the old Romanesque churches look dark and impenetrable.

The rebuilding of St Denis marked a turning point in the history of western architecture. Suger's new edifice was Europe's first truly Gothic church; and it was not long before it found imitators. Among the first was the archiepiscopal cathedral of Sens, rebuilt in the 1140s. It was from there that in the next generation the new style was brought to England, to Canterbury, where a disastrous fire in 1174 occasioned the rebuilding of the cathedral which Becket had known. The man entrusted with the commission was one William of Sens – whose name betrays his origins – and the design he produced was one almost without precedent in Britain. Reactions to it were predictably mixed. The apsidal eastern termination, for example, found little favour in a land where already a preference was emerging for a flat end wall into which a great window could be inserted. But in its overall conception the new design was still influential, not to say revolutionary, and architecture in the British Isles was never to be the same again. St Hugh's choir at Lincoln (begun 1192) was inspired by it; so too was the Chichester retrochoir; and in the next generation an indirect debt was paid by the chancel and transepts at Dryburgh in Scotland and the presbytery at Ely in England. In a sense, therefore, the reaction in England and Scotland to the new Gothic style may be said to have been an epitome of the reaction in those countries to continental influences generally – one of eclecticism: picking and choosing those aspects which suited the national mood and rejecting those which did not. European currents greatly enriched British culture, but they did not in any way diminish its individuality.

XIV
A PROSPEROUS PEOPLE
THE ENGLISHMAN ABROAD

When John of Salisbury went to France in 1164, he was immediately struck by the prosperity of the people:

> I admired with joy the wealth and abundance on all sides . . . When I saw the abundance of food, the light-heartedness of the people, the respect paid to the clergy, the majesty and glory of the whole Church and the various employments of the seekers after truth, I looked on it as a veritable Jacob's ladder with its summit reaching to the skies and the angels ascending and descending . . . Then that line of poetry came to my mind – Happy is the exile driven to this place.

Three hundred years later, when another Englishman – the lawyer and Lancastrian partisan Sir John Fortescue – found himself in France, as a political exile, the impression formed was very different:

> The people live in no little misery. They drink water daily, and they taste no other liquor unless at solemn feasts. They wear frocks of canvas like sackcloth. They do not use woollens, except of the cheapest sort, and they wear no hose, unless to the knees, exposing the rest of their shins. Their women are barefooted, except on feast days; the men and women eat no flesh, except bacon lard, with which they fatten their pottage in the smallest quantity. They do not taste other meats, roast or boiled, except occasionally the offal and heads of animals killed for the nobles and merchants . . . If anyone grows in wealth at any time, and is reputed rich among the others, he is at once assessed for the king's subsidy (tax) more than his neighbours, so that forthwith he is levelled to their poverty. This, unless I am mistaken, is the condition of the plebeian people's estate in the realm.

There are difficulties in the way of comparing these two accounts with each other. Fortescue's purpose was to demonstrate the oppressiveness of taxation in an absolute monarchy; he was not questioning either the fertility of the French soil or the productiveness of the French people. John of Salisbury, on the other hand, did not mean to deny that the English enjoyed a high standard of living. What he felt was lacking in his own country was 'liberality' – that readiness to put wealth to good uses which made the French *look* better off.

Thus the difference between these two accounts is probably a good deal less than it first appears. But all the same it is real enough and should not be underestimated. A major change in perception had occurred: whereas in the twelfth century it had been the French who had appeared the happier and more prosperous people, in the fifteenth it was the English. Just when this change came about is unclear, but there are signs that it may have been as early as the turn of the thirteenth and fourteenth centuries. While visiting England in 1327 a Hainaulter called Jean le Bel was greatly struck by its wealth. Reflecting on a six weeks' stay at York, he wrote that he 'never ceased to marvel at how so great an abundance could have arisen there'. This was a sentiment to be echoed many times over subsequently by visitors to England. Montesquieu in 1729 spoke of 'the solid luxury' which the people of England enjoyed, and Tocqueville in the 1830s affirmed that he had never been anywhere where the level of wealth was greater. England was clearly perceived as a rich country – far richer in per capita terms than her neighbours. The origins of those riches are to be found in the expansion of the economy in the Middle Ages.

A PLAIN FULL OF PEOPLE

Behind that expansion lay the growth in population. More hands meant more work. Additional resources were available for tilling the soil, driving the plough and doing all the other tasks that needed to be done. Everywhere in the British Isles the level of economic activity was on the increase.

Reliable population figures for the Middle Ages are hard to obtain. Registers of births, marriages and deaths were not kept before the sixteenth century, and national population censuses were not undertaken before the nineteenth. Estimates of population have to be derived therefore from indirect sources, principally those connected with taxation. In regard to England two of these are of particular interest. One is Domesday Book, the great survey of the realm undertaken by William the Conqueror in 1086; the other is the series of poll tax returns from the years 1377–81. Together these provide us with approximate figures for different points in the Middle Ages – of some 1.75–2 million in 1086 and 3–4 million three centuries later. But what we really need to know is the level of population at its peak on the eve of the Black Death in 1348. To arrive at this it is necessary to work backwards from the figure for 1377. It is generally assumed that mortality in the Black Death was somewhere between a third and a half. If the population was 3–4 million in 1377, then, it must have been at least 5–6 million thirty years earlier; there is a possibility that it may even have been more.

Remarks about the level of population in medieval England involve a certain amount of conjecture; those about population levels in Wales and Scotland, however, are little better than guesswork. For these parts of the British Isles fiscal sources are few. Estimates have to be made largely on the basis of likelihood and probability. A figure of perhaps 300,000 at the end of the thirteenth century has been posited for Wales, and of a million for Scotland. How reliable these figures are it is impossible to tell. Probably they are chiefly of value in comparative rather than absolute terms. In other words, they show how much less populous these more mountainous parts were than England. It was in England, particularly in lowland England, that the rate of demographic growth was fastest.

In an economy still relatively undeveloped – as medieval Britain's was – rapid population growth carried with it dangers. If sustained over a long period, it could have outstripped the growth of production and precipitated a crisis of subsistence. Crises of this kind were not uncommon on the continent of Europe. In Italy in 1328–9, for example, there was a famine so severe that at Siena the hungry went on the rampage and the governors were afraid that they would sack the city. At the great city of Florence there were also outbreaks of famine in 1339–41, 1346 and 1347 – the last two causing the deaths of nearly four thousand people – while at Pistoia, a little to the north, there were famines or epidemics in 1313, 1328–9, 1339–40 (when allegedly a quarter of the population died) and 1346–7. In Britain mortalities were neither so frequent nor so severe as these. The only great famine to strike with nation-wide incidence in the early fourteenth century was that of 1317–18, following two summers of heavy rain which washed away the crops. Set-backs tended to be more localized in character. By and large the terrible and recurrent disasters that laid low the Italian cities were foreign to British experience. One reason for this was to be found in Britain's more equable climate – though then, as now, this was subject to aberration, and probably in the early fourteenth century getting worse. Of greater importance, however, was the more even spread of wealth in these Isles. There were fewer large centres of population dependent on food supplies from the surrounding countryside. Only London could match the great cities of Italy in size, with a population of nearly 100,000 in 1300; every other town was small by comparison. Only in London, then, was there the possibility that an interruption to the food supply would provoke the calamitous consequences that it did in Italy: but even here the threat was potential rather than actual; not even in the 1330s and 1340s is there evidence of the terrible suffering inflicted on Florence at the same time.

When finally a devastating blow *was* dealt to society, the cause lay outside and not within the system. In June 1348 the Black Death arrived in England – carried by rodents on board ships that docked at Melcombe Regis (now Weymouth), Dorset. Its symptoms were large swellings in the groin, neck or armpit – ashy in colour, according to one contemporary – which gave off a repulsive smell, and within five or six days proved fatal. 'So vast a multitude was carried off', wrote William de Dene, a monk of Rochester, 'that nobody could be found who would bear the corpses to the grave. Men and women carried their own children on their shoulders to the church and threw them into the pit.' The existence of such pits and cemeteries – a large one was found in London on the site of St Mary Graces – attests the enormous scale of the mortality. In the eighteen months that it ravaged England it claimed the lives of some 2 million people. Most of these were drawn from the poor and the destitute who lived in the unhygienic surroundings frequented by the bacillus-carrying rats. But the clergy too were badly affected, because they came into contact with the diseased and the dying. The well-to-do, on the other hand, escaped very lightly.

Contemporary preachers interpreted the plague as evidence of the wrath of God: the Almighty in their view was visiting this terrible punishment on His people because they had failed to lift themselves out of the state of sin. Whether or not this was so – and whether or not their listeners believed that it was so – the plague was in reality less retributive than cathartic: it purged the country of its surplus population and restored a healthier balance between land and people. The result was a welcome and rapid increase in the level of peasant living standards. Wages rose as a result of the shortage of labour, while rents fell in line with the demand for land. Small wonder that the chronicler Froissart, noting the tendency to peasant assertiveness at the time, spoke of 'the ease and riches that the common people were of'. If ever there was a golden age of the English – indeed, of the British – peasantry, it was in the century or so that followed the Black Death.

THE ADVANCE OF THE PLOUGH

The rapid growth in population in the central Middle Ages acted as a spur to the advance of rural colonization. Everywhere the margin of cultivation was being pushed forward. New fields were created on the edge of villages, allowing more complex systems of cropping and cultivation. Spectacular incursions were made into the swathes of forest that covered the landscape. The Pennine fells were tamed by the arrival of Cistercian monks at abbeys like Fountains (NT), Bolton and Roche. In sum, the various endeavours amounted to a not inconsiderable movement of settlement and colonization. Even more spectacular, however, was the policy of winning land from the marshes and silt-fens along the coast. Along the estuaries of the Exe, the Clyst and the Taw in Devon, of the Humber in Yorkshire, and on the levels of Pevensey in Sussex, land was being reclaimed, and 'inned' or embanked to prevent it from being inundated again by the sea. In the wapentake of Elloe in South Lincolnshire, where activity was at its most intense, no fewer than 50 square miles were reclaimed in this way; and to that should be added a large but unquantifiable figure for land reclaimed from the sea itself. It was not in the seventeenth century, therefore, that the movement to drain the Fens got under way; it was four centuries earlier in the Middle Ages.

The uses to which the reclaimed lands were put were various. Sometimes, as in the Fens, they were enclosed by dykes or hedges and made the basis of self-contained farms: this is evident from a contemporary account which tells how the men of Holland, having reclaimed land in the three manors of Moulton, Weston and Spalding, subsequently met to divide it up between themselves for each man to till as he saw fit. Sometimes too, particularly on the monastic estates of northern England, they were organized around centres called granges, from which a colony of monks would organize the tilling of the soil and management of the sheep flocks: the barn at Great Coxwell (NT) in Oxfordshire survives from the grange built there by the monks of Beaulieu. But more often they were absorbed into the village fields and integrated into the communal system of arable cultivation.

The origins of this system – known as the 'open-field' system – are unclear. But that it had come into existence by the twelfth century at the latest cannot be doubted. In a typical village the lord's lands – the 'demesne' lands – and those of his tenants were distributed across some two or three large fields in the form of strips which intermingled and interlocked with each other. Because these strips were too small to serve as units of ploughing they were grouped together in larger units known as furlongs or selions, each one of which, measuring some 22 yards by 220 yards, was reckoned to represent one day's ploughing for a horse or ox team. Cropping was organized either by the field or, more commonly, by the furlong. In a three-course system one portion of the land would

GREAT COXWELL (Oxfordshire) (NT), the tithe barn.
The barn was built by the monks of Beaulieu Abbey in the thirteenth century to serve the needs of one of their outlying manors

'Give us this day our daily bread . . .'

Evidence for the study of diet for the early Middle Ages is decidedly thin; and what there is is chiefly archaeological. For the fourteenth and fifteenth centuries, however, the evidence thickens: there are recipe books and household accounts which illuminate the dietary habits of the upper classes, and maintenance agreements, or corrodies, which do likewise for the middling and well-to-do peasantry. Only for the very poor is there anything resembling a documentary blank; and in their case the deficiency is more than made good by Langland's vivid evocation of their plight in Piers Plowman.*

Langland's experience of poverty was direct and personal. The cold meat and stale fish which he describes the poor as eating are the foodstuffs which he and his wife were condemned to eat for most of their lives; and the farthing's worth of mussels that were a treat for them were just as much a treat for him. All the same, the power of Langland's writing should not mislead us into thinking that hunger was on the increase in his day. It was not; rather it was on the retreat. A run of good harvests ensured that corn prices stayed low right into the fifteenth century, and per capita consumption was probably higher at this time than ever before.*

Having said that, however, it is true that the general character of the peasant diet remained much as it had always been. The daily staple was the loaf of bread – be it a wheaten loaf in the better-off households or one baked from barley or oats in those of the poor. This was supplemented by various pottages, which consisted of pulses, oats or some other corn boiled up and left to solidify; while for liquid refreshment there was ale, which was brewed either from barley or, more likely, from oat malt.

A FEAST
From a marginal illustration in the early fourteenth-century Luttrell Psalter

Thus the peasants' diet was one heavily weighted towards carbohydrates. Whether this resulted in a serious protein deficiency is hard to say because too little is known about the intake of protein from other sources. In the woodlands there was always game to be had, albeit illegally. But in most of the British Isles it was probably vegetables which constituted the main supplement to the daily fare: beans, cabbages and peas, grown sometimes in the fields, but more often in garden plots.

Far more exotic, but not necessarily more wholesome, was the diet of the upper-classes. If the recipe books are to be believed, they consumed an extraordinary variety of concoctions, many of them to our way of thinking not only incongruous but repellent. Ingredients were mixed irrespective of whether they complemented one another; and each course of a meal was conceived as an isolated, self-contained unit devoid of any relationship to the courses before and after. Typical of the menus of the period is this one, from a supper party given by the Wardens of the Goldsmiths Company of London: for the first course, roast capon, pike and baked venison; and for the second, cream of almonds, rabbit with chicken, turbot, pigeons and tarts. With each course, strawberries and sugar were also served.

Meat and fish were well represented at this dinner, as they were at all medieval feasts. But vegetables were not represented at all – for the simple reason that they were regarded by medical opinion as injurious to the health and fit only for the lower-classes. Variety was provided instead by the use of spices and fresh fruit. Spices were enormously popular in the Middle Ages, partly because of their association with exotic parts of the world and partly because of their value as flavouring. They were served sometimes with the meal and sometimes after it. Chaucer's Franklin liked them in one of his favourite dishes, 'sop-in-wine'. This was made by cutting up pieces of bread or cake, and pouring over them a sauce of wine, almond milk, saffron, ginger, sugar, cinnamon and cloves. Other cooks used spices to decorate their delicacies. According to one recipe, the pastry of a pork pie should be painted with saffron and baked to a deep gold. According to another, a chicken stew should be 'powdered with a spice that is light red coriander and set with pomegranate seeds and edged with fried almonds'. The result in each case would have been sure to gratify the diners to whom it was served.

Choosing a menu was not a matter in which the chef and his master had a completely free hand. Throughout the year their range of choices was limited by the alternation of fast and feast in the Church's calendar. Fridays were designated as days of fast – though all that this meant in practice was a switch from meat to fish; and before Christmas and Easter there were the long periods of fasting in Advent and Lent which lasted four weeks and six weeks respectively. In Lent there was not only a change of diet; there was also a limitation in the number of meals taken each day. In the Middle Ages there were typically two meals – dinner at about noon, and supper at about four. But in Lent they were reduced to one, just dinner. Not surprisingly, this degree of austerity was unpopular, and ways were sought of mitigating its rigour. One such was by making more than usually lavish use of sweetmeats and spices, which were not forbidden. But, even so, the coming of Easter Sunday must always have been eagerly awaited, not least by the children.

As for the actual manner in which a meal was eaten, manuals and manuscript illustrations suggest that this was fairly rough and ready. The food was heaped up on dishes laid down the middle of the table, and the diners were expected to help themselves. In a sophisticated household they would be given a wooden platter to eat from; elsewhere they would take a thick slice of bread, known as a trencher, and eat from that. A fresh trencher was cut for each course, the remains of the previous one being either tidied away or tossed to a dog. The most commonly used utensils were spoons and knives; forks do not appear to have become fashionable, at least in Britain, until the seventeenth century. As a result meats had to be chopped up beforehand into small, easily digestible portions, and grains and other foods pounded into a mess that could be sipped from a spoon. Guests were expected to bring their own cutlery. The host did not provide it himself: it was too expensive be given over to winter wheat or rye, another to spring barley, oats or legumes, and the third left fallow. The winter wheat, being the more exacting as well as the more valuable crop, was mostly grown on land fresh from the fallow, while the barley or oats was grown on land which in the previous year had carried a winter crop.

Harvesting, whether undertaken in the spring or the summer, was a job which the villagers had to do all at the same time, because when it was completed the animals were grazed on the stubble; and the risk of some of the crops being eaten obviously had to be avoided. For this reason alone, the agrarian life of the village had to be subjected to a measure of communal supervision. This was provided through the manorial court. At its regular monthly or bi-monthly meetings regulations were made concerning the all-important matter of grazing, and also about a host of other matters, like cropping and the clearing of ditches, and officials were appointed to enforce them. Given the collaborative nature of open-field farming, it was inevitable that the individual would find his freedom of action to some extent curtailed. But with this in the end he could cope: after all, he could still buy and sell land, and organize exchanges with his neighbours if he wanted to consolidate his holdings. To a far greater degree his freedom was curtailed by the power of the lord. If he was as a villein – that is, of unfree condition – he would have suffered a number of disabilities: he would not have been allowed to leave the manor; he would have had to pay a fine on inheriting his tenement; and, most important of all, he would have had to perform labour services on the lord's demesne – so many days a week throughout the year, and almost every day at harvest-time. No amount of good ale disbursed at the subsequent 'bedrips' (harvest supper) would compensate him for these interruptions to his own agricultural routine at such a busy time of the year.

It has often been remarked that open-field farming was a system of agriculture only extensively practised in the English lowlands: that in the north and in Scotland and Wales methods of farming were more varied. Up to a point this is certainly true. The open-field system in its classic form was a characteristic of the central and east midlands. Further north and west it became less common. Villages and hamlets varied increasingly in shape and size; and so too in consequence did their field systems. In the north of England and in Scotland fields were often made up of furlongs, divided in turn into strips, blocks of assarted land (sometimes enclosed), and intervening patches of meadow and pasture. In the same areas there were also many scattered settlements to which small, compact holdings were attached. The origins of these regional differences lay in the varying types of agriculture practised. Central and eastern England were classic arable areas; in the far north and the west, where the terrain was hillier, the raising of stock played a bigger role. In the north Welsh commote of Cafflogion in 1292 two-thirds of the taxable wealth of the taxpayers derived from their animals, and it is likely that a roughly similar proportion obtained in areas of similar economy. It is not insignificant that renders of cows were often a major element in the rent paid by upland communities in Wales.

While recognizing these distinctions, we should not exaggerate the distinction between the rural economies of the various parts of Britain. In the river valleys and lowlands of Scotland and Wales arable cultivation was actively practised throughout the Middle Ages; and, as time went on, it was to play an ever more important part in the rural economy. In Wales by the thirteenth century native law-texts abound with references to joint ploughing and to penalties for trespassing in corn. In Scotland by the fifteenth century there is evidence that shares in the common arable were periodically reallocated by the practice of 'run-rig' (the rigs being the strips in the fields). Cereal production, and by implication open-field farming, was a characteristic of rural life in almost every part of Britain.

The open-field system reached the peak of its development in the thirteenth and early fourteenth centuries when population was still rising. Peasants were actively producing corn both for their own needs and to raise cash, while lords were doing the same to satisfy demand in the market-place. Every available acre was put under the plough – even when it was patently unsuitable for the purpose, as on the chalk downlands of southern England. By the late thirteenth century there are signs that the balance between arable and pastoral was being upset. Hayfields, because they were so precious, were becoming relatively more expensive. At Laughton (Sussex), for example, 78 acres of meadow were valued in 1292 at £8.11s.6d., but 213 acres of arable at only £3.5s.2d. An imbalance as acute as the one suggested by these figures posed dangers for the rural economy. On every manor there were large numbers of livestock – ploughbeasts, pigs and of course the ubiquitous sheep – which had to be over-wintered, and in an age when rootcrops were unknown and grain was hardly to be spared, hay was almost the only fodder available. If it was not to be had, the animals went hungry. Only when the pressure on the soil eased, as it did after 1348, was the imbalance corrected. Marginal land was allowed to pass out of cultivation, and a lower ratio was established between arable and pastoral. Then and only then did a 'mixed' agriculture become truly mixed.

One result of the greater availability of pasture was a major shift in land use. Animal husbandry became more prominent. Sheep flocks were built up on a large number of estates. At Blockley, a manor of the bishops of Worcester, the number of head of sheep rose from fewer than 1,000 in the 1380s to between 1,400 and 1,760 half a century later. On Sir William de Etchingham's manor of Beddingham (East Sussex) it rose rapidly from 260 in 1307 to over 800 in 1311 and fluctuated between 700 and 1,000 in the later decades of the century. Sheep grazing had a number of attractions, most notably that it was less labour-intensive than arable husbandry: one shepherd could manage a normal flock of 200–300 animals, whereas a full-time staff of three was required to run even the smallest demesne. But it also had one major drawback. The prevalence of the variety of diseases described in the accounts as 'murrain' meant that mortality was high. At Claverham (East Sussex) the flock which Sir Andrew Sackville (ancestor of the Sackvilles of Knole) had carefully built up was decimated by a single visitation in 1367: 110 of his 367 ewes and 401 of his 931 lambs were lost. In the opinion of many far greater profit was to be made from the grazing of cattle. John Brome (d. 1468), owner of Baddesley Clinton (NT), waxed rich fattening stock for the markets of Warwick and Coventry. A lawyer by training, he had seen where money was to be made, and had invested in 300 acres of pasture and 200 acres of woodland at Baddesley. The income he enjoyed was roughly £40 per annum – enough to support knighthood, had he wished to assume it; and the house that he built, which forms the core of the present mansion, is evidence of his standing in local society. His example was not lost on his neighbours, many of whom, like the Lucys of Charlecote (NT), also turned from arable to the grazing of sheep or cattle. The markets they served were not always very large – Coventry, indeed, was a town in decline in this period. But, with the rapid rise in living standards, the per capita consumption of meat went up. People were able to buy foodstuffs beyond the basic necessities of bread and pottage. Underlying graziers' prosperity, then, was that of the peasants and townspeople whom they supplied.

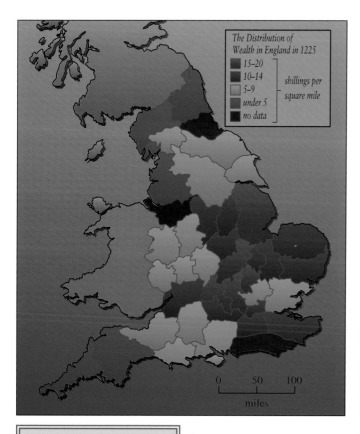

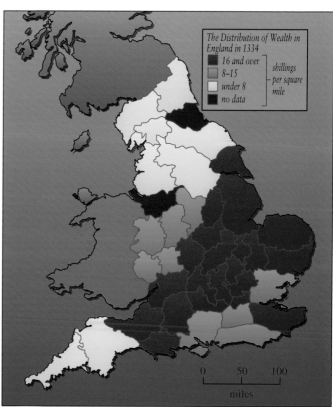

MAP 22: THE
DISTRIBUTION OF
WEALTH IN ENGLAND IN
1225 AND 1334

*The two maps are based on the
assessments for the levying of a
tax of one-fifteenth of
moveable property. What
emerges is that at both dates
the wealthiest parts of England
were the predominantly arable
areas of the midlands and
south-east. Within these areas,
however, a shift occurred in the
relative position of the various
counties. Wiltshire, Somerset,
Gloucestershire and Essex were
catching up on traditionally
wealthy areas like Norfolk. It
was in these counties that the
cloth trade was growing most
vigorously.*

THE DISTRIBUTION OF WEALTH

The changes we have observed in rural society were reflected in a significant shift in the geographical distribution of wealth in England. At the beginning of the thirteenth century that wealth was concentrated in a band of counties running from the Severn to the Wash. A little over a century later it was more widely distributed. Areas to the north and south of that band were sharing in the prosperity (map 22). How did this shift come about?

In a general sense it was a result of the vigorous growth of the economy in the interim. Population had risen, and with it the area under cultivation. More people were producing more wealth, and doing so too in parts of the country which had hitherto been lightly settled. Everywhere economic activity was on the increase, and prosperity was brought to areas which till then had lacked it.

Population growth, however, is at best only a partial explanation. It shows why the overall level of wealth was increasing; it does not show why it was increasing at different rates in different parts of the country – and why in particular it was increasing at such a spectacular rate in counties like Wiltshire and Norfolk. For an answer to these questions it is necessary to look not at the demographic developments of the time but at the changing fortunes of the cloth industry.

Cloth had for long been a staple English export. Since the twelfth century if not earlier it had been traded as far afield as Italy and Spain. In the mid-thirteenth century 'stamfort' cloths were listed in official records in Valencia and Montpelier. In 1253 Northampton 'plains' and 'rays' (striped cloths) were included in a list of maximum prices fixed in the kingdom of Portugal. In 1268 scarlets from Lincoln were assessed in a Castilian price schedule as more valuable than the supposed luxury cloths woven in Flanders. Evidently English products were holding their own wherever cloth was on sale. The names of some of the cloths afford a clue to their places of origin. Stamford was obviously a major centre, to judge from the use of the term 'stamforts'. 'Scarlets' are referred to as a Stamford speciality as early as 1204, but they were also made at Lincoln. Cloths of other varieties were made at Northampton, Louth, Beverley and elsewhere in eastern England. 'Burnets' were particularly associated with Beverley, and 'Russets' with Colchester. The industry, it is clear, was in a healthy and flourishing state in the late twelfth and early thirteenth centuries. But then quite suddenly in the late thirteenth century it went into decline. Interruptions to the trade caused by foreign wars, fierce Flemish competition and a failure to control rising wage costs all took their toll. By the mid-fourteenth century some vigorous cloth-making communities were reduced to petitioning the king for relief.

Relief of a sort did come. Remission of taxation was granted to a few of the worst hit towns, and reduction of tax farms to others. But measures of this kind were at best palliatives; they did not create new jobs to replace those that had been swept away. More effective in promoting revival was the stimulus given to the trade by the English war effort. With the onset of hostilities against Scotland in the 1290s and France in the 1330s, a large and continuing demand was generated for soldiers' uniforms – uniforms like the distinctive ones in red and white which the veteran campaigner Sir John Fastolf was to order from his tenants in Castle Combe (Wiltshire) in the early 1400s. At the same time, to raise money for war, the government imposed a tax on exports of wool which, quite unintentionally, served as a tariff wall behind which the trade could recover. Long-standing competitors like the Flemings now had to pay vastly more for a commodity which the English themselves were able to get net of tax. The result was that the English were able to undercut their competitors in a whole range of markets where the latter had once reigned supreme.

Specializing as they had to in cheaper cloths, the English found it vital to control their costs. But with time this was becoming more difficult because the weavers and other artisans had formed themselves into guilds to protect their interests. Employers' efforts to reduce wages and end restrictive practices therefore met with resistance and even the outright withdrawal of labour. The employers' response was to move the trade from the towns into the countryside – where labour was cheaper and less well organized. Looms were set up in villages where the right skills were to be found, and these places quickly acquired the character of small towns. Some of the most successful were ones in the valleys of Gloucestershire and Wiltshire – Stroud and Minchinhampton in the former county, Bradford-on-Avon and Castle Combe in the latter; for here were the fast-flowing streams that could drive the wheels for the fulling mills. But equally prominent were the settlements of Essex and East Anglia – places like Sudbury, Lavenham and Long Melford. It is the growing wealth of these communities and their counterparts in the west that accounts for the more even distribution of wealth across England in the late fourteenth century. The cloth industry created a boom in the countryside. Like all booms, this one was eventually to pass; but the prosperity that it generated can be savoured still in such buildings as the guildhall at Lavenham (NT) and the clothiers' houses of Bradford-on-Avon and Lacock (NT) in Wiltshire.

THE PATTERN OF INDUSTRY

Cloth was unusual among English manufactured products in being marketed so widely abroad. The majority of goods in all parts of the British Isles were disposed of at home. Bells, stained glass windows and altar vessels were snapped up by ecclesiastics and pious benefactors, tombs and brasses by people seeking commemoration, and pottery, pewter and precious metalwork by the nobility and gentry for their manor-houses. Raw materials like marble, alabaster and stone found a ready market among craftsmen who turned them into finished products.

The factors which influenced the location of industry were various (map 23). One was proximity to raw materials. In an age of slow communications it made sense wherever possible to work on materials at source – at or near the Purbeck quarries in Dorset, for example, in the case of marble. A second factor was the need to minimize the nuisance caused to local residents. A number of trades, such as tanning and metalwork, were banished if not to open country then to the suburbs because they were too

MAP 23: INDUSTRY AND TRADE IN THE LATE MIDDLE AGES

Industrial activity was found in both town and country. Mineral extraction tended to be based in the countryside; manufacturing was centred more in the towns. The major towns are shown here with a note of their specialities. For the relative ranking of the English towns see map 24.

BRASSES OF SIR JOHN D'ABERNON AND SIR WILLIAM DE ETCHINGHAM (opposite)

These two beautifully executed brasses are characteristic products of the main London workshops of their day. D'Abernon's, at Stoke d' Abernon, Surrey (above), used to be dated 1277 but is now thought to have been made nearer 1330. Sir William de Etchingham's, at Etchingham, East Sussex (below) dates from 1389. Sir William's head had gone by the eighteenth century

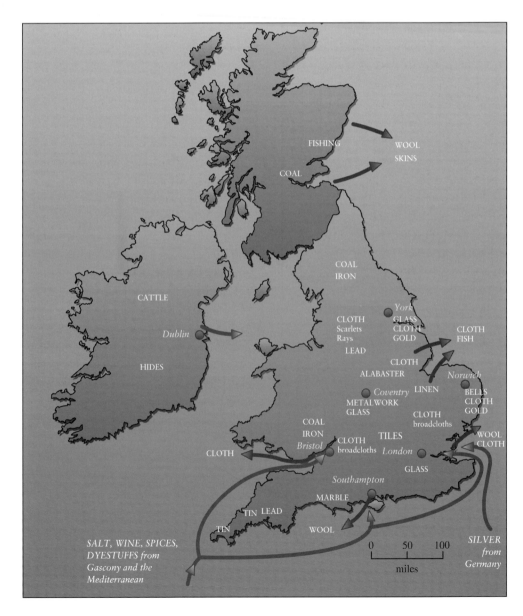

noisy or too noxious to be tolerated for long in towns. Thirdly, there was the need for access to a pool of skilled labour. While there were arguments of convenience for operating in the countryside, it was often only in the towns that the skills and know-how were to be found. In that case it was usual for manufacturing processes to be broken up – the earlier, simple processes being undertaken in the countryside, near the raw materials, the later, more technical ones, in a town.

For the most part medieval industry was organized along corporatist, not to say monopolistic, lines. Control of a trade was vested in an élite of masters. Entry was restricted to those who had served a long apprenticeship, and competition was subordinated to the overriding need for market regulation. In practice, however, the working of industry was a good deal less restrictive than this summary might suggest. There was considerable diversification across boundaries. In the retail trade, for example, men like the pepperers engaged not only in the pepper trade but in spices in general: just as, in the manufacturing field, someone describing himself as a brazier might make everything from cutlery through harnesses to iron-work for doors. The reasons for diversification were twofold. The first was the simple desire for profit. Men like pepperers had the market contacts to allow them to branch out into other lines of business, and they took full advantage of them. The second was the attraction of establishing control over sources of supply. In the cloth industry it was this control that led the dyers, who stood at the end of the manufacturing chain, to gain an ascendancy over those further back – the weavers, carders and fullers. The dyers' position was not dissimilar to that of modern employers.

The emergence in cloth-making of a dominant élite can be paralleled in other trades, where the need to control supplies was not so paramount. An obvious case is the commemorative trade. Here the London marblers quickly established an ascendancy which squeezed out not only the latteners, the dealers in raw 'latten' or brass, but also the marblers in the provincial workshops. Their success was allied to changes in the pattern of demand. With the steady increase in material wealth there was a growing demand for a type of memorial that suited all sizes of pocket. This the London marblers were able to satisfy by mass-production of the elegant, refined, if slightly monotonous, brass effigies of the type represented by those at Stoke d'Abernon (Surrey) and Etchingham (East Sussex). Other producers simply could not compete. One by one they went out of business, and they did not recover until the beginning of the fifteenth century.

None the less, for all their success, the cloth-making and marbling industries were the exception rather than the rule. Not many industries operated on the same scale. Glass-painting may have been one, bell-founding perhaps another. More typical of medieval industry as a whole were the innumerable potteries and tileries in the countryside. These were generally modest in scale and under-capitalized. For this reason their life-spans were fairly short – fifty years or less if they were called into being by a particular building project (say, a cathedral), longer if they served a wider local market. Remains of their fabrics are rare above ground, but footings have often been uncovered in excavations. Those at Limpsfield Common (Surrey) (NT), which were probably thirteenth century in date, stood on a site that had been in use from Roman times.

TOWN AND COUNTRY

When so much industry was located in the countryside, it is obvious that the towns must have performed a very different function from the one that they perform today.

They were not, as they are now, primarily centres of manufacture; they were rather centres of administration and exchange – nodal points around which local society cohered.

In one sense it was in this period that towns really came into their own. In the early and high Middle Ages a good deal of trade had been handled not in the towns – or not at least in the town centres – but at fairs on the edge of the countryside. Across the Channel there were the great fairs of Champagne and Flanders, which specialized in the exchange of luxury goods. At home there were those of Boston, Stamford, St Ives and Winchester, which served more local needs. By the late thirteenth century, however, for a number of reasons the fairs were in decline, and traders were congregating instead in the rapidly growing towns. London in particular benefited from this change, for it was there that the dealers in the main luxury goods – the mercers, goldsmiths and so on – made their headquarters. But other, smaller towns benefited too. Shops with workshops attached sprang up along the narrow streets, and something like the modern town centre came into being. Towns became places to which people went to do their shopping. In Sussex, for example, the servants of the Etchingham family are found going to Shoreham to buy fish and to Seaford to collect uniforms for two lads whom the lord was sending to school in Lewes. In East Anglia the Pastons are found sending their servants on similar expeditions to Norwich.

By comparison with today's towns, those of the Middle Ages were small. The larger provincial centres, like York, Norwich, Bristol and Newcastle, mustered at most 10,000 people each in the early 1300s, the lesser towns perhaps 3–5,000 each or fewer. The Scottish towns, such as Glasgow, Edinburgh, St Andrews and Aberdeen, were smaller still. Only London could have compared in size with the great cities of the continent. At its peak in the early fourteenth century it probably sheltered as many as 100,000 people, which would have made it the equal of such centres as Paris or Florence. In the aftermath of the Black Death, of course, it came down in size – probably to some 50–60,000 – though this shrinkage would have been compensated to a degree by immigration from the countryside. A combination of demographic decline and shifts in prosperity played havoc with the population levels of other towns (map 24). The major provincial centres of Bristol, York and Norwich maintained their positions relatively if not absolutely – Bristol indeed gained a little, because of its trading links with Ireland and Gascony: wine was imported there and cloth exported. Other towns, however, declined in both absolute and relative terms. Among the worst casualties were the former cloth-making towns of eastern and southern England, which suffered from the industry's move into the countryside. While not all of their tales of woe should be taken at face value – their purpose after all was to secure remission of taxes – a good many were the product of genuine hardship and distress.

The effect of, on the one hand, shrinkage of population in the towns, and, on the other, the accretion of urban characteristics by villages was to blur the distinction between town and country. The difference between the two became less one of function or size than one of status. A town in the legal sense – that is, a borough – was somewhere that enjoyed the privilege of self-government. The terms of this privilege were generally set out in a charter, or constitution, which the townsmen obtained from their lord – in the case of most of their number, that is, from the king. One of the first such charters to be granted was that for London, in the reign of Henry I. But others soon followed, those for Beverley and Lincoln being among the most influential. By the end of the century almost every important town had its charter, the only exceptions being places like St Albans and Bury St Edmunds which were held in tutelage by the lordship of powerful Benedictine abbeys.

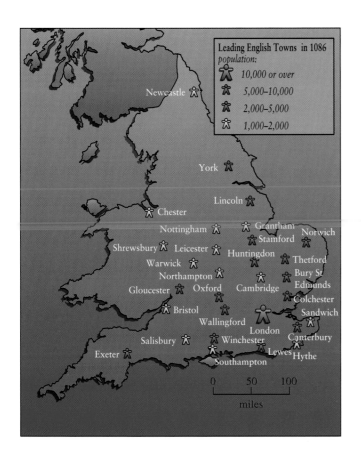

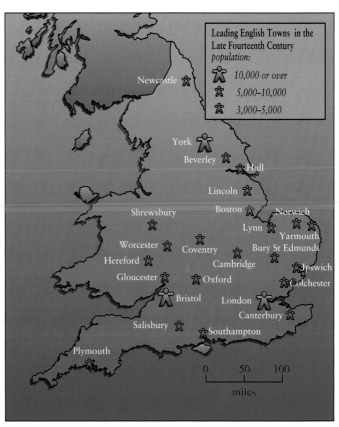

In the short run the granting of borough status cost lords income, which is why they were often reluctant to acquiesce in it: the dues and tolls which they had collected in the past were theirs to collect no longer. In the medium term, however, it had a different effect: it actually brought them new income. The granting of privileges attracted traders, and traders produced wealth. This is why so many lords at the time were keen to establish towns: they realized that there was money to be made in them. Typical of their number was the Bishop of Worcester, who founded Stratford-upon-Avon (Warwickshire). He laid out the streets and granted the standard privileges – the right to hold a market, exemption from tolls and so on – and before long his generosity reaped its reward. Settlers flocked in from the surrounding area, and a healthy income was generated in rents. Other founders were blessed with similar success, notably the Bishop of Lincoln at Thame (Oxfordshire) and Edward I at Conwy and Caernarfon – but by no means all were. For their initiative to pay off, a number of conditions had to be met: the location had to be right; there had to be good communications; and the immediate hinterland had to be clear. If any or all of these were missing, then the future could be bleak. Edward I discovered this when he established the town of Bere on a barren mountainside in Merioneth in the 1290s. The place was doomed from the start, and by the end of the century was deserted. Not even the king's backing could help it to overcome the disadvantage of its location.

In layout and appearance towns varied a great deal. Those of organic growth tended to develop in a loose, rather haphazard way. Their plans lacked coherence: streets twisted and turned for no apparent reason; they intersected at odd angles; they varied in length and breadth. York is the classic example of such a place; Northampton and, on a smaller scale, Rye are others. The planned towns, however, present a different

MAP 24: THE LEADING ENGLISH TOWNS IN 1086 AND THE LATE FOURTEENTH CENTURY

Comparing towns in size over a long period is difficult because of problems with the data. All the same a number of points emerge clearly enough from these maps. London was always pre-eminent. York, Bristol, Norwich and Newcastle-upon-Tyne were the main provincial centres. Boston, Yarmouth, Ipswich and Colchester were the fastest growing towns in the fourteenth century. Because of lack of evidence it is impossible to compile similar maps for Scotland in this period.

WORCESTER, *Greyfriars, Friar Street (NT)*
The overhanging storeys of this fifteenth-century and later dwelling would have been common in a medieval town

aspect. Generally, as at Stratford, they were laid out on a chequer-board pattern, with streets intersecting neatly at right angles. At the centre of the grid would usually be a market-place or, as at Winchelsea, a parish church. Lining the sides of the grids would be the tenement plots of the burgesses. Though a number of these planned towns were the lineal descendants of Roman towns – Winchester and Canterbury, for example – there is no reason to suppose that their plans were directly derived from these earlier settlements. The Saxons revived the art of town planning in the ninth-century 'burhs', and the tradition was kept alive in the centuries that followed.

Since towns were often surrounded by walls and space was at a premium, there was constant pressure to build upwards rather than outwards. Houses rose steadily higher, each storey projecting out from the one below to give more floor-space – hence the dizzying appearance of street façades like those of The Shambles at York or Friar Street at Worcester. Eventually it was impossible to build any higher, and lateral expansion had to be allowed. Towns then began to sprout suburbs, and it was here that the poor lived. The rich, by contrast, stuck together in the centre. Right down to modern times they held state there in houses that were often spacious and well constructed. Their accommodation consisted of shops and work-rooms on the ground floor and living rooms upstairs. These latter were furnished with chairs, stools, settles and wall-hangings, as can be seen at Paycockes (Essex) (NT), while adequate sanitation was ensured by the provision of garderobes. Before the thirteenth century the majority of such properties were of timber-frame construction, and they were for long to remain so in the towns of the West Midlands and North-West where wood was the staple building material. However, from the thirteenth century there was a tendency in many parts of Britain to rebuild in stone, for two main reasons. Firstly, there was a concern with fire risk: stone is less combustible than wood. And secondly, there was the matter of prestige. A stone-built house was a status symbol. It marked out its owner as a man of wealth and standing. The occupants of such properties as Grevel's House at Chipping Campden (Gloucestershire) or the slightly later Tudor Merchant's House at Tenby (NT) in Dyfed were clearly numbered among the leaders of their communities. Outward magnificence was their way of proclaiming that fact.

DESERTION IN THE COUNTRYSIDE

The social and demographic changes that transformed the urban geography of late medieval Britain left their most profound mark in the countryside. Between 1300 and 1500 over three thousand settlements disappeared, and many more were greatly reduced in size. The majority of these were in a broad swathe of territory stretching from Wiltshire north-eastwards to Yorkshire. In east Warwickshire, north Oxfordshire and Northamptonshire the rate of contraction was particularly severe. Immediately north of Wormleighton (Warwickshire) a group of no fewer than eight contiguous villages just vanished. Even today, after population has recovered, this area seems a strangely remote one. There are no towns for miles around, and churches stand alone in the fields with only the sheep and cattle for company. How did the process of contraction come about? And why was it so severe in the Midlands?

In a broad perspective the late medieval desertions should be seen as an episode in the long and constantly shifting history of settlement patterns. Villages were never fixed in either shape or location. They were for ever developing and regressing, reviving and decaying. In the seventh century, for example, the village of West Stow (Suffolk) was suddenly deserted after being occupied for a period of at least 250 years. Six centuries later, in the 1200s, Knapwell (Cambridgeshire) had to be moved from one trackway to another when shifts in traffic patterns threatened to leave it high and dry. These are only a couple of the many examples that could be quoted. Expansion, contraction, desertion and migration were part of the experience of almost every village in pre-modern Britain.

A general explanation of this sort, however, does not account for the rapid increase in the number of desertions in the late Middle Ages. Between 1300 and 1500 nearly a third of England's villages vanished from the scene. The reasons for this were many and complex. But there was one factor above all that mattered, and that was the fall in population. The Black Death of 1348–9 brought England's population down from roughly 5–6 million to some 3–4 million. A series of later visitations added to the problem by striking in particular at the young, thus preventing population from recovering. So for more than half a century, from 1349, the demographic curve was set firmly on a downward trend; and even after it had stabilized it showed little sign of moving up again. The result was a lengthy process of retreat. Villages which had never prospered ceased

A Tale of Two Towns: Rye and Winchelsea

*D*uring the 200 years from 1100 to 1300, roughly 170 new towns were established in England and Wales. Some were founded wholly or partially for military reasons – notably those planted by the Normans in Wales and the Marches – others much more for financial gain. But all owed their appearance to royal or seignorial initiative.

Rye and Winchelsea, in East Sussex, were both the plantations of an absentee landlord, the Abbot of Fécamp in Normandy. The motivation behind their establishment was only to a slight degree military. Certainly the need to protect the sea route to Normandy was one element in it; but it was not uppermost. Far more important was the abbot's appetite for profit. He wanted traders to come and take up residence on his estates. This he did by establishing a couple of boroughs on sites near the confluence of the Brede and Tillingham rivers. One he placed on a hill to the east of the Tillingham, near to the ancient settlement of Rye. The other – Winchelsea – he placed a mile or two to the south-west by the sea.

Rye was in existence by 1086, when the 'novus burgus' is mentioned in Domesday Book; and Winchelsea probably came into being no more than a year or two later. But of the circumstances attending the creation of the two towns virtually nothing is known because no documentation has survived. The only evidence to have come down to us from this time is that of the layout of the streets, which in the case of Rye follows the characteristic gridiron pattern. The abbot's new town was not just planted, then; it was planned.

Rye was guaranteed a fairly secure existence on the top of its hill. But it was otherwise with Winchelsea. Lying as it did on the marshes close to the sea it was in constant danger of inundation, and after serious flooding it was decided in the late thirteenth century to remove it to a less vulnerable site on a hill three miles further inland. In 1281 Edward I appointed Sir Stephen de Penchester, Itier of Angoulême and Henry le

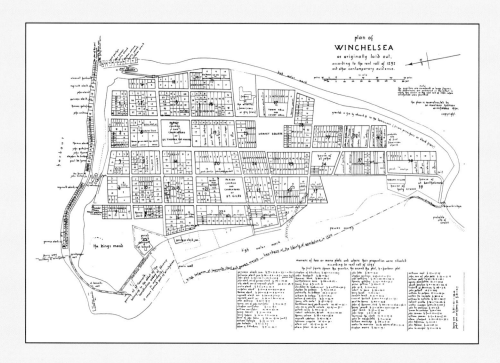

WINCHELSEA (East Sussex)
A reconstruction of the layout of Edward I's new town of the 1290s. It is doubtful if all of the plots were ever taken up

Waleys to measure out the new burgage plots and to let them at a fixed rent to the 'barons' or citizens of the town. Itier and Waleys were men of wide experience in the art of town planning. They had been closely involved in the programme of 'bastide' building undertaken by Edward in the Duchy of Gascony, and the expertise which they acquired in the course of their work there they put to good use in the Sussex new town. For example, they adopted in an exceptionally thoroughgoing form the chequer-board layout, which was all but universal in the duchy. Streets were made to intersect at right angles, so dividing the town up into some thirty-nine rectangles or 'quarters' (see plan). In one quarter the church was placed, in another the friary, and in another again the market. All the rest were divided up into plots which were assigned to the residents. Outside the walls and at the bottom of the hill adjoining the quay additional tenements were laid out which are referred to in the documents as 'subpendentes'. These were probably the sites of the warehouses. Storage space would have been essential in a major wine-importing town like Winchelsea. Provision for it was made as well within the walls in the form of spacious cellars, which are still one of the glories of the town (NT).

Whether the ambitious plans for the New Winchelsea were ever fully realized is unclear. The church of St Thomas, as it stands today, is a fragment consisting only of the chancel. It is possible that a nave was, in fact, built and then destroyed in a French raid; but equally it is possible that one was never built at all, for prosperity at Winchelsea was to be short-lived. Within a century or less of the town's removal the sea which had engulfed its predecessor began to retreat, leaving its harbour inaccessible to sea-borne traffic. The life-blood of the town ebbed away. People left to seek work elsewhere; tenements fell into decay; and sheep and cattle moved in to graze where business and enterprise had once flourished. Winchelsea became a backwater – still regularly returning its two Members to Parliament down to 1832 – but a backwater none the less. Rye was the ultimate victor in the contest for supremacy between the two towns. And long after it has ceased to be a port of any significance, it still flourishes as a market town and tourist centre.

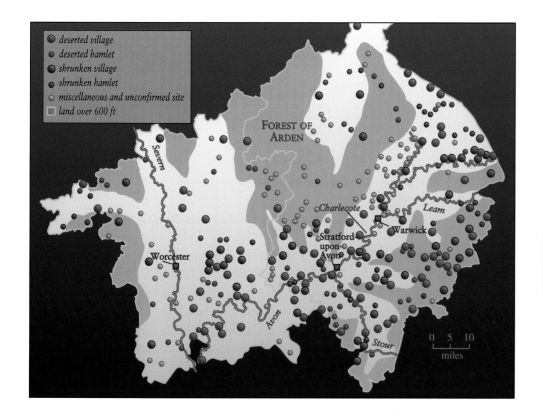

- deserted village
- deserted hamlet
- shrunken village
- shrunken hamlet
- miscellaneous and unconfirmed site
- land over 600 ft

MAP 25: DISTRIBUTION OF DESERTED AND SHRUNKEN SETTLEMENTS IN WARWICKSHIRE AND WORCESTERSHIRE

New deserted or shrunken settlements are still being identified, and the map records the state of knowledge at the end of the 1970s. Note the high incidence of desertion in the Avon valley and south of Warwickshire.

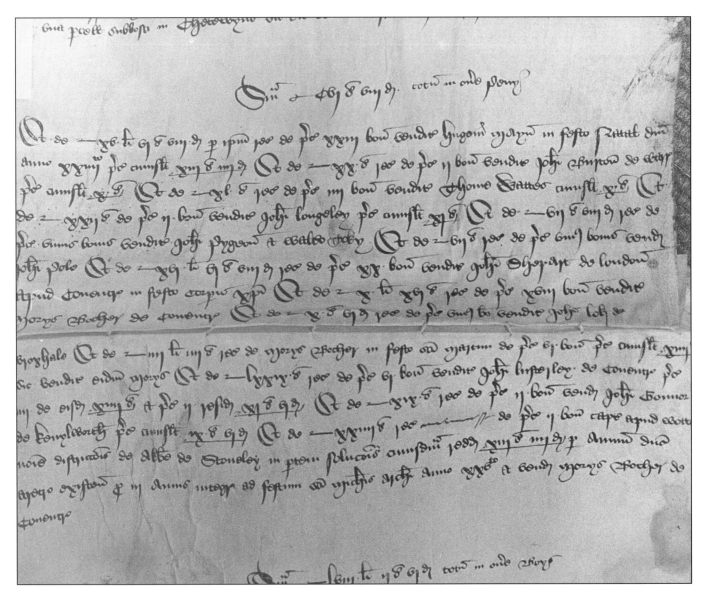

BADDESLEY CLINTON (West Midlands) (NT)
A section of an account roll of the manor for the year 1445–6 showing sales of stock to butchers of Coventry and Warwick

to exist, while ones which had prospered but had experienced excessive growth underwent severe shrinkage. All over the country land was being abandoned or turned to other uses.

As striking as the overall process of retreat, however, was its uneven progress across the British Isles. Some areas were worse hit than others, and in those which were hit worst there were districts which escaped almost unscathed. Scotland escaped relatively lightly. South of the border, in the midland counties of Warwickshire and Worcestershire, the valleys of the Avon and Stour suffered very badly, while the forested areas to their north were hardly affected at all (map 25). The reasons for this unevenness are not always clear, but an important clue is to be found in the history of land use. The areas of most acute desertion were those which had specialized in arable husbandry. With the reduction in demand for grain after 1370 their populations went over to a form of mixed husbandry with a growing emphasis on pasture. In the north Warwickshire woodlands this change could be accommodated quite easily because there was much enclosure and mixed land use already. A fully-fledged open-field

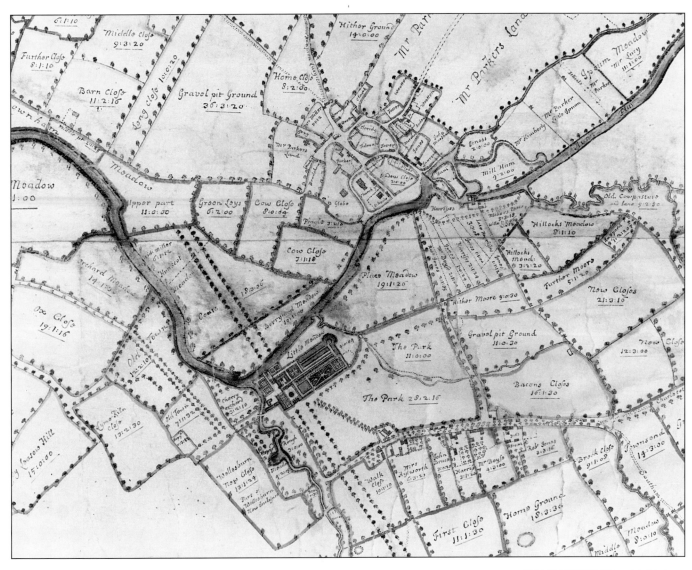

CHARLECOTE (Warwickshire)
(NT)
*A map of the park in 1736
recording the site of the former
settlement on the left as 'Old Town'*

system, however, like that operating in the south of the county, responded less readily.
Conversion of arable strips to pasture, piecemeal enclosure and increases in the number
of animals led time and again to acrimony, dissatisfaction and eventually to the demise
of the village as a community.

The attraction of pasture, of course, was that it could be used for grazing – in particular, in areas like south Warwickshire, for the grazing of sheep. A kind of specialist
economy emerged in which sheep grazing assumed a dominant role. Characteristic of it
was the Lucy family estate in which the fields of no fewer than six former villages –
those of Alscot, Fulbrook, Goldicote, Hunscote, Willicote and, most famously,
Charlecote (NT) – were turned over to this use. By the beginning of the sixteenth century no fewer than 2,676 beasts were grazing on the family's well-nourished pastures
near Stratford-upon-Avon.

It was the relentless advance of the sheep that led contemporaries to accuse families
like the Lucys of being the prime movers of depopulation. It was said against them that
they found it more profitable to have sheep on their lands than people, and that they
expelled the latter to make way for the former. The position in reality was more

complicated. Landlords generally turned to sheep-grazing only when the people had already gone. If no rents were being paid, then some other way had to be found of generating an income. Sheep-grazing was favoured because it made little use of labour. But financially it was by no means the panacea it was once thought to have been. Wool prices were low for most of the late Middle Ages, and as a result profits were too. Only by comparison with the still lower profits from corn-growing could those from sheep-grazing be considered in any way attractive. In other words, it was not so much avarice that drove families like the Lucys to enclose as desperation. If a village was swept aside – or, as in Charlecote's case, relocated at the gates of a park – it was because its life-blood had already drained away.

XV
THE RANKS OF SOCIETY

The economic developments of the Middle Ages had the effect not only of adding to the stock of the nation's wealth, but also of widening the gulf between rich and poor. Growing inequality of income brought about an increase in social differentiation; and the vocabulary of rank and status was by stages adapted and then extended to take account of this. To reduce this society to some two or three groups is to risk misrepresenting it; but the risk has to be taken if any generalizations are to be made about its character.

THE LORDS

The lords were the descendants of the Norman knights who had triumphed at Hastings and subsequently colonized the greater part of the British Isles. As John de Warenne, Earl of Surrey was to tell Edward I's commissioners of enquiry while brandishing his sword: 'Here, my lords, is my warrant. My ancestors came with William the Bastard and conquered their lands with the sword, and by the sword I shall defend them.'

The association between arms and privilege to which John drew attention was one which had its origins in the rise of cavalry warfare in the eleventh and twelfth centuries. Fighting on horseback was an activity in which only an élite could indulge. It entailed a régime of training so rigorous that only those freed from other occupations could undertake it, and it necessitated a financial outlay – on mounts and on armour – so heavy as to preclude participation by all but the very rich. In other words, the exercise of arms was slowly but inevitably being turned into a professional activity that was paid for by the labours of a dependent peasantry. The *corps d'élite* of the battlefield was on the way to becoming a social élite too – dominant politically as well as militarily, and supported by the tenurial structure of feudalism.

The values espoused by these men were the ones stressed in the epic literature of the time: prowess, valour and loyalty. These had their roots in the heroic age of pagan antiquity, and they lived on into the following age of Christian enlightenment. But with the passage of time, and particularly in the late eleventh and twelfth centuries, they underwent a subtle transformation. For one thing they were softened by a change in sensibility that made it possible to envisage the notion of service to a woman as well as service to a lord; and for another they were given a Christian overlay which turned the wanderings of the knight errant into something in the nature of a quest for truth and a test of personal worth. These values were still recognizably the values of a knightly élite – hence the use of the word 'chivalry' to describe them. But now, subtly modified, and subordinated to ends of which the Church could approve, they were given a more mystical flavour and were made the means of imposing a measure of restraint on the wilder and more unruly elements of the class.

In a sense chivalry acted as a substitute for the discipline imposed by loyalty to the state. Because such loyalty was only imperfectly developed in the Middle Ages an alternative form of restraint had to be found, and chivalry was seen as filling the gap. In practice, of course, it was a somewhat ineffectual substitute. It did little to mitigate the horrors of war or to bring peace to the areas that suffered them. But it did generate in the knights a mutual respect which transcended national divisions. It encouraged them to behave towards each other with a decency which might otherwise have been lacking; and it made it easier for them to come to terms again when hostilities were over. These may not have been large gains; but they were better than no gains at all.

The feelings of solidarity felt by the military élites of all European societies were strengthened in the late Middle Ages by a growing emphasis on lineage and nobility of blood. By the fourteenth century these had come to count for more than knighthood itself as qualifications for admission to the charmed circle. Provided a young tiro could show that his father and ancestors had been knights and had borne arms valorously, that was proof enough of status; there was no need for him to be knighted himself. The effect of this shift of emphasis was simultaneously to narrow and yet to broaden the base of the aristocratic class. It narrowed it by making admission more difficult for those who lacked pedigree. It widened it by making it possible for all the offspring of a lord or knight, and not just those who were themselves knights, to inherit his status. Whether the former or the latter tendency triumphed depended on the social and legal traditions of particular societies.

France represented one such tradition. There the nobility were defined by law. They had to be, because they enjoyed certain privileges – notably exemption from taxation on the grounds that they otherwise supported their country by providing personal military service. Therefore those were considered noble who were born the sons of nobles. The result was a large, but relatively impoverished, *noblesse* whose claim to nobility was attested less by their style than by their legal condition.

England and Scotland, on the other hand, represented a different tradition. Their nobilities were not defined by law: there was no reason why they should have been, because they carried no fiscal privileges. They were defined only by possession of wealth. To that extent they were more accessible than were their counterparts across the Channel. Entry into them was open to anyone with sufficient means; and there were no legal impediments to be surmounted en route.

In Scotland another sign of the relative fluidity of society was the absence of any titles to distinguish the greater from the lesser nobility. 'Lord' and 'laird', respectively, were the words which were used; but, of course, they are actually the same word, and the distinction between them was one of degree not of kind. 'Lairds', like lords, lived in castles or tower-houses of the kind we still see at Drum (NTS) and Kellie (NTS); and lords and 'lairds' sat together in a single assembly when summoned to Parliament. They

DRUM CASTLE (Grampian) (NTS)
On the left is the 'tower house' of
the original castle. It was built by
Richard Cementarius, first provost
of Aberdeen, in the late thirteenth
century

were both members of the second estate, so no greater terminological precision was required.

In England, however, it was otherwise. By the end of the Middle Ages a sharp distinction had emerged in the former undifferentiated nobility between a higher nobility or parliamentary peerage on the one hand and a lesser nobility or gentry on the other; and on both sides of the divide the process of stratification was carried still further by the gradual formation of internal hierarchies – those of duke, marquess, earl, viscount, baron in the nobility, and of knight, esquire, gentleman in the gentry. In part this proliferation of ranks was simply a by-product of the greater complexity of English society, and reflected people's need to make sense of it by reducing it to a series of manageable groups. In part, it was also a by-product of the singular development of representative institutions in England.

Parliament had come into existence by the thirteenth century as an instrument of royal government. Its purpose was to advise the king on matters of policy and to set his need for money against his subjects' need for redress of grievances. At first, attendance was restricted to ministers, judges, bishops and the great magnates, all of whom were there in response to a royal summons. But as the king's demands impinged on ever more of his subjects, so it became necessary to arrange for the presence of an elected

More than Embroidery: The Role of Women in Medieval Society

The growth of chivalry had important consequences for the position of women. Not least among them was a lowering of their status as landowners. In the early Middle Ages aristocratic women had enjoyed a position of considerable legal independence. But in the eleventh and twelfth centuries this was undermined as land was increasingly subjected to liability for knight service. Women tenants could not perform this service themselves; so provision had to be made for others to perform it on their behalf. In the case of minors it was generally carried out by someone nominated by the lord from whom the estate was held, and in the case of those women of mature age (and assuming that they were married) by the husband. The need to ensure the adequate performance of military service provides the background to the gradual increase in the eleventh century in the rights enjoyed by the husband over his wife's property. In England, by the end of this process, the married woman ceased to have any independent personality at law. Loss of status could hardly have gone further than that.

However, the regard in which women (well-to-do women particularly) were held was enhanced by the growth of the cult of the Virgin Mary. The cult operated at two levels. At one the Virgin was presented as an example of humility and courtesy, and a model of virtue to which ladies could aspire. At another she was presented as the Queen of Heaven. Pictures and statues depicted her as possessing an unmistakably royal appearance; and while, of course, suggestions of similarity to any earthly women were played down, she was made to appear as someone to whom homage and allegiance were due.

The Virgin Mary was by no means the only exemplar of womanhood presented by the Church. At the opposite extreme there was Eve, the temptress. But in terms of the influence that she had on perceptions of women the Virgin was the more influential of the two, and her cult contributed powerfully to the shift in attitudes towards women that occurred in the twelfth century. It was at roughly this time that women began to be regarded by their menfolk with an amorous longing that had been absent before. In the past it had been the love of man for man which had been celebrated in literature – that of Roland for Oliver in the Chanson de Roland, for example; but in the twelfth century it was the love of man for woman. Provençal troubadours are heard singing of the valorous deeds performed by young knights for their ladies. The yearning felt by these men is evoked with a tenderness never before expressed, as is the anguish that tore them when their love was not reciprocated. Love is seen in this poetry as a uniquely ennobling force – as both 'a source of virtue and a cathartic ecstacy'. As such, of course, it is being idealized. But so too is womanhood itself. The lady beloved is invariably represented as being superior in qualities of mind to the knight who is courting here. At the same time, however, she is portrayed as remote and inaccessible. She keeps her suitor waiting in agony before disclosing her intentions to him. She does not allow a whiff of warmth and compassion to enter into the sentiments she utters. Obedience and submission appear to be the sole objects of her desire. She is 'la belle dame sans merci'.

In which case what is being described is not a 'love affair' as we today would understand the term; it does not involve a relationship between equals. Rather it resembles the relationship between mistress and lover – as is only to be expected of a society in which marriages, arranged as they commonly were for material motives, were often loveless. Romantic relationships had necessarily to be conceived in adultery. So the language in which they were expressed was that of obedience and submission. Small wonder, then, that for the lady, love's greatest reward was the establishment of lordship over the suitor.

All of this bears out the truth discovered by the knight in the Wife of Bath's Tale – that what women desire most of all in the world is the same dominion over their husbands as they had over their lovers. In saying this the knight was speaking for the Wife herself. In the course of a long and active life she had established dominion over no fewer than five husbands, and the Prologue to her Tale is a rondo burlesque in which she describes how she ruled over them:

> I'd tackle one for wenching, out of hand,
> Although so ill the man could hardly stand,
> Yet he felt flattered in his heart because
> He thought it showed how fond of him I was.
> I swore that all my walking out at night
> Was just to keep his wenching well in sight.
> That was a dodge that made me shake with mirth;
> But all such wit is given us at birth.
> Lies, tears and spinning are the things God gives
> By nature to a woman, while she lives.
> So there's one thing at least that I can boast,
> That in the end I always ruled the roast.

No one conforms better than the Wife to the medieval stereotype of the noisy, bullying woman. But someone with a good claim to be a runner-up is surely the virago depicted on a misericord in Chester Cathedral. Caught in the act of giving her husband a sound drubbing, she is shown lifting him by the top of his head and preparing to set about him with a washing beetle. The poor man is obviously helpless in her hands and he does not stand a hope of escaping.

THE BATTLE OF THE SEXES
A henpecked husband is beaten about the head by his virago of a wife. (A misericord of the 1380s in Chester Cathedral)

The implication of this and other evidence is that male supremacy was somewhat more uneasily maintained in practice than exclusive attention to the letter of the law would lead us to suppose. Women, though physically weaker than their husbands, yielded nothing to them in spirit. They could and did run businesses. Katherine Lightfoot, a Londoner, is known to have been a builder's merchant prior to her marriage to the mason Henry Yevele; and there were others like her. Indeed, their numbers may well have increased in the years after the Black Death when there was a shortage of labour. Moreover, women could and did run landed estates. In widowhood and during the periodic absences of their spouses they simply had to. Margaret of Brotherton, Duchess of Norfolk, for one, acquitted herself with distinction in this capacity long after she had seen two husbands into the grave.

If we turn from upper-class to peasant society we find that women were engaged in an even greater variety of employments. In the fields they did all the jobs that men did – haymaking, weeding, mowing and so on; and at home they were also occupied in various forms of commercial activity, notably in brewing and money-lending. If any two areas are to be regarded as their domain, it is probably these. In some villages in the Midlands nearly a half of all those engaged in brewing were women, and the income which they earned from their work gave them a considerable measure of economic independence. Indeed, taking all the evidence in sum, it seems likely that women in peasant society enjoyed a greater degree of freedom and occupational independence than did their counterparts in the aristocracy. In other words, the lower down in society we go, the more equality between the sexes we find.

KELLIE CASTLE (Fife) (NTS)
The core of the castle is a fifteenth-century tower-house typical of those built by the Scottish lairds in the late Middle Ages

element that could speak for the people as a whole. This was the lower house, the future House of Commons. Its members were chosen by the shires (hence the use of the term 'knights of the shires' to describe them), and they saw themselves as the spokesmen of their communities. They met separately from the lords; and within a short time their ranks were swelled by the addition of representatives of the towns as well – the folk who in France would have sat by themselves in the so-called 'Third Estate'.

The fact that the knights were thus separated from the nobility, who might be supposed their natural partners, and thrown together with the townsmen, with whom they might be supposed to have had less affinity, had major consequences for the development of English society. It led to the formation of the 'class' we call the country gentry. It fostered the identification of gentry with shire (and thus in a later age stimulated the writing of county histories by gentlemen of antiquarian inclination), and it broke down the social barriers between town and country. It may even have reconciled the gentry to seeing their younger sons go into trade (assuming that they needed to be reconciled). Richard Whittington, to think only of the most famous of English merchants, was the younger son of a Gloucestershire squire, William Whittington of Pauntley.

Although the higher and lesser nobility – the peers and the gentry – ended up for parliamentary purposes in different houses, and thus in a sense constituted separate 'classes', relations between them continued to be close. There were good reasons why this should have been so: they moved in the same circles; they were brought up in one another's households; and they subscribed to the same ethic, the ethic of chivalry. In addition, there were more tangible interests that drew them together. The gentry saw in the nobility possible patrons and protectors – men who would help them and assist them – and in their households they saw possible sources of employment and ladders of social advancement. The nobility, on the other hand, saw in the gentry possible allies and supporters – men whose local eminence would be of assistance in the establishment of their own territorial hegemony. Commonly this convergence of interests found expression in the making of indentures of retainer, or 'manrents' as they were known in Scotland, which formed the basis of a contractual relationship between the two. A good example is provided by the indenture which John of Gaunt made with Sir Maurice de Berkeley of Uley (Gloucestershire) in 1391. Maurice was retained to stay with the duke for life in peace and war. When summoned, he would attend the duke, from whom he would receive food and drink in common with the other knights of his rank. In return he would receive annually a retaining fee of £20, to be paid in two instalments at Easter and Michaelmas. Gaunt by this instrument gained the services of a dependant in a part of the country where his following was otherwise small, and Berkeley the support of a patron who was second only in importance to the king.

Retaining – or 'bastard feudalism' as it is often known – became the standard means by which local society, in Scotland as well as in England, was organized to the mutual benefit of magnates and gentry. The scattered distribution of most magnate estates – a characteristic begun by the Conquest and made more pronounced by subsequent acquisitions by marriage and inheritance – made it imperative for their owners to draw gentry, resident in more distant parts, into the business of protecting and managing those estates. For a magnate as richly endowed as John of Gaunt this meant recruiting in almost every county. For a lord like Sir Thomas de Berkeley, whose estates were both smaller and more concentrated, it was sufficient to recruit only in those counties in which his estates lay – in his case Gloucestershire and Somerset. Sir Edmund de Clevedon, the builder of Clevedon Court (NT), was one who was drawn into his service. Others included Sir John Tracy of Toddington, Sir Simon Bassett of Uley and Sir Thomas de Bradeston of Winterbourne – the last being the probable donor of the great east window of Gloucester Cathedral. Sometimes these retainers became rich and important men in their own right, as the splendour of Bradeston's gift so amply shows. Sometimes they even rose into the ranks of the peerage themselves, as did Gaunt's servants, the Hungerfords. When that happened, they were ready to start looking for retainers of their own.

THE TOWNSMEN

Society in the towns in the Middle Ages divided sharply into two – those who enjoyed the privilege of freedom, and those who did not. The latter were easily in the majority. They included the servants, the labourers and artisans who thronged the upper storeys of the tall, jettied buildings and gathered in the slums – in other words, all those whose hopes and fears were so memorably captured by William Langland in *Piers Plowman*. Among their number were a fair proportion of immigrants from the countryside (urban mortality being what it was, the towns could hardly have replaced, let alone increased, their populations without recruitment from outside). The 'new towns', obviously, had the highest proportion of immigrants, the great majority of them coming from within a

*KING'S LYNN: ST GEORGE'S
GUILDHALL (Norfolk) (NT)
The front of the largest surviving
guildhall in Britain. Begun in the
late Middle Ages, the hall exhibits
work from a number of periods*

10–15 mile radius. But established towns, too, drew heavily from without. At Bristol, Gloucester and Worcester at the beginning of the fourteenth century, roughly a third of the taxpaying population had place-name surnames, suggesting that they or their immediate forbears were immigrants, and recent ones at that. Interestingly, the fact that these men were taxpayers shows that they had not ended up as down-and-outs. If the medieval streets were not paved with gold, they at least pointed the way to where gold could be found.

The governing élite of the towns was recruited from the ranks of those who were of free condition – that is, the well-to-do citizenry who owned property and were exempt from tolls. Generally, the privilege of freedom was gained by one of three routes: patrimony, apprenticeship or redemption (paying a lump sum down). In the twelfth century the idea still lingered that town air made free – in other words, that a year and a day's residence in a town enfranchised a villein – but by the fourteenth century this idea was wearing thin, and the commonest routes to freedom were redemption and apprenticeship. How many people might typically be free is hard to say, as the number varied from place to place and from time to time. In London in the fourteenth century only about one in four of adult males were free – and the males themselves comprised only half of the population. Although in some towns the rules were relaxed to admit more to the élite, there can be little doubt that for the most part urban government was strongly oligarchical in nature.

The men who ruled the towns were by all appearances a self-confident group. The magnificent guildhalls that they built at places like Coventry, Lavenham (NT) and King's Lynn (NT) in Norfolk bear witness to the feelings of pride and solidarity that they had. But alongside the self-confidence there was also a measure of insecurity. They felt – some of them quite strongly – the lack of that respectability which only the ownership of land could confer. For this reason it was not uncommon for them to invest a proportion of their capital in the purchase of a country estate. Laurence de Ludlow, the wool merchant who negotiated the wool custom of 1294 for Edward I, established himself at Stokesay (Shropshire), where he built the fortified manor-house which still survives. Half a century later the London draper Sir John Pulteney bought the Penshurst estate in Kent, and built a house there which would have been (and later was) fit for a duke. These were of course exceptional purchases by exceptional men, and they can hardly be accounted representative. Most burgesses who established themselves as landed proprietors were men of less ample means who invested at a more modest level by buying estates worth no more than £10–£15; and their aim was less to make a complete break with their urban roots than to win parity of esteem with the gentry. Up to a point they were successful. If intermarriage is taken as an index of social acceptance, they may be said to have won measured approval. The gentry were happy enough to take the hands of their daughters, and happier still to take the dowries they brought. But what they were not prepared to do was to offer their own daughters in return – apparently because they were reluctant to sacrifice them to what they saw as 'the insecurity of life without land' (Thrupp).

This was not simply a disguise for prejudice, for the mutability of human fortunes was a favourite theme of the moralists of the time. It was expressed in the image of the wheel of fortune, which raised up the successful as it was later to cast them down again. Eloquent proof of its workings was to be found in the experience of those who lent money to the Crown. Time and again they were bankrupted – first the Italian banking houses, and then the English syndicates that succeeded them. But there was another sense in which urban life was insecure. It lacked the dynastic stability valued so highly by an élite whose claim to respect was based on heredity. Only rarely did burgess families maintain their pre-eminence for longer than three or four generations. Indeed, more often it was only for one or two. Usually they fell victim to extinction in the male line – because to an even greater extent than the nobility they were deficient in producing male heirs. But sometimes too there was a failure of business capacity, a failure that could have been cushioned had there been land to fall back on. Thus it may be no coincidence to find that in one city – York – the dynasties that lasted longest were the ones that had such an endowment of land.

Burgess fortunes may have been short-lived, but while they lasted they could certainly be large. The London merchant Gilbert Mayfield is known to have amassed capital of nearly £1,500 – equivalent to the annual income of an earl – before he went bankrupt in the 1390s. His contemporary, Richard Whittington, appears to have amassed even more – perhaps as much as £2,000–£3,000. Both Mayfield and Whittington significantly were mercers, because it was in mercery that the biggest profits were to be made. The market for textiles was so much bigger than in most other lines of business, and the opportunities to be seized so much greater. Those who were successful, then, tended to be outstandingly so, and went on to convert their wealth into power, by taking control of the governing councils of the towns in which they lived. At York in 1420, out of a governing body of twenty-nine, no fewer than twenty-two were merchants; only five

Lordship and Lineage: The Life-Style of the Nobility

F or much of the Middle Ages the nobility led a peripatetic life-style (map 26). Driven by a seemingly irrepressible restlessness, they itinerated from manor-house to manor-house, dragging their servants with them. Humphrey Stafford, Duke of Buckingham travelled between houses as far apart as Writtle (Essex), Maxstoke (Warwickshire), Thornbury (Gloucestershire) and Stafford itself. His inheritance was a particularly scattered one. But at a less exalted level even a lord whose estates were more concentrated covered a fair number of miles in a year. Sir William de Etchingham, for example, a Sussex knight, was constantly on the move between his properties in the east and west of the county. According to an account roll of his manor of Beddingham, near Lewes, he passed through, or stayed overnight in, that village almost once a month in the year 1310–11: in January and February; in late April while on his way to Chichester; in June en route to his wife's manor of Stopham; again in July and August; and finally in September at harvest-time for a full week.

The roots of this itinerant life-style lay deep in the early medieval past. Moving from manor to manor, and consuming the surplus of each in turn, had been the means by which the nobility had fed themselves in an age when they had no choice but to be self-sufficient. In later times, when the use of cash allowed them to satisfy their needs in the market, they kept it up because it enabled them to supervise their officials and to give visible presence to their lordship. There was, therefore, much to be said in its favour. But it suffered from one main disadvantage, and that was its cost. A whole host of manor-houses had to be maintained and kept in readiness for the lord's descent. With the onset of inflation in the early thirteenth century, and the more gradual rise in the cost of living that followed, this was more than many families could afford. Thus increasingly they tended to settle down at one or, at the most, two of their houses and bring these up to the desired levels of comfort.

Manor-houses of the late Middle Ages were, therefore, generally larger and more spacious than their predecessors. The older, more modest type of property which they superseded is represented by Old Soar in Kent (NT/English Heritage), a knightly dwelling of about 1290. As it stands today, it consists of a two-storey solar block out of which a chapel projects at one end and a garderobe at the other. The hall which would once have run west from it is now lost (its place being taken by a Georgian house). Only the private wing remains. Its walls inside are now bare, but in their heyday they would have been plastered and decorated with paintings of the kind that can still be seen at Longthorpe (Northamptonshire).

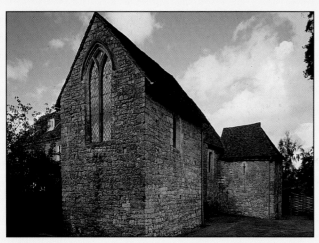

OLD SOAR *(Kent) (NT/English Heritage)*
The solar block of the Culpepers' manor-house, built in about 1290

The larger type of house that became fashionable in the late Middle Ages is represented by Ightham Mote (Kent) (NT), a property which in origin consisted of the familiar hall and solar block, but which was gradually added to until it assumed its present courtyard plan. Some of the additions were commissioned largely for effect – the gate-tower, for example, and the early Tudor chapel. But others were occasioned by the more practical needs of providing more rooms for the private use of the lord and his lady, and of finding accommodation for visiting lords and their retainers. The level of comfort and decoration in these rooms varied according to their use. In the servants' quarters standards were fairly low; but in the hall and private quarters they were higher. Furnishing even here was fairly sparse, but a note of opulence was struck by the hanging of tapestries. Two such pieces still adorn the hall today. It is at Cotehele (Cornwall) (NT), however, that the overall impression created by these cloths can best be savoured. Room after room in the house is hung with them, creating an impression of rich but sombre magnificence.

IGHTHAM MOTE (Kent) (NT)
One of the finest moated manor-houses surviving from the fourteenth and fifteenth centuries

The tapestries at Cotehele, as so often elsewhere, are not contemporary with the house; they are seventeenth-century replacements of lost originals. But the presence of such hangings in houses in the late Middle Ages is amply attested by inventories of the period. In the hall of his castle at Caister in Norfolk, for example, Sir John Fastolf is known to have had pieces depicting the Assumption of the Virgin, the Siege of Falaise and scenes of hunting and hawking. These were 'cloths of Arras' – that is, tapestries imported from the town of that name in Artois. They were luxury items, expensive to buy. People of lesser means had to content themselves with cheaper cloths woven at home. A number of these are mentioned in an inventory of the possessions of the Sussex knight Sir Andrew Sackville, compiled just after his death in 1369. Near the head of the list are some 'curtyns tapicies' with apparel that went with his best bed and were valued at a fairly modest 40s. Lower down come two sheets or coverlets of 'Reyns' and two coverlets in the keeping of one John atte Nash. And towards the end, though worthy of a higher place given their likely splendour, come two costers of Worsted depicting the career of Alexander the Great.

Even more interesting than the list of cloths, however, is the inventory of the contents of Sir Andrew's wardrobe, likewise tagged on at the end of the list. Three of the garments were called 'gounes': there was a short one of scarlet furred with 'gris', the grey back of the squirrel's skin, another short one in black and white mi-parti also furred with 'gris', and a longer one furred with 'calabria', an imported skin. Over one of these 'gounes' Sackville would probably have worn a cloak. Two are mentioned in the inventory, one of sanguine-coloured cloth furred with 'gris', the other parti coloured in red and black and furred with miniver. The final garment listed, however, was without doubt the most splendid. This was a white surcoat furred with miniver, with which went long ermine cuffs or sleeves. Considering that according to the sumptuary legislation of only seven years before ermine was reserved to the higher nobility and royal family, its appearance here occasions some surprise. The garment to which it belonged was probably one that he was given rather than had purchased himself. It may have been a robe of livery – that is to say, a robe granted to him as part of his annual fee by a lord by whom he was retained. At different times in his life he had been a fee'd retainer of the Earls of Arundel, Salisbury and March; and the last named he had served in the capacity of household steward. He was evidently a man worth rewarding, and rewarding well.

In some respects Andrew Sackville's career anticipates that of his more famous descendant Thomas Sackville, Lord Buckhurst. Like him, he was a careerist. Like him, he was able and ambitious. But, unlike him, he never made it into the peerage; he remained a knight, a member of the gentry. Indeed, with him the Sackville line very nearly came to an end, for Sir Andrew's only son and heir, Andrew the younger, predeceased him. The family faced extinction. But by his mistress the knight had sired two illegitimate children, Thomas and Alice; and, as he entered old age, he conceived a plan whereby he might transmit his estates to the former. It was a risky business. Bastards were common in upper-class society, because so many men had mistresses, but they enjoyed no right of succession at common law. Had there been any Sackville collaterals who could have challenged young Thomas's right to succeed, the result could have been ruinous litigation. But, as it happens, there was none. Sir Andrew was lucky, and Thomas succeeded without difficulty. It is from this boy – the bastard – that the Sackvilles of Knole, Kent (NT) are descended.

were drawn from the ranks of the manufacturing crafts. And even more significantly almost all of these men had held office before. Thus the government of the city had fallen into the hands of an élite, and a self-perpetuating one at that.

The cohesiveness of a group such as this was reinforced by their pattern of residence. They all tended to live together, in the same parish, or even in the same street. At Southampton, for example, they gathered in the area to the west of English Street and to the south of Broad Lane. In this small but select district of the town lay a group of some half a dozen tenements that passed down from one generation to another of its wealthiest burgesses. On the corner itself was the great house that Walter le Fleming had built in the early thirteenth century, and which was held subsequently by William le Horder, John le Fleming, Henry de Lym, John atte Barre and various members of the Montagu and James families – all of them men influential in the town's affairs. Close to it were tenements with similar stories of ownership. They were the centres of political as well as of economic power in Southampton. And appropriately they were sited right at the town's very heart. In the Middle Ages, as we have seen, it was the rich who lived in the inner cities, not the poor.

THE PEASANTRY

The rural masses, from whose number so many of the townsmen were drawn, formed the greater part of the population in all parts of the British Isles. By what proportion they outnumbered the inhabitants of the towns is impossible to say. But certainly it was by a large margin. And even when industrial activities spread into the countryside, as they did in the fourteenth and fifteenth centuries, the majority of the rural populace were still largely dependent on husbandry for their livelihood.

Sheer variety of circumstance makes it difficult to generalize about the condition of the rural peasantry. In 1279 in a small part of Cambridgeshire Edward I's commissioners recorded the presence of *liberi tenentes, liberi homines, sokemanni, liberi sokemanni, custumarii, custumarii tenentes, mollond, tenentes in villenagio, villani, bondi, servi, cotagii, cotarii, liberi cotarii, croftarii, coterelli, liberi coterelli, croftmanni* and *cotmanni*. And a few miles further north in south Lincolnshire they were able to add *consuetudinarii, pleni villani, molemen, monedaymen, bordarii, bordi, werkmen* and *operarii*. Such bewildering complexity puts into perspective the achievement of the Domesday commissioners in reducing the ranks of rural society to only four – the *liberi homines* or sokemen, the *villani*, the bordars and cottars, and the slaves (who were shortly to disappear).

The differences between many of these groups must of course have been slight. Indeed, the groups often overlapped. In a society as rich in localism as medieval Britain's there was an almost limitless number of ways of describing exactly the same people: in Scotland in the fourteenth century the terms *nativi, bondi, nayfs, carls* and *cumlaws* were all employed to describe the same group of rural unfree. Yet it has to be said that for all the occasions when the niceties of terminology did not matter, there were nearly as many when they did. Distinctions of status or condition not only affected a man's standing at law, they were also a vital determinant of his ability to earn a living. This was why Edward I's commissioners had to be so precise in their use of terms.

The distinction that mattered most was, once again, that between those who were free and those who were unfree. In England its origins lay in the late Anglo-Saxon period, when growing insecurity drove the more vulnerable in society into a state of dependence on the lords. They were beholden to them for their land, for their house, even for the tools of their trade. They could not leave the manor without their permission; and they were required to perform week-work on their demesnes. The free, on the other hand, managed to retain their independence. They could come and go as they pleased; they could sell their land; and they were free from the burden of labour services.

The distinction is shown at a further stage of development in Domesday Book of 1086. Here we find the free still in possession of their freedom. But the unfreedom of the remainder is more blurred. They are bound to the manor, as they always were, but their liability to perform labour services is far from universal; and quite commonly they are allowed to pay money rent instead. Insofar as labour rent was equated with loss of freedom, their lot was somewhat improved.

By the beginning of the thirteenth century, however, that period of respite had come to an end. Labour services were being exacted more comprehensively than ever, and the other burdens incident upon unfree tenure were being intensified. The distinction between freedom and unfreedom, which had previously been a largely empirical one, was being sharpened into one of legal definition. For this it seems that the deteriorating economic situation was largely to blame. By the late twelfth century incomes were being eroded by inflation, and landowners found it imperative to reduce costs. This they did through the reimposition of labour services – that is, by providing themselves with a pool of cheap labour. Tenants unlucky enough to be burdened sometimes took their lords to court, but little good did it do them. Decisions invariably went in the lords' favour, and in the course of time a body of case law evolved which we know as the 'law of villeinage'.

Villeinage (from the Latin word *villanus*) varied in intensity between estates. On some its burdens were quite heavy; on others, much less so. Generally, the more important and the longer established the lord, the heavier the burdens were going to be (on the estates of the great Benedictine abbeys, like St Albans, they were very heavy indeed). But in the manner of their enforcement a degree of flexibility often crept in. Not all the labour services nominally due were needed every year, and those which were not were 'commuted' for money. In the early fourteenth century a lot of services were commuted in this way. In the wake of the Black Death, however, when wage labour became more expensive, lords found it in their interest to reimpose them. Widespread, if localized, resistance followed, and when government ineptitude provoked the more general uprising known as the Great Revolt, in 1381, the abolition of villeinage was in the forefront of the rebels' demands. To persuade the rebels to disperse, charters of emancipation were granted; but soon afterwards they were revoked, and in the end it was economic reality and not militant resistance that was to win people their freedom. With the rise in the cost of labour large-scale husbandry became less and less attractive to landowners. They began to put their demesnes out to lease; and, as they did so, demands for labour services were inevitably relaxed. Villeinage was becoming an irrelevance; and by the fifteenth century it was well on the way to being replaced with the form of tenure later known as copyhold.

Though status was probably the main determinant of a man's relations with his fellows, in the Celtic lands it was at least matched in importance by ties of kinship. Here, to a greater extent than in England, it was the kindred that provided the essential network of support. If a man were found guilty of a trespass, it was the kin who stood surety for his behaviour; if he were the victim of an act of homicide, it was the kin who

MAP 26: TRAVELLERS AND TRAVELLING IN THE FOURTEENTH CENTURY

This map plots a combined (and simplified) itinerary of four English kings – John, Henry III, Edward I and Edward II – alongside the road system shown in the Gough map of c. 1360. It is remarkable how little the two overlap. The road system linked towns, the kings' itineraries centred on palaces and hunting-lodges.

the royal itinerary

the road system on the Gough map

F   Freemantle
K   Kings Langley
O   Oxford
Od   Odiham
R   Reading
W   Windsor
Wa   Wallingford
Wk   Woodstock

Berwick and Scotland

Carlisle

Darlington

Northallerton

Scarborough

Lancaster

York

Beverley

Pontefract

Doncaster

Lincoln

Chester

Boston

Nottingham

Walsingham

Stafford

Derby

Lynn

Norwich

Shrewsbury

Leicester

Stamford

King's Cliffe

Ely

Cambridge

Thetford

Ludlow

Bury St Edmunds

Newmarket

Cardigan

Worcester

Northampton

Hereford

Towcester

St Davids

Tewkesbury

Leighton Buzzard

Gloucester

Wk

Brill

Ware

St Albans

Abingdon

O

K

Wa

W

London

Bristol

R

Rochester

Canterbury

Od

Guildford

Leeds

Marlborough

F

Farnham

Dover

Salisbury

Winchester

Southampton

Dorchester

Ringwood

St Ives

0   50   100

miles

156

avenged his death; if he were to die before his son was of age, it was the kin who acted as guardians during the minority. In the highly localized and closely-knit societies of Celtic Britain the kin took on many of the responsibilities later assumed by the state.

The two determinants of status and kinship had their inevitable effect on people's living standards. Those who were free were likely to do better in the world than those who were unfree, just as those well endowed with kin were better shielded from insecurity than those who were not. But the relationship between living standards and status or kinship was rarely a mechanistic one; it was always modified by individual and local circumstance. A man with the advantage of free birth might end up in penury, while his neighbour of unfree condition might overcome his disability and prosper. In every vill there were those who were raised up on fortune's wheel and those who were cast down. How many there might be in each category we have no means of telling. The improved quality of peasant housing, however, suggests that not all were cast down. In the thirteenth century a fair number of timber dwellings were rebuilt in stone. Generally these were of the longhouse type with a cottage at one end and a byre and grain store at the other; sometimes, however, they were large enough to assume court-yard shape. Properties of this type were of course never more than a minority of the whole. The majority were fairly flimsy dwellings, fashioned from wood and thatch. Their life-spans were usually short – fifty years typically, a hundred at the most. For this reason few have survived (or have survived in recognizable form) outside the stone belt. Excavations at deserted sites like those of Goltho (Lincolnshire) and Wharram Percy (North Yorkshire) have uncovered their foundations and permitted the reconstruction of their layouts. But for the visitor a major effort of imagination is required to picture them as they were lived in. Modern luxuries such as running water and glazed windows were unknown. Such heating as there was was provided by a fire in the middle of the room, the smoke from which trailed out through a hole in the roof. Privacy (a modern concept anyway) was impossible. All the family – and it might be one extending to two or three generations – lived together in one room. Proximity bred frustration and enmity, and arguments and fights were common. Not untypical was the case of Agnes Flower of Shuckburgh (Warwickshire), who was indicted in 1390 for a variety of petty thefts and acts of violence; she was driven from the village for her misdeeds.

XVI
THE LIFE OF THE CHURCH

Nestling beneath the Cotswold escarpment are the remains of the Cistercian abbey of Hailes (Gloucestershire) (NT, in guardianship of English Heritage). Slight though they are, they bear witness to the former grandeur of the place. The doorways opening off the cloister are richly moulded, and the windows that flank them have the remains of fine tracery. In the museum the roof boss depicting Samson breaking the jaws of the lion is one of the most spirited examples of the carver's art. It is all work of exceptional quality – rich and sophisticated, elaborate and exuberant: as far removed as could be imagined from the simple buildings of the early Cistercians. There is no sign of the restraint enjoined by St Bernard, the founding father of the Order, no sign of the austerity and asceticism that he preached. All is vigorous and self-indulgent, full of *joie de vivre*. Hailes is a study of monasticism in decline – or, if not of monasticism in decline, then corrupted by wealth.

Humbler by far is the other church at Hailes – the parish church across the road. Predating the abbey by a century or more, this is a simple Romanesque structure, entirely lacking in subtlety or grandeur. It has its rewards, of course, as every medieval church does – notably some wall paintings and a fine collection of tiles – but architectural distinction is hardly to be counted among them. As a building it is as humble as the abbey was once grand.

The contrast between these edifices raises a number of questions about their history. Why was the one so much more splendid than the other? Why did the parish church remain so small? Why was it never enlarged over time? The answers to these questions are not hard to find. Size in the Middle Ages, as in any period, was largely a factor of wealth, and at Hailes the abbey was far richer than the church. Founded by Richard of Cornwall, Henry III's brother, it was endowed on a lavish scale with a string of manors in southern England and a cash grant of 1,000 marks for the purchase of yet more. In the next generation it was given the means to become still richer when Earl Richard's son bestowed on it a drop of the Blood of Christ – a relic that attracted countless pilgrims with all the possibility of donations. The parish church, on the other hand, had to manage on what the parishioners could give, and that was relatively little. The parish was neither a large nor a particularly prosperous one, and it lacked a resident manorial

HAILES ABBEY (Gloucestershire) (NT/English Heritage), the cloister. The arcades, though fragmentary, give an indication of the grandeur of the late medieval buildings

lord who could make up for the relative poverty of the tenants. So the church remained small, very small, while the abbey grew bigger.

The explanation, then, for the disparity is clear. But it is an explanation which in its turn begs another set of questions. How could a Cistercian house see fit to display such ostentatious wealth? Why was a relic a source of such wealth and power? Was Hailes exceptional in being served by such a small parish church? A search for the answers to these questions requires a consideration of some of the major themes of Church history, and it is with the monasteries that we must begin.

THE NEW ORDERS

In the eleventh century, in Britain as in the rest of Europe, all monastic communities professed the Benedictine obedience. The source of their inspiration and the foundation of their daily routine was the Rule composed in the sixth century by St Benedict of Nursia. As it was interpreted in the central Middle Ages, this Rule wore a rather different aspect from that intended by its author. The balance which he envisaged between

HAILES CHURCH
(Gloucestershire)
The simple two-cell structure would have been overshadowed in the Middle Ages by the great abbey nearby

celebration of the liturgy, private study and manual labour had gradually given way to a concentration on the first two, with manual labour disappearing almost entirely. At the same time the monastic movement had spread so far geographically that considerable diversity had crept into patterns of observance. Local traditions and characteristics developed which gave monasticism in one part of Europe a very different flavour from that found elsewhere. Subject to this qualification, however, it can be said in all fairness that monastic life was always and everywhere Benedictine monastic life. But, by the early years of the twelfth century that was no longer true. The Benedictine monopoly had gone.

What took its place was a variety of approaches to the monastic vocation. Instead of one Order there were now several: the Cistercians, the Carthusians and the Premonstratensian Canons on the one hand, the Cluniacs on the other, and the Augustinian Canons somewhere in between. These Orders were of widely different character and background. But they had one thing in common – a desire to recapture the purity of the original monastic ideal. They were in that sense backward-looking. Their object was not to promote change in the positive sense, but to recover what had been lost – namely, that simple and ascetic way of life associated with Christ and the Apostles. In the course of seeking this end they explored possibilities which were to transform the way that monasticism was to develop in the late Middle Ages.

The origins of this upsurge in activity lay in the mood of doubt that gripped Europe at the time. Men were preoccupied with the consequences of sin. They feared for the salvation of their souls and contemplated with horror the prospect of the eternal torments of hell. They knew that if they stayed out in the world they would never be saved: the burden of man's debt to God was so great that it could scarcely be repaid in the space of a normal lifetime. The only sure course was to withdraw from the world into a monastery, where they could devote themselves to a life of prayer. It was for this reason that the monasteries were so popular (and so full) at this time. They brought a glimmer of hope to a people filled with despair. Pursuit of the contemplative life, for those who embraced it, offered an early end to the pains of purgatory. And the richer and more reflective the quality of that life, the sooner, it was assumed, would the pains be ended.

Benedictine monasticism was in many ways the natural expression of this set of beliefs. It offered order, beauty and stability. It answered the needs of a fairly static society which found reassurance in the security of a single, all-embracing religious system. Its liturgy was a perfectly fashioned vehicle for drawing down the mercy of the Almighty. Its one weakness was a tendency to stifle individual devotion beneath the sheer weight of routine – so that, when an instinct developed for the pursuit of greater individualism, its régime was found wanting. Such a moment appears to have come at the turn of the eleventh and twelfth centuries. Society by then was breaking out of the shell which had nurtured it for so long. It was growing richer and fatter on the proceeds of an increasing volume of trade. It was developing greater diversity in modes of expression and ways of life. Beliefs and practices which had long been cherished were challenged and called into question. Traditional Benedictinism was no longer taken for granted as offering the only, or even the best, way of achieving the *vita apostolica*. A variety of ways was considered possible, each of them valid according to the aims laid down for it. Some men chose a path of compromise with the world, so that they could assist a little in the relief of its suffering. Others felt moved to distance themselves more firmly from its wickedness than they had done in the past. In short, every taste was catered for.

The least assuming of the new Orders was that of the Augustinian Canons – so called because their observance was based on a set of guidelines originally composed by the fifth-century theologian, St Augustine of Hippo. Unlike the regular monks, the Canons were allowed to divide their time between the cloister and the world. The full liturgical round in the church was required of them; but in the time remaining they were permitted to perform pastoral duties in the local community. Many of their houses – those at Oxford, Colchester and Smithfield in London, for example – were sited in or near major centres of population, and they performed a useful service in ministering to the poor, bringing relief to the sick and providing burial for the deceased. Despite their obvious 'usefulness', however, the Canons never grew wealthy. Their houses were numerous rather than splendid. The ruins at Lilleshall (Shropshire) and Kirkham (East Yorkshire) suggest structures which in their heyday would have been fairly solid, even functional in character, but modest in scale; and if the surviving naves at Canons Ashby (Northamptonshire) (NT) and Brinkburn (Northumberland) are any guide, their churches would have been noble but unadorned. Moderation may be said to have been the hallmark of their architecture as well as of their way of life.

Though the Cistercians, like the Canons, made a virtue of poverty, they did so from choice rather than from force of circumstances. In almost every respect they were the

Canons' exact opposite: the Canons compromised with the world, the Cistercians rejected it; the Canons often settled in or near towns, the Cistercians always in the countryside; the Canons were noted for the looseness of their organization, the Cistercians for the tightness of theirs. The Cistercians took their name from the abbey of Citeaux in Burgundy, which had been founded in 1098 by a group of dissidents from Molesme. It was a small and isolated house, and after a few years it looked doubtful if it would even survive. But then in 1112 the young Bernard of Fontaine came knocking on its door. From that moment on its future was assured. St Bernard, the future abbot of Clairvaux, was one of the most brilliant figures of the age. It was his genius which above all else transformed the fledgling institute into the most influential Order in Europe. By the sheer power of his oratory he won the backing of Popes, kings, lords and princes. And by the force of his example he inspired many who knew him only by repute to follow his chosen path.

There can be no doubting the impact of the early Cistercians on the members of the older monasteries. In 1132, when the first of them arrived in northern England, at Rievaulx, they precipitated a crisis at the Benedictine abbey of St Mary in York. A group of monks, persuaded that their house was too complacent by far, went to the abbot to ask for reform. Discussions dragged on for months without anything being settled, and eventually the dissidents took their case to the archbishop. A visitation followed, and disorder broke out. The archbishop placed St Mary's under an interdict, and offered the dissident group refuge at Ripon. From there he led them out in December to some wasteland three miles to the west, in the valley of the River Skell. It was a barren spot: one that appealed to the ascetic streak in these men; but the presence of some springs in the rocky hillside made it habitable. There they settled, and erected a wooden structure that would serve as a church.

Such is the story of the foundation of Fountains Abbey (NT). It is a tale which finds echoes in the annals of a number of other communities, not all of them Cistercian. At Llanthony in the Black Mountains, in a house which when regularized took the Augustinian Rule, it was the desire of a disillusioned knight to renounce worldliness and to retreat to 'a desert place' that was the motivating force in the establishment of a community. Undeniably life for these pioneering monks was hard, and the régime rigorous. For some it was too much. At Calder (Cumbria) the monks packed their bags after three years, and a second attempt had to be made to establish a colony. But more often the story was one of success. Rievaulx in particular grew with phenomenal speed. Within ten years of its foundation the combined number of monks and lay-brothers was said to have been 300, and by the 1160s it had risen to 140 monks and over 500 lay-brothers. The admiration widely felt for the community led patrons who wanted to found monasteries of their own to draw settlers from its ranks. In this way Rievaulx was prevailed upon to establish daughter houses at Melrose (Borders) and Dundrennan (Dumfries and Galloway) in Scotland, and Warden (Bedfordshire) and Revesby (Lincolnshire) in England. Fountains nurtured as many as eight such houses – one in far-off Norway, the rest in central and northern England (map 27). In Wales nearly all of the Cistercian foundations were offshoots of the now vanished abbey of Whitland in Dyfed.

Given the rapid growth in the Order, it is not surprising that in 1152 the General Chapter at Citeaux should have decided to call a halt to new foundations. By that time there were in fact 328 in existence; and thanks to the Chapter's willingness to permit exceptions, more were to follow, notably Sweetheart (Dumfries and Galloway) in

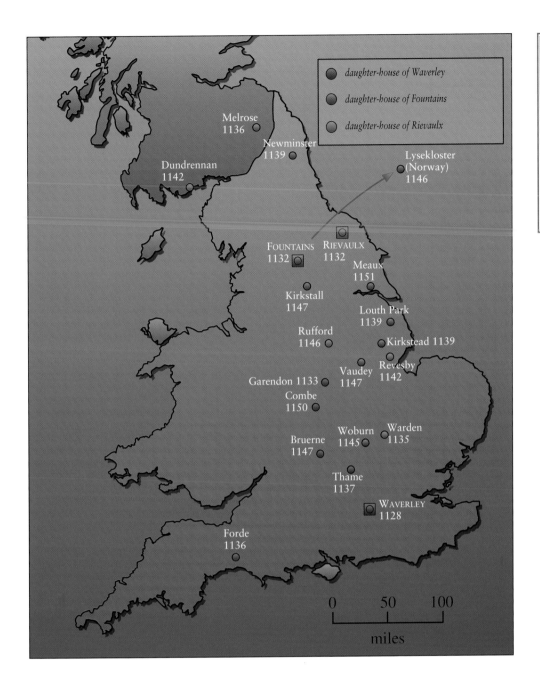

MAP 27: THE EARLIEST
CISTERCIAN
MONASTERIES IN BRITAIN

*The map charts roughly the
first generation of growth.
Some of the daughter-houses –
Melrose in Scotland, for
example – themselves
established new colonies.*

daughter-house of Waverley

daughter-house of Fountains

daughter-house of Rievaulx

Melrose
1136

Newminster
1139

Dundrennan
1142

Lysekloster
(Norway)
1146

FOUNTAINS
1132

RIEVAULX
1132

Meaux
1151

Kirkstall
1147

Louth Park
1139

Rufford
1146

Kirkstead 1139

Vaudey
1147

Revesby
1142

Garendon 1133

Combe
1150

Woburn
1145

Warden
1135

Bruerne
1147

Thame
1137

WAVERLEY
1128

Forde
1136

0   50   100

miles

Scotland and Beaulieu (Hampshire) and Hailes in England, the latter two being both royal foundations. The obvious appeal of the Order was based on its rejection of materialist values. It came into existence as a reaction against the visibly increasing level of wealth in society and to the debilitating influence of that wealth on the life of the Church. The emphasis on poverty was absolutely central to its being. It was for that reason that St Bernard was insistent on prohibiting his communities from ownership of feudal or manorial sources of income.

So rigorous a doctrine, of course, would have been hard to maintain without the provision of due safeguards, and these were sought in the creation of an elaborate system of government based on the principle of mutual visitation by abbots of each others' monasteries. But even so, the initial inspiration proved difficult to maintain. The more successful the Cistercians became, the harder they found it to live up to their original

The Citadels of Prayer

Medieval monasteries were rarely if ever built by the monks themselves. The belief, once common though now discredited that they were, derives from a misreading of statements made by the chroniclers. When these say, as they often do, that this or that part of the church was rebuilt by such-and-such an abbot, it is not meant that the abbot personally directed its construction, only that he commissioned it: responsibility for design and construction was always entrusted to a professional master mason and his team.

Nevertheless design was a matter too important to be left to architects. It had to take account of monastic observance as well as stylistic whim. The buildings in which a community lived were an expression of its ideals and identity; and as such they bore witness to the changing interpretations placed over the centuries on St Benedict's Rule. Those erected by the Cluniacs were characterized by their elaboration and magnificence; those erected by the Cistercians by their austerity; and those erected by the Augustinians by their sheer diversity. Wealth apart, the particular observance of a house was probably the biggest single influence on its architecture; and it is for that reason that a study of monastic remains provides so revealing an insight into the aspirations of those who dwelled within them.

MOUNT GRACE PRIORY *(North Yorkshire) (NT/English Heritage)*
The cells around the great cloister, to the left, provided most of the accommodation. A further six cells were grouped around the outer court, to the right

The Benedictines had traditionally disposed their buildings around a cloister-garth. On the northern side was generally placed the church which, as at Worcester and Ely, sometimes doubled as a cathedral church; on the east were placed the chapter-house and dormitory (the latter usually at first-floor level); on the south the refectory; and on the west the abbot's quarters and guest chambers. This is essentially the layout visible today at such sites as Durham and Westminster.

At the hands of the Cistercians, however, it was subjected to a degree of modification occasioned by the need to accommodate the 'conversi' or lay-brothers. These men, not being fully professed, could not enter into every aspect of community life; they were required to live and to eat apart from the monks, even to worship apart from them. So one whole range of the cloister was set apart for their use – generally, as at Fountains, the western side. From there they could make their own way into the church for services. The part of the church which they used was the nave – that is, the part which in a Benedictine abbey would have been given over to the local parishioners. In the Cistercians' churches, as in the Benedictines', it was separated from the monks' choir by a solid stone screen.

The Cistercians, though they broke free from the Benedictines, believed that they were re-establishing the original purity of St Benedict's Rule. The Carthusians, on the other hand, sought to return to a more primitive model – that of the eremitic tradition. The Carthusian monks, instead of eating and sleeping together as the Benedictines did, lived in solitude in separate cells. They did not even meet very often in the church: many of the offices were recited in the cells. So in a Carthusian house the church was small, almost oratory-like. At Mount Grace it stands inconsequentially between two large courts around which the cells are grouped. The cells themselves, though small, were not incommodious. They were built on two floors and contained a lobby, living room, study and bedroom. They even had a fireplace and garderobe; and there was a garden at the rear.

The solitude of life at Mount Grace had its consolations, then: by earlier standards the level of comfort enjoyed by the monks there was high. On the other hand, there was not a whiff of worldliness about the place. The late medieval drift towards self-indulgence that we see elsewhere – in the cloisters at Lacock (NT), for example – passed it by. To some extent this was because the monks never acquired the means to indulge themselves: they were simply too poor. To some extent as well it was because their links with their patron weakened. Other communities cherished and fed upon the link with the founder and his kin. At Hailes, for example, it provided the monks first with a valuable relic – some drops of the Holy Blood – and then with a magnificent new choir in which to display it. For both gifts they had to thank the king's cousin, Edmund of Cornwall (see p. 158).

Most monasteries, of whatever Order, turned periodically for assistance to their patron. Payment for new buildings would have been impossible if they had not. Their income from land – that is, from rents and sales of produce from the demesnes – paid for current expenditure and for such agrarian investment as the building of barns. But for major capital spending much more had to be raised, and the patron was the obvious person to approach. Sometimes, however, what he could provide was not enough, in which case an appeal would have to be launched. Most of the great structures we admire today were paid for by one or other of these means, or both. Appropriately it is by resort to broadly similar methods that they are maintained today.

ideal. The more gifts they attracted from benefactors, the higher their standard of living became, and the further they drifted from the austerity of the founding fathers. It was a familiar dilemma in the history of the Religious Orders, and certainly not one unique to the Cistercians – witness, for example, the splendour of the late medieval cloisters of the Augustinian nunnery of Lacock (Wiltshire) (NT). But it was one posed all the more acutely in the Cistercians' case because of the greater intensity of their vision. Thus Abbot Huby's tower at Fountains, erected only decades before the Dissolution, may be a tribute to the dignity of its builder and to the pre-eminence in the English Cistercian family of his house. But its spirit ran clean counter to that of the early statutes, which forbade the building of high towers over the Order's churches.

One Order only remained immune from these developments – that of Chartreuse, commonly known as the Carthusians. They were never a large family, and to that extent never had to deal with the problems of success. Therein lay one reason for their continued austerity. The other was provided by the nature of their internal régime: for, unlike the Benedictines and the Cistercians, they did not lead a communal life. They lived in isolation in cells around the cloister. In England their heyday came in the later fourteenth century when no fewer than five new houses were called into being. One of them – Mount Grace (North Yorkshire) (NT, in guardianship of English Heritage), founded by Richard II's nephew Thomas Holland, Duke of Surrey – offers by far the best preserved site of a Carthusian house, and illustrates well how its ground-plan differed from those common to houses of the other Orders.

Carthusian asceticism was the acquired taste of a small circle of patrons, most of them either retired soldiers or courtiers like Holland. It failed to establish a broad appeal, principally because its heyday came too late. By the fourteenth century the idea of retreating from the world had passed out of fashion – or, rather, had been found wanting in one important respect: though it might assure the inhabitants of the cloister of salvation, it did nothing for those who remained outside. The founder and his kin

LACOCK ABBEY (Wiltshire) (NT), the cloister

A fifteenth-century rebuilding which attests the wealth of this highly favoured community

might be remembered in the monks' prayers; but what hope was there for everyone else? It was the failure of traditional monasticism to offer satisfactory answers to questions like these that led another great figure in western religious history, St Francis (d. 1226), to suggest a new approach to the 'apostolic life' – one that would offer more to the poor and the needy. St Francis' brothers (Latin *fratres*, hence friars) were to go out into the world to preach and to set an example by the modesty of their life-style. They were not to own property, and they were to support themselves on the voluntary offerings of others. And if they needed possessions like books, which were essential to them in their work, these were to be held for their use by the Pope.

St Francis' ideas were more radical and more comprehensive than even the Order of the Cistercians. They aroused enormous interest in his native Italy, and before long his followers were to be numbered in thousands. But an ability to organize was not one of his strengths, and the whole movement would have grown out of control had not the Papal authorities obliged him to draw up a Rule. At the same time, however, a Spaniard by the name of Dominic was thinking along similar lines, and by the 1220s a parallel but slightly different organization had come into being under his leadership. These two Orders were to be known, after their founders, as the Franciscans and the Dominicans or, respectively, the Friars Minor and the Friars Preachers.

The Franciscans owed their early success – they had arrived in England by 1224 – to their humility and their ability to identify with the poor and the downtrodden. They reached out to people ignored by the other clergy; they circulated in areas to which the parochial system did not extend; they taught, they helped, they ministered; above all, they preached. At preaching crosses like the one to be seen at Hereford they drew enormous audiences. Sometimes these were so large that the parish churches were left empty, and the secular clergy, who had first welcomed the brothers' arrival, thought the better of it and turned against them. The friars' relations with the regular clergy, then, were sometimes strained; but within their own ranks, too, tensions appeared. There were disagreements over the interpretation of the doctrine of poverty. Some wanted to modify it in the light of experience; others insisted on following it literally. Eventually, in 1323, Pope John XXII imposed his own solution by restoring to the brethren the full ownership of their property.

Despite the undoubted criticisms that were levelled against them, it seems clear that the friars retained their popularity into the late Middle Ages. The enormous naves that they built for their churches bear witness to the size of the congregations that they expected. Likewise the bequests left to them in wills afford a clear indication of where people's sympathies lay. These were always modest bequests: the friars did not need or expect more. At Northampton the sums of 40s. left to the Dominicans, and of 20s. to the other Orders of friars, by Elizabeth, widow of Sir Robert de Grey of Grey's Court (NT) are fairly typical. But the recipients were evidently thought deserving. Had they not been – and had they all been like the corrupt, fun-living friar whom Chaucer portrayed in the *Canterbury Tales* – they would have received nothing at all.

CULTS AND SHRINES

Chaucer's choice of setting for the *Canterbury Tales* takes us to the heart of medieval religion: for the pilgrimage to the shrine of a saint, which Chaucer made the vehicle of his story-telling sequence, was one of its most characteristic manifestations.

FOUNTAINS ABBEY (North Yorkshire) (NT/English Heritage) One of the earliest and most celebrated Cistercian foundations in Britain. This view from the west shows the long western range with the cellarium below and lay-brothers' quarters above

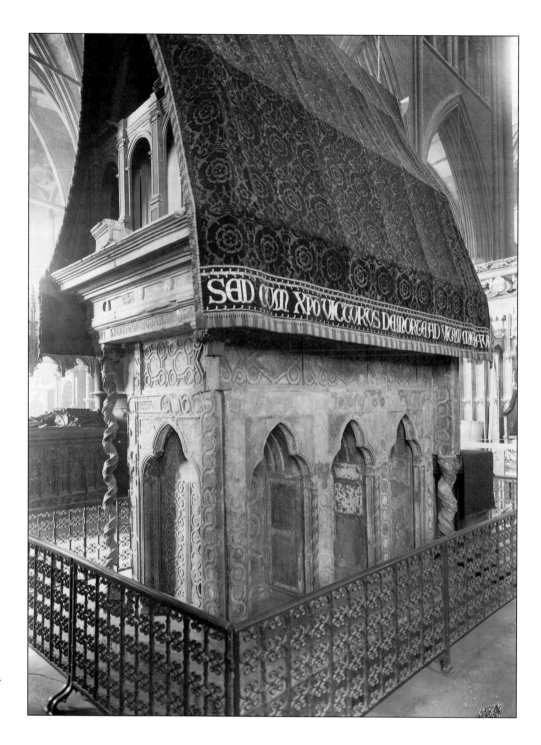

SHRINE OF EDWARD THE
CONFESSOR, WESTMINSTER
ABBEY
*Edward the Confessor was
canonized by the Pope in 1161.
Only the lower stages of his shrine
survive. They are Italian work of the
1260s, reflecting the cosmopolitan
taste of King Henry III*

The cult of relics, and the connected practice of both visiting and collecting them, was the counterpoint of the contemporary obsession with the consequences of sin. The remains of a saint, said a twelfth-century theologian, were the means whereby the faithful might resist the power of evil in the world: they gave health to the bodies of men and absolution to their souls. By virtue of the holiness of his life and of his nearness to God, the saint was held to be capable of interceding with the latter on the penitent's behalf; and the working of a miracle was taken as evidence of the success of that intercession. A belief in the miraculous came easily to people. Given their limited understanding of the workings of the universe, much of what today can be explained in natural terms was then explained in providential ones. Besides, the Bible, the record of God's dealings with His people, was full of miraculous stories; and there was no reason to suppose that the age of miracles was passed.

Relics were not only a source of hope to the faithful. They were a source of wealth and power to those who owned them. Their presence in a church lent it distinction, and secured for it the saint's protection, ensuring that supernatural as well as natural penalties could be visited upon despoilers of that church's lands. No less importantly, relics attracted pilgrims; and the greater their number, the richer the church was likely to become. As a result it was in the interests of the clergy of every important sanctuary to gain possession of a set of relics, and some stooped even to theft in order to achieve that end. The bones of St Benedict himself were stolen from Monte Cassino in Italy at the end of the seventh century by a French monk who brought them to France; and many important relics, including the elbow of St Stephen and pieces of the True Cross, were looted from Constantinople after its capture by the Crusaders in 1204.

The assembling of a relic collection, when it was undertaken by honest means, was a process that took time and effort. Not every church was lucky enough to possess the body of a figure long venerated for his sanctity of life, as Durham had, for example, in the remains of St Cuthbert – very few in fact; and some of those that thought they did were to find themselves disabused after the Conquest when their saints were denied recognition by the Normans. At Canterbury a host of Saxon saints were struck from the calendar by Archbishop Lanfranc on the grounds that their cults were fraudulent.

Indeed, by the twelfth century the process of securing recognition of a saint was everywhere becoming more difficult. Canonization now required Papal approval, and increasingly this was given only after careful scrutiny of the evidence. Churches with a case to advance, therefore, had first to compile a dossier of miracle stories and then to forward it to Rome. Commissioners would then be appointed to investigate the claims, and whether or not canonization was granted depended largely on the outcome of their deliberations. Given the power that they had to confer or withhold recognition, it was inevitable that they would be subjected to intense lobbying. In the 1310s, for example, both they and the Pope were lobbied by Earl Thomas of Lancaster in support of the cause of the recently deceased Archbishop of Canterbury, Robert Winchelsey, and the Pope had to explain that the matter was not one that could be hurried, but had rather 'to be debated in consistory by experienced persons'. Earl Thomas' efforts proved unavailing. Archbishop Winchelsey's reputation was thought to rest too much on his history of opposition to the Crown; and canonization, though actively prosecuted, in the end eluded him.

The fourteenth century saw attempts to promote the claims of a number of other political candidates – for example, the same Earl of Lancaster after his execution in 1322 for rebelling against Edward II, and of course Edward II himself. In neither case was canonization secured. But popular recognition, at least for a while, made both Lancaster's tomb at Pontefract and Edward II's at Gloucester, significant centres of pilgrimage. At Gloucester, particularly, the volume of traffic in the 1330s must have been huge, to judge from the splendour of the rebuilding programme set in motion there only a decade after the king's death and financed in part from offerings at his tomb. But cults, whether official or unofficial, rarely lasted for long, and half a century represented the life-span of most of them. Even Becket's at Canterbury was tailing off badly in the late Middle Ages. Offerings dwindled from a peak of £1,142 per annum in 1220, the year of the translation of the relics, to a paltry £36 on the eve of the Dissolution.

*The most popular shrines in
medieval England were those
of St Thomas at Canterbury,
St Cuthbert at Durham and, by
the fifteenth century, Our Lady
at Walsingham. Unofficial
cults, however, flourished for
relatively short times around
the tombs of Earl Thomas of
Lancaster at Pontefract and
Edward II at Gloucester.*

centre of unofficial cult with
date that it flourished

pilgrimage centre

DUNFERMLINE
St Margaret of Scotland

ST ANDREWS
St Andrew

GLASGOW
St Kentigern

EDROM
1390s

WHITHORN
St Ninian

DURHAM
St Cuthbert

RIPON
St Wilfrid

YORK
St William

BEVERLEY
St John

PONTEFRACT
1320s

LINCOLN
St Hugh

WALSINGHAM
Our Lady

CHESTER
St Werburgh

BROMHOLM
Holy Rood

LICHFIELD
St Chad

CROWLAND
St Guthlac

WORCESTER
St Wulfstan

ELY
St Etheldreda

NORWICH
St William

HEREFORD
St Ethelbert
St Thomas Cantilupe

HAILES
Holy Blood

ST ALBANS
St Alban

BURY ST
EDMUNDS
St Edmund

GLOUCESTER
1330s

OXFORD
St Frideswide

WESTMINSTER
St Edward the Confessor

WELLS
1300s

GLASTONBURY
St Dunstan
St Joseph

WINCHESTER
St Swithin

CANTERBURY
St Thomas

SALISBURY
St Osmund

CHICHESTER
St Richard

0   50   100

miles

SANTIAGO DE
COMPOSTELLA

ROME

JERUSALEM

GUERNSEY
St Apolline

Hereford's experience was typical of those churches with relics of lesser fame. Offerings at the shrine of that cathedral's saint – Thomas Cantilupe (d. 1282), a former bishop – reached their peak in the early fourteenth century at the time of his canonization, but were already dwindling by 1336, and by 1388 came to only £1.6s.8d.

The scale of money offerings is admittedly not always a reliable measure of the duration of a cult, because generosity found expression in the donation of jewels and plate as well as of cash. All the same it seems impossible to deny that many cults passed quickly in and out of fashion. Most obviously this was so in the Celtic parts of Britain: at Pennant Melangell (Powys), for example, there is a superb twelfth-century shrine which bears witness to the temporary fame of a St Monacella whose name is now forgotten. But in England the same phenomenon is also to be observed. Bury St Edmunds in East Anglia was definitely out of fashion by the late Middle Ages, whereas further north Bromholm, with its piece of the Holy Rood, and Walsingham were in. Both were favoured by the Pastons and their correspondents; and John Paston I chose to be buried in the church of the former. But the necessity of actually visiting these shrines was not as paramount as it once had been because many had relics in their own homes. Sir John Fastolf had the hand of St George, a finger of John the Baptist and (like many other people) a fragment of the True Cross. By the fifteenth century there was evidently such a market in these bits and pieces that anyone with the means to pay could pick up a few.

But what did their owners make of them? Fastolf thought enough of his fragment of the True Cross to 'keep it daily about his neck'. Yet less than a century later Bishop Latimer could describe as 'an unctuous gum' and 'a compound of many things' a relic – in this case the Holy Blood of Hailes – the authenticity of which had, three centuries before, been vouchsafed by no less a figure than Pope Urban IV. Relics as a whole, and not just certain of them, were evidently passing out of fashion. In this respect, as in others, expressions of piety were apt to change direction with the passage of time.

THE PARISH CHURCHES

By 1400 the cathedrals and greater churches visited by the pilgrims stood largely as we see them today. Only at Winchester and Canterbury were ambitious programmes commenced (in each case involving reconstruction of the nave) which dragged on into the fifteenth century. Elsewhere little remained to be done. It was on the parish churches that the masons were henceforth to find their chief employment.

The pace and chronology of parish church building varied greatly from one part of the British Isles to another. In some areas like the south-west and East Anglia practically every church seems to have been rebuilt in the fifteenth century. In others like Hampshire and Sussex very few were. In others again, notably in Wales and Scotland, generalization is almost impossible because the buildings are of such simple design they afford few clues to dating. But whether it is to Scotland, Wales or England that we look, it is a measure of the scale of building activity that went on in the late Middle Ages that relatively so few Romanesque churches should have come down to us unaltered.

The earliest parish churches in England had been founded in the tenth and eleventh centuries, when the hold of the minster or 'missionary' churches was beginning to weaken. Generally they were built by ealdormen and thanes for the use of themselves and their tenants, and their strongly proprietorial character is well conveyed by the arrangements known to have existed at Stoke d'Abernon (Surrey). Here the seating for the lord and his lady was provided in a gallery at the west end of the nave from which they could look down on the congregation. Social differentiation was hardly to be taken further in the Georgian age.

Except in the case of churches which laid claim to minster (or in Wales *clas* status) the earliest parochial fabrics were usually small. In the towns they were often diminutive – the tenth-century church of St Mary's, Tanner Street, Winchester consisted simply of two adjacent houses knocked together – and in the countryside they were rarely much larger. But once population began to grow, as it did in the late eleventh century, then the need arose for more accommodation, and a process of piecemeal enlargement got under way. First of all the nave would be extended westwards by a bay or two; then an aisle would be added on the side, and later perhaps another one opposite it; and finally, in the fourteenth or fifteenth century, the tower would be heightened and a clerestory raised above the arcade, the two lending a touch of dignity to the building.

But in many places this story of piecemeal enlargement and aggrandisement was brought to a halt by the Black Death. With population now going into decline there was no longer a need for so much space, and difficulty was often experienced in filling what there was. In parishes where the shrinkage was greatest the fabric was sometimes cut down in size. At Wharram Percy, for example, the aisles built in the thirteenth century were demolished in the late fourteenth or fifteenth century. And elsewhere, proposed rebuildings, if carried through, were scaled down to conform to the diminished expectations of the new age.

Not often, however, was the relationship between the size of a church and the size of its congregation as direct as this sort of chronology would suggest. Many factors other than population had a bearing on a church's growth. Not least among them were changes in liturgical practice, which had the effect of focusing increased attention on the chancel. In the late Middle Ages this part of the church took on many of the attributes of a shrine. There was a growing belief, of which the doctrine of transubstantiation was part cause and part consequence, that the Host embodied the Real Presence. In the *Lay Folks' Mass Book*, a devotional manual of *c.* 1170–90, it is laid down that, when the host and chalice are elevated in the canon of the mass, the lay worshipper should lift his eyes and gaze at God's body and blood being re-created before him. God's presence in the sacrament enhanced the character of the chancel as a sanctuary. Increasingly it was cut off from the nave by means of high screens which restricted the view eastwards of the laity; and its affinity with a reliquary was emphasized by growing sculptural adornment and architectural embellishment. Piscinas were set in the wall near the altar for the washing of the chalice and paten, and, close by them, aumbry cupboards for the keeping of books and vessels. Against the wall opposite there was often a set of seats known as the sedilia for the use of the priest, deacon and archdeacon. At the same time there was an increase in the elaboration of the ritual attending the celebration of Easter. The practice of 'reservation' of the sacraments became more common, and in many churches a sculptured Easter Sepulchre was commissioned to hold the consecrated wafer between Maundy Thursday and Easter Sunday. Sometimes, as at Hawton (Nottinghamshire) and Beverley Minster, this might be combined in surroundings of great magnificence with a benefactor's tomb. It is hardly surprising, in the light of these developments, to find that many of our grandest chancels date from the late thirteenth and early fourteenth centuries.

*HAWTON CHURCH
(Nottinghamshire)
The founder's tomb and Easter
Sepulchre, built with the rest of the
chancel by Sir Robert de Compton
(d. 1330)*

Typically, however, it is not the chancel but the nave and tower which dominate the skyline. These were the parts of the fabric which were maintained by the parishioners; and the willingness with which they accepted their burden forms a sharp contrast to the reluctance with which the parson often accepted his in respect of the chancel. For the laity the church was much more than a place of worship. It was the focal point of their ambitions and aspirations; and it was an expression of the solidarity which they felt as a community. Thus embellishing it was for them a means whereby they could honour themselves as well as honour God. A community's pride was invested in the fabric of its church, and if that fabric showed up badly by comparison with that of a neighbouring one, then self-esteem demanded that it be brought up to scratch. As a result, an element of competitive rivalry crept into the rebuilding process as towers grew ever higher and clerestories ever more fantastic. To suggest, however, that the inspiration behind this work was purely, or even mainly, worldly in nature would be to mislead. It was not. It sprang from feelings of genuine piety. It affords the best possible evidence for the view that late medieval Catholicism was a movement with genuinely popular roots.

In many parishes the clearest sign of that popularity was the developing association

Tithes and Temporalities

The clergy serving a church usually lived in a cottage or house close by. In a well-endowed parish this could be quite a substantial property. The Clergy House at Alfriston (East Sussex) (NT), for example, is a typical 'Wealden' style dwelling of the type inhabited by the well-to-do yeomanry of the district. It has a lofty hall rising the full height of the house, flanked on one side by a service wing and on the other by a two-storey chamber block, the whole being covered by a single high roof. The decorative detail is of above average quality; and only the isolation of the service range from the hall (to separate the clerks from the maidservants) reminds us that it was occupied by clergy not gentry.

Alfriston dates from the late fourteenth century. It was probably built and paid for by the rector of the day (one possibility being Peter de Hoo, a servant of Sir Andrew Sackville); but that is not to say that it was necessarily the rector who lived in it. Here, as so commonly elsewhere, the rector might well have been non-resident. In which case responsibility for taking the services in the church would have devolved upon a curate, assisted by a deacon or archdeacon; and it would have been he (or they) who resided in the Clergy House.

On a more formal basis this was the arrangement that obtained at another country parsonage that has come down to us, the Priest's House at Muchelney (Somerset) (NT). The rectory of this parish was acquired in 1308 by the monks of Muchelney Abbey. Naturally, being confined to the cloister, they were unable to perform the cure of souls themselves, so a vicarage was instituted; and it was for the use of the vicar and his staff that the Priest's House was built. It is an early fourteenth-century structure, sturdy and solid, and of roughly the same size as the Clergy House at Alfriston. Its inhabitants clearly enjoyed an unusually comfortable life-style by the standards of most of the lesser clergy of the day. Vicars often complained of being poorly paid and poorly housed. On the latter score, at least, the clergy of Muchelney had no reason to grumble.

Those who did best out of the system, however, were the holders of the rich cathedral prebends – men like the rector of Martock, for example, whose house at Martock (Somerset), known as the Treasurer's House (NT), recalls its occupant's dignity as treasurer of Wells. It is a substantial property fitted out as the country retreat of a clerical high-flyer. In the centre, opposite the entrance, is the great hall; to one side of it is the solar, and then beyond that the kitchen. Its layout

ALFRISTON CLERGY HOUSE *(East Sussex) (NT), the interior of the hall*
Though the residence of a parson, the Clergy House has the character of a gentleman's manor-house

MUCHELNEY PRIEST'S HOUSE (Somerset) (NT)
A vicarage built by the monks of Muchelney, and little altered since

is clearly modelled on that of a knightly manor-house; and a manor-house is in effect what it was. The treasurer was a man with a position to maintain, and perhaps as well a person of importance in the royal administration. What he needed was a house that bore witness to his standing in society; and that most certainly is what the property at Martock did for him.

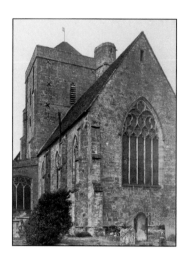

ETCHINGHAM CHURCH (East Sussex)
The church was rebuilt in the 1360s by the lord of the manor, Sir William de Etchingham, who is buried before the high altar (for his brass, see above p. 133)

between the guilds and the church. As a result of seeing to the decent burial of their members the guilds had long been involved in the life of the church. But in the four-teenth century, when it became popular for testators to ensure the safe repose of their souls by endowing commemorative masses, their commitment greatly increased. They assumed responsibility for the maintenance of altars where these masses could be cele-brated; and if funds permitted they paid for the building of side chapels for the exclu-sive use of priests appointed by themselves. Hence the identification of chapels with particular guilds, as at St Michael's, Coventry, where there was a Drapers' Chapel, a Dyers' Chapel, a Mercers' Chapel and so on. The church was on the way to being con-verted into a gigantic memorial chapel for those who had been of the guilds' fellowship.

Evidence of communal involvement in church building tends to be strongest in the towns. In the countryside it often takes second place to lordly patronage. Even in a church that owed as much to the cloth trade as Lavenham (Suffolk), the boars and mul-lets of the de Vere earls of Oxford, who were lords of the manor, are as prominent as the merchant marks of the town's woolmen and clothiers. In places where industrial wealth was slight or non-existent the lord was necessarily the largest single benefactor; and even if it was the parishioners' needs that prompted a rebuilding, it was his wealth and his ambitions that made the most visible impression on the fabric. In no church can the point be better illustrated than at Etchingham (East Sussex).

The reconstruction of this building in the fourteenth century followed hard on the parishioners' initiative in seeking permission to bury their dead there rather than at Salehurst three miles away. Etchingham, being a dependent chapelry of Salehurst, lacked a cemetery of its own. But in 1357 authority was given for one to be laid out, and five years later the lord of the manor, Sir William de Etchingham, made available the land that was needed. Twelve months after that he entered into contracts for the complete rebuilding of the church. That he and he alone was paying for the job is evi-dent from an action which he brought in the courts in 1368 against one of the masons for failing to make the window tracery according to agreed specifications. Indeed, his hand is visible at every point in the design – in the heraldry that fills the windows, in the presence of the Etchingham arms in the weather-vane on the tower, and most strik-ingly of all in the tombs and brasses that dominate the chancel. This was a church con-ceived less to provide seating accommodation for the faithful than to provide burial space for the lords of the manor. There, in front of the altar, lies Sir William himself, and a little to the west of him his son, another Sir William, and his son in turn, Sir Thomas. It is a sight that can be paralleled in a host of other churches, notably at Cobham (Kent), rebuilt by Sir John de Cobham at almost the same time as Etchingham, and now famous the world over for its series of brasses to him and his kinsmen. In these churches-turned-burial chapels the gentry created a setting for worship that mir-rored their own values and aspirations. Their consciousness of lineage, their sense of fellowship with the other gentleborn and of course their sense of pride all found due expression. And so too did their assertiveness. No longer were they content to be buried in the local abbey or friary, next to their feudal overlord and his kin; they wanted a burial place of their own. It was their way of saying that they had 'arrived'.

XVII
A LITERATE SOCIETY

LANGUAGE AND THE GROWTH OF LITERACY

The extensive migrations of the ninth to the eleventh centuries added greatly to the linguistic complexity of medieval Britain. In most parts of Britain by 1100 as many as three or four languages were spoken side by side – in England French, Latin and the Old English vernacular, and in Wales, Scotland and Ireland Latin, English, French and the various Gaelic vernaculars. In all parts of the British Isles Latin had become the language of the Church and of the formal documentation of government. French at the same time became the language of the Anglo-Norman aristocracy. In the twelfth century, when the aristocracies of Scotland and Ireland were Normanized, it became the language of the élite of those parts too. French in a sense was the *lingua franca* of the upper-classes of medieval Britain much as it was to be of the European élite in the eighteenth and nineteenth centuries.

Gradually, however, over time the linguistic pattern became simpler. By the thirteenth century French was beginning to lose ground and the upper-classes resumed use of their local vernaculars. The process appears to have proceeded at its most rapid in Scotland – partly because there were fewer Norman settlers there than south of the border and partly because the long period of war with England from the 1290s gave a spur to the growth of national consciousness. Appropriately one of the most remarkable poems of the period is Barbour's *Bruce*, composed in 1375, which celebrates the deeds of the great Scottish leader. In Wales too in the same period a spur was given to vernacular writing by the experience of suffering in war. In the wake of the Edwardian conquest Welsh poetry acquired a new vigour and the odes of Dafydd Benfras and Llygad Gwr delighted in the use of the native tongue.

The part of Britain in which French survived for longest as a language of literature and speech was probably England. This was because the English aristocracy had much the closest contact with France and the French nobility. However, a change in linguistic habits can be observed from the mid-thirteenth century onwards. This is strikingly illustrated in the arrangements that were made for the publication of two major constitutional documents of the period – Magna Carta and the Provisions of Oxford. In June 1215 Magna Carta was written out in Latin and French. Just under half a century later the Provisions of Oxford, when similarly published, was written out in French and

Schools and Studies

*I*n the years of instability that followed the collapse of the Roman Empire, organized education owed its survival almost entirely to the monks. The obligation laid on them in the Rule to spend some 3–4 hours a day in study ensured that reading occupied a position of central importance in their way of life. The purpose of this reading was supposed to be self-improvement – to point the way towards individual salvation; but inevitably a movement developed to see that its fruits were shared with the oblates, or young boys, who were offered for profession to the habit, and accordingly schools were often grafted on to many of the larger foundations. Probably the earliest such school to have been established in England was the one founded by Archbishop Theodore at Canterbury in the 670s.

The permanence of these institutions was threatened by the Viking onslaught of the ninth and tenth centuries. Schools were destroyed and their teachers dispersed. In his introduction to Pope Gregory's Pastoral Care, King Alfred lamented that learning had declined so far in England that there were few men south of the Humber who could understand divine services in English or translate a letter from Latin into English – and probably not many the other side of the Humber either. To remedy this situation the king launched a programme of reform. Important Latin texts were translated into the vernacular; new monasteries were founded; and a new school was established, as part of the royal household, for the education of the king's children and those of the nobility. These were remarkable measures for the king to contemplate while the enemy was not yet beaten; and in a sense their time had not yet come. Most of the new monasteries, for example, failed to take root. But the basis had been laid for a more comprehensive programme of reform which bore fruit in the reign of King Edgar (959–75). Under the guidance of Edgar and his archbishop, Dunstan, monasteries were refounded and new schools established. Their purpose, as before, was still chiefly that of providing instruction for the oblates, but there is also evidence to suggest that a fair minority of the pupils were youngsters not destined for the cloister.

The eleventh century saw the heyday of the monastic schools. By the twelfth century they were facing a dual challenge: from critics within the Monastic Order, who questioned the relevance of teaching to the life of prayer; and from secular teachers outside, who sought through their own efforts to satisfy the growing demand in the Church for a qualified, educated clergy. In the older monasteries the schools survived, but increasingly it was by those in non-monastic establishments that society's needs were met. Most of these were attached to cathedrals, for the simple reason that here there were prebends (endowments) which enabled teachers to provide instruction free to all comers. But such was the demand for learning in the twelfth century that before long teachers were established in a good number of non-cathedral towns, notably Northampton and Oxford. Eventually these various establishments were to sort themselves into a functional hierarchy: at the summit was the community of masters licensed to teach at the highest level – the university as we call it today; beneath it the grammar schools, so called because the study of Latin grammar was the lynchpin of their syllabus; and at the foot the 'reading' or 'song' schools, to which children were sent from about the age of seven (map 29).

Oxford and Cambridge were, of course, the only universities established in England prior to 1400. The ruthless use to which they put their influence in high places ensured that no rivals were allowed to threaten the joint monopoly which they quickly built up. In Scotland there were no universities at all before 1400, but in the fifteenth century no fewer than three were founded, at St Andrews, Glasgow and Aberdeen.

In both countries, as elsewhere in Europe, the function of the universities was to train an élite for service in Church and state. Admission was at the tender age of fourteen or fifteen to a Liberal Arts course which was divided into the 'trivium' (grammar, rhetoric, logic) lasting three years, and the 'quadrivium' (arithmetic, *geometry, astronomy and music) lasting another four. By his seventh year a candidate was ready to supplicate for the degree of MA, for which, as for all degrees, he was examined orally. After that he could seek presentation to a benefice; or alternatively he could pursue a further period of study leading after five years to the degree of B. Theol. and after two more to the doctorate. In either event he needed a patron. Presentation depended as much on connections as on qualifications, and further study cost money which, in the absence of parental backing, only a benefactor could provide. The cost of living in a medieval university – at least in medieval Oxford, for which figures are available – was not high: board and lodging could be had for less than 4¾d. a week. But undeniably the training was long, and the régime hard; not surprisingly the drop-out rate was high.*

What entrants into the higher faculties needed above all was financial security; and it was this which the earliest colleges were intended to give them. Merton and Balliol in Oxford, Peterhouse and King's Hall in Cambridge, were founded and endowed specifically with a view to providing Fellowships for struggling students. Undergraduate teaching played no part in their design. Undergraduates lived, as they had always done, in houses or 'halls' scattered around the town. Exeter College, Oxford was the first to break with precedent by admitting them – but then only in their third year, and without offering them instruction. It was not until the foundation of New College in 1379 that the provision of undergraduate teaching was included in the foundation statutes of a college.

The most widespread and characteristic of all medieval schools were the 'grammar' schools. By the mid-thirteenth century establishments answering such description had sprung up in almost all the cathedral cities and in many smaller towns. Those attached to cathedrals were expected to provide instruction free because the schoolmaster was provided with income from a prebend. Those lacking such endowment were necessarily obliged to charge fees; and accordingly they may have lacked the permanence of the more securely based institutions. But whether or not this was so, the thirteenth and fourteenth centuries appear to have witnessed a considerable expansion of educational provision. Some of this was admittedly ancillary to foundations such as chantries which were primarily religious in purpose. But in the late fourteenth century two schools were founded which were important for the emphasis which they placed on teaching above religious and devotional observances. The first of these, and much the grander, was William of Wykeham's Winchester, founded in 1382 for the instruction of seventy scholars who would spend four or five years there until they qualified for admission to New College, Oxford. The other, perhaps more influential in the long run for being more modest, was the 'House of Scholars' at Wotton-under-Edge (Gloucestershire) founded by Lady Katherine Berkeley in 1384. Like his colleagues at earlier foundations, the schoolmaster at Wotton had to sing masses for the souls of the foundress and her relations; but his main duty was to give free instruction in grammar to the two poor scholars who received free board and lodging and to any others who might attend. Wotton was to be the archetype of many similar endowed schools in the late Middle Ages.

Something of the character of medieval school life can be captured from the documentation that has come down to us. Classes were larger than they are today – probably numbering forty or more – and hours were longer. Judging from early Tudor regulations, the day would begin at 6 or 7 in the morning, and, after lengthy breaks for breakfast and midday dinner, would culminate in a long haul from 1 till 5 in the afternoon. Perhaps to keep his pupils on their toes, the schoolmaster was free in his use of the cane. The schoolboy in Chaucer's Prioress's Tale *promises to learn the song to the Virgin:*

> *Though they should scold me when I cannot say*
> *My primer, though they beat me thrice an hour.*

As for the provision of urinals (to end on an irreverent note) it seems that the boys were supposed to go outside to some recognized spot – too often, according to one Oxford schoolmaster who complained that, as soon as he went into the school, 'this fellow goith to make water, and he goith oute to the comyn drafte'.

A TEACHING SCENE
(British Library, MS Cotton
Augustus V, fol. 103r).
It is doubtful if every lecture in the
Middle Ages was as formal as this
idealized scene of Aristotle lecturing
to his pupils (mid-fifteenth century)

WINCHESTER COLLEGE
(Hampshire)
The cloister of the great college
founded by William of Wykeham in
1382. The architect was William
Wynford, whom Wykeham
employed to build the twin
foundation of New College, Oxford

English (though a Latin text may have been issued as well). This was the first time since the Conquest that an official government document had been circulated in English. It was now recognized that beneath the aristocracy there was a politically conscious class, probably of gentry rank or just below, whose first language was English.

Nevertheless change, when it came, came slowly. It is not until the reign of Edward III (1327–77) that much solid evidence is afforded of a shift in the linguistic tastes of the aristocracy. Of particular interest in this connection is a religious treatise written by a royal duke, Henry of Lancaster (d. 1361), the king's cousin. This treatise, the *Livre de Seyntz Medicines*, is written in French; but its author craved his readers' indulgence because – so he said – being English he was not used to writing in the French tongue. This statement probably was not just a case of false modesty. Writing a quarter of a century later John Trevisa, the chaplain to the Berkeley family, commented that it was the practice in the schools now to translate from Latin into English and not Latin into French. Significantly it was at this very time – the 1380s and 1390s – that Chaucer was writing *The Canterbury Tales*, the first great poem in English for a courtly audience.

The extent of literacy in medieval Britain (in whichever language) is difficult to measure. Before the twelfth century it was clearly very limited. The strength of the association between writing and sacred texts had the effect of confining it almost entirely to the clergy – hence the equation, which the clergy themselves coined, of 'clericus' with 'literatus' and 'laicus' with 'illiteratus'. But in the course of the twelfth and thirteenth centuries literacy underwent an expansion. In England the production and retention of written records by the government departments encouraged sheriffs and other officials to develop literate skills; and the revolution in justice in the reign of Henry II, which

MAP 29: THE GROWTH OF LEARNING IN MEDIEVAL BRITAIN

In the twelfth and thirteenth centuries schools were established all over Britain. Some lasted for no more than a few years. Others flourish to this day. The symbols on the map illustrate these schools' earliest attested existence.

introduced a legal system operated by the serving of writs, obliged all who wished to bring suits in the king's courts to be conversant with written forms. By the reign of Edward I it is clear that royal or seignorial writs were reaching every bailiff in the land and drawing men well below the gentry into the fold of literate society. But equally important in a different way was the growing use of account rolls in estate management, because this required proprietors (if they were to make any sense of them) to be numerate as well as literate.

For all these very practical sorts of reasons laymen were beginning to master skills which had once been the monopoly of the clergy. Gradually that monopoly was broken down. From the time of Henry I (1100–35) it could be assumed that the king was literate – literate, that is, in Latin. From the time of Henry II or John it could be assumed that most of the nobility were, and probably a good proportion of the more active gentry. In 1334 – admittedly a good while later – when Glastonbury Abbey called upon thirty-three of its local tenants to testify on its behalf in a court case, slightly over half were said to have been literate (in Latin and presumably therefore in English too). Doubtless those who were illiterate did not recommend themselves as witnesses; and to that extent the figure cannot be taken as nationally representative. But it does at least make possible the suggestion that in the mid-fourteenth century an overall literacy rate of some 40 per cent was achieved.

If this was so – and it is worth remembering that in the early sixteenth century Sir Thomas More claimed a rate of more than 50 per cent for his fellow-countrymen – then there can be little doubt that literacy was more widely diffused in English society than in Scottish or Welsh. In Scotland the institutions of government lacked the range and sophistication of their English counterparts, and consequently they did not generate the same familiarity with the use of official documents. Nor was the involvement of laymen in the business of administration so widespread. Though the office of Chancellor was often given to members of the nobility, the lawyers were all Churchmen, and there was no equivalent of the English Inns of Court to provide a training for the laity independent of the ecclesiastical educational system. On the other hand, the Scottish élite was not uncultivated. They were familiar with social and intellectual currents in the wider world, not least through their many links with France. We are told, for example, that Robert Bruce read French romances to his followers while they were fugitives in 1306. Certainly their literacy in Scots, and to a certain degree in French and Latin, can be assumed by the fourteenth century. The literacy of the lairds – the gentry – on the other hand, is more problematical. This may have been widespread by the fifteenth century, but probably not before. As the most recent historian of late medieval Scotland has written, the spread of literacy was 'probably considerably slower, later and less comprehensive than it was in England'.

In both countries the process was greatly assisted by the linguistic simplification which reduced the number of tongues a person needed to master. But even by the fifteenth century literate skills appear to have been unequally distributed between the sexes. Men, it seems, could master both reading and writing, but women – to judge from the evidence of the Paston Letters – only reading. Margery Paston, admittedly only a youngster at the time, had to employ a clerk of her father's to write a Valentine to her lover; and even so businesslike a women as her mother Margaret was in the habit of dictating the great majority of letters that went out in her name. Reading and writing were not automatically coupled in the Middle Ages. Writing was a skill distinct from reading because the use of parchment and quills made it technically demanding. It therefore became the preserve of a class of professional scribes whose services could be hired as and when required. Reading, on the other hand, was simply an extension of hearing and speaking. And it could be mastered by people quite unable to put quill to parchment. The reputation of certain late medieval duchesses for their devotion to religious literature bears witness to their ability to read for themselves as well as to listen to works read out to them.

READING FOR PLEASURE

Among the laity of both sexes the demand for reading matter greatly increased in the later Middle Ages. Romances, chronicles, histories and ballads were all sought out by patrons who wanted to enjoy them in the new-found privacy of their solars. Volumes of this nature were not expensive to buy. Unlike the de-luxe manuscripts of the twelfth century, which were the products of monastic scriptoria, they were mass-produced in stationers' workshops in London, Oxford, Cambridge and elsewhere – but particularly in London. Frequently they took the form of quires or booklets which the owner could then put together in composite volumes – as Sir John Paston did his. Expensive binding seems in general to have been avoided. In the interests of both economy and practicality it was considered sufficient to stick them together in paper covers.

Being objects of little value, these books were readily circulated between friends and relatives. The Pastons, for example, are often found lending books to each other. Sir John, a great bibliophile, writing to his mother, asked her to arrange for her chaplain's books to be left in London, at the George by Paul's Wharf, where they would be safe until he could collect them. The George, whither members of the family regularly repaired on visits to London, was quite commonly used by them as a place for either leaving or collecting books. What clearly emerges from these and a multitude of other references is that the age of oral transmission of poetry was over. The famous illustration in the Corpus Christi College manuscript which shows Chaucer reciting his poetry to a courtly audience is an evocation of the past. The contemporary reality was very different. Poetry was now read privately and in silence; and it was transmitted in written copy. Already in 1400 there was a reading public in England. Three-quarters of a century later Caxton was able to launch his printing business because a market for his books was already in existence.

Poet and Peasant: Chaucer and Langland

Geoffrey Chaucer and William Langland were living and working at about the same time within a few hundred yards of each other in London; yet for all that they had in common they might have lived worlds apart. With Langland, an obscure cleric, we enter into the sufferings and grievances of the labouring classes; with Chaucer, a king's esquire, we move in the polite society of the 'courtly makers'.

Of Langland's career and background little is known beyond what he himself reveals in his great poem Piers Plowman. As a boy, he tells us, he was provided with some schooling in the scripture at the expense of his father and some friends. But when these friends died, he was left without a patron. He moved from the West Midlands and wandered a great deal, eventually settling in London. There he supported himself by singing the Office of the Dead. It is doubtful if he ever proceeded beyond Minor Orders, because on his own admission he had a wife and daughter – Kitty and Colette respectively – with whom he lived in a cottage in Cornhill. He found himself absorbed into the ranks of the unbeneficed clergy – of whom there was no shortage thronging St Paul's and the other great churches. The experience shaped his entire outlook, and provides the essential background to an understanding of his poem. Langland knew poverty at first hand. He could understand the feelings of the poor because he was one of them himself. On the other hand, he was no social revolutionary; his outlook was as far removed from that of the rebel leaders of 1381 as it was from that of the nobility. He sought a moral not a political reformation. He was concerned with inner reality, not with day-to-day policy prescriptions. He looked to the Holy Trinity to give structure to human thought and action. The Trinity, he believed, was in everything – in man and in the mind of man; and Piers was its manifestation in human form.

Chaucer's attitude, on the other hand, was that of a man who viewed the world with detachment. The political struggles through which he lived, between Richard II and his opponents, find no echo in his work. Nor do the contemporary religious controversies involving John Wyclif and the Lollards. Chaucer was influenced to a far lesser degree than

GEOFFREY CHAUCER
A portrait of the poet in Thomas Hoccleve's Regimen of Princes, *written in 1412, painted in accordance with Hoccleve's own memory of his appearance*

Langland by the consolations of religion: indeed, he is the first great English poet whose work is not religious in either purpose or content.

An explanation for this detachment is probably to be found in the development of his career, which allowed him to move freely between worlds that were often separate. His background lay in the mercantile élite of the capital, where his father was a vintner; yet most of his adult life was spent in aristocratic households and at court. He never rose high in the social pecking order; yet he had plenty of opportunities for travel, and he is known to have made at least two visits to Italy. He was a royal civil servant first and foremost; yet he managed to combine this life with that of a country gentleman. He kept houses in London and Greenwich, then in the countryside; and a sinecure post as a sub-forester of North Petherton (Somerset) gave him the financial security that he needed in order to engage in literary pursuits. From about 1387, then, he was able to give most of his time to the composition of his magnum opus, The Canterbury Tales.

The idea behind the poem is ingenious. On the suggestion of the Host, Harry Baily, the pilgrims assembling at the Tabard Inn at Southwark agree to tell a couple of tales each on the outward journey to Canterbury and a couple on the return. In the event the scheme turned out to be too ambitious, and less than a quarter of it was executed. But what there is is a masterpiece. In the Knight's Tale of Palamon and Arcite, the Reeve's Tale of Simpkin, the crooked miller . . . and all the others, the whole panorama of human life is made to unfold before us. Chaucer's wit and sense of irony give the tales a vitality all of their own. Without exception they bear witness to that universality of sympathy which puts him on a par in English poetry with Shakespeare.

SOUTHWARK, THE GEORGE INN (NT)
Upper portion of the galleried inn. The Tabard Inn, immortalized in Chaucer's Canterbury Tales *would have been very similar in appearance*

The Tabard sadly has gone; but the George (NT), also at Southwark and a similar galleried structure, gives an idea of what it would have been like. Chaucer's chief monument is obviously his poetry, which is the first substantial corpus in the English tongue which can be read in the original and not in translation. Unlike Langland, who wrote in the old alliterative mode, Chaucer wrote in the newer style of rhyming couplets. In other words, he was the first of the long line of 'courtly makers' stretching down to Sir Thomas Wyatt in the sixteenth century. It is particularly fitting, therefore, that this most attractive man should be the first of our poets to be buried in what was to become Poets' Corner in Westminster Abbey.

XVIII
WAR AND SOCIETY
ENGLAND AND THE ANGLO-NORMAN LEGACY

Though England had often been overrun in the Anglo-Saxon period, she had always managed to win back her independence. Even when she had been absorbed into Knut's dominions in 1017, she managed to break free again a generation later. But in 1066 her luck ran out. Defeat at Hastings spelled absorption into a continental empire and subordination to the needs of a French-speaking dynasty. English morale was shattered. Nostalgia took the place of hope, and fear the place of confidence.

The character of Norman rule was determined by the need to preserve and strengthen the link between England and the duchy. Almost from the moment of its creation that link was under threat from one or other of the Normans' many enemies. In the Conqueror's reign it was Denmark's might that menaced (though after the failure of the projected invasion of 1085 that might looked a good deal less menacing than it had). In the longer term it was the challenge from France and Anjou that came to the fore. To the King of France the sudden elevation of a vassal of his to the rank of king was not only a personal affront, it was a threat to his power; and it became his paramount objective to seek its reversal. Through patient diplomacy he built up an anti-Norman coalition, and by the early 1100s he was in a position to mount a full-scale invasion of the duchy. That invasion proved to be a failure, as did others after it. But eventually his and his successors' persistence earned its reward, and the fortunes of war changed. In the reign of King John the Anglo-Norman resistance crumbled; and on 24 June 1204 Philip Augustus of France entered Rouen.

As a result of the creation of the cross-Channel state, England was drawn into a series of continental conflicts in which her colonial status condemned her to the role of a milch-cow. Never-ending demands for money were met by tapping her abundant resources. The feudal and judicial prerogatives of kingship were exploited to the limit; justice was sold to the highest bidder; new forms of taxation were invented and developed; the currency was debased; and on one occasion, so the Worcester chronicler tells us, the monasteries of England were searched for wealth which could be transferred to the royal treasury. To facilitate collection of the king's income new departments of government were established. Of these the most important was the Exchequer – the accounting office, which in the reign of Henry I was grafted onto the old Anglo-Saxon treasury. The rigour of its procedures was notorious. According to Richard FitzNeal, the treasurer in Henry II's reign, even tough-minded sheriffs quaked with fear when summoned before it. But in their case the suffering was short-lived: they could recoup themselves at the expense of those in their grip at home. It was the ordinary people who were the real losers. Small wonder that they were always grumbling. But until the reign of King John they did no more than grumble. Angevin kingship offered compensating benefits which made the burden worth bearing. Only when the Crown passed into the hands of John did oppressiveness tip over into tyranny. The weakness of the subject's defences against the prerogative was all too painfully exposed, and recourse was had to rebellion. The imposition on the king of the charter of liberties we know as Magna Carta was the result.

One effect of England's continental involvement was therefore to stimulate the growth of taxation and to encourage the development of agencies capable of collecting it. Another was to divert its rulers from the objective which they might otherwise have had of conquering the non-Anglo-Saxon parts of the British Isles. In the Anglo-Norman scale of values priority was always going to be given to the defence of Normandy over the claims of continuing conquest in Britain. So Scotland and Wales were spared immediate absorption, if only by default; it was left to the more gradual processes of settlement and colonization to draw the two nations more closely into the Anglo-Norman orbit.

ENGLAND AND THE CELTIC LANDS

Infiltration in fact was to prove itself as powerful an agent of change as conquest. By the second quarter of the twelfth century the coastal lowlands of Wales from Glamorgan westwards had been taken over by the Normans and made subject to their authority. Lordships were established and a pattern of feudal landholding laid upon the landscape. Castles, such as those at Pembroke and Cilgerran (NT), were built to overawe the populace and, as soon as conditions allowed, boroughs were founded and the outlines of an administrative structure delineated. By the 1090s some of the more adventurous barons like Bernard de Neufmarché were already penetrating up the river valleys into the interior. Footholds were established on the Usk at Brecon and on the Monnow at Skenfrith (NT), and colonizing activity was extended outwards to the less hospitable terrain of the hinterland. Life in these areas was nothing if not dangerous, but over time the uneasy military superiority was converted into a society more strongly civilian in character, and a measure of understanding was reached with the local population. In the late twelfth century Rhys ap Gruffydd of Deheubarth, Lord of Dinefwr (NT), is caught exchanging pleasantries with Norman barons at Hereford, and Owain Cyfeiliog of Powys delighting Henry II with his wit at dinner in Shrewsbury. The many opportunities available for contact and mutual influence helped to soothe the bitterness and resentment built up in earlier years. And even if there were only a few Welshmen who were entrusted by the Normans with military commands, as Bleddyn ap Cydifor was at Laugharne, there were certainly a good number of others who learned the benefits of compromise and respectful co-existence with the intruders.

In Scotland it was a not dissimilar story. Society was subtly transformed by the arrival of Norman settlers who brought with them the ways of continental Europe. But the Scottish experience differed from the Welsh in one major respect – for here in the

CILGERRAN CASTLE (Dyfed)
(NT)
Aerial view of the thirteenth-century castle of the Marshal family, Earls of Pembroke

north changes were not brought about forcibly by alien intervention; they were sponsored by the Crown itself. From the time of Edgar (1094–1107) and his brothers onwards a line of rulers showed themselves eager to augment their military strength by attracting the service of knights from Normandy and other parts of France. The influx reached its peak in the reign of David I (1124–53), but continued at a lower level for another 150 years. How many Normans and Frenchmen settled in Scotland is difficult to say: the evidence is too incomplete to admit of quantitative analysis. But south of the Forth, certainly, and in the southern valleys (Galloway excepted) there is scarcely a village which cannot afford evidence of colonization: while the impact of the migration on the future direction of Scottish history can be judged from the presence, among the new arrivals at King David's court, of Robert of Bruce, ancestor of the future champion of Scottish independence, and Walter fitz Alan, ancestor of the Stewarts (Walter's father was a steward), the family that succeeded the Bruces on the throne.

In the course of the twelfth century, therefore, Scottish government and society were reshaped along lines that would have been familiar to visitors from south of the border. Tenure of land by military service was introduced; sheriffs were appointed, on the

DUNSEVERICK CASTLE (County
Antrim) (NT)
*The fragmentary but evocative
remains of a cliff-top fortress
looking across the sea to Scotland*

English model; and castles were constructed in the up-to-date Norman fashion. In addition, the social structures of the northern and southern kingdoms were knitted together by the existence of an important group of lords, led by King David himself, who held lands on both sides of the border. Robert Bruce, for example, held Cleveland in England in addition to Annandale in Scotland; and Hugh de Morville the younger – one of Becket's murderers – held the lordship of Westmorland under Henry II as well as the county of Lauderdale in Scotland, where he was also hereditary constable. England and Scotland, though separate states, were not yet totally separate societies. At the highest levels they overlapped; and in the ecclesiastical sphere there was a good deal of inter-penetration. Ailred, the future abbot of Rievaulx, was brought up at the Scottish Court, though he was of English birth; and years later, after he had been elected abbot, he was to make regular visits to Rievaulx's dependent houses in Scotland at Melrose and Dundrennan (map 27). Moreover, his friend and patron King David was instrumental in bringing monks of the Reformed Orders into Scotland. He established houses for Augustinian Canons at Jedburgh and for the Cistercians at Melrose. Melrose was largely rebuilt in the late fourteenth century, but Jedburgh survives mainly as its builders left it. It is a noble Romanesque building, and bears eloquent witness to the cosmopolitan nature of King David's Scotland.

The long period of peace on the borders in the later twelfth and thirteenth centuries gave the Scottish kings the chance they needed to extend their rule into the northern and western parts of the country (map 30). These were the areas furthest from the seat of government; they were also the areas where the Gaelic strain ran deepest and where the Norse impact had been strongest. By this time, however, Norse power was on the wane; and the sudden collapse of royal authority in mainland Norway was one factor which precipitated Scottish intervention. The other was a threat as yet only perceived rather than real – the growing power of the English in Ireland as represented by mighty castles like those at Carrickfergus and Dunseverick (NT) which looked across the sea to Scotland. There was a feeling that Scotland might one day find herself encircled.

The Anglo-Norman presence in Ireland, like that in Wales out of which it had grown, was initially a private enterprise affair. But in 1171 Henry II took over a large army numbering some 500 knights and 3–4,000 archers to put the stamp of his authority on the settlement. Strongbow – the leader of the settlers – accepted the royal will, and the Irish chieftains competed with one another in their eagerness to offer loyalty. 'There was almost no one of any repute or influence', wrote Gerald of Wales, 'who did not present himself before the king or pay him the respect due to an overlord.' 'The whole island', he continued, 'remained quiet under the watchful eye of the king and enjoyed peace and tranquillity.'

But in Ireland peace and tranquillity were rarely to be enjoyed for long, and for this the settlers were perhaps more to blame than the Irish themselves. The knights' appetite for land led to recurrent hit-and-run raids on the domains of chieftains with whom they were supposed to be at peace; and the attitude of contempt with which all but a few of the colonists regarded the natives bred mutual distrust and frustrated any possiblity of peaceful co-existence. 'The Irish have not progressed at all from the primitive habits of pastoral farming', wrote Gerald of Wales again. 'They despise work on the land, have little use for the money-making of the towns, and condemn the rights and privileges of civil life . . . Dedicated only to leisure and laziness, they are a truly barbarous people.' Gerald's views were echoed by other English writers who commented, however briefly, on the Irish. William of Newburgh compared Ireland's political structure unfavourably

SKENFRITH CASTLE (Gwent)
(NT)
The thirteenth-century perimeter
wall of the castle built by Hubert de
Burgh, Henry III's justiciar

with that of Anglo-Norman England, and William of Malmesbury spoke of the country's backwardness. Gerald, as always however, had the last word. 'The Irish', he said, 'are a filthy people, wallowing in vice.'

Whether or not these denunciations were justified, they represented the view that most of the Anglo-Normans had of the native Irish; and they provided the justification for continued English expansion in the country. In a sense it was the first manifestation of the English 'civilizing mission'. And for a while it worked. In 1210 King John led an expedition to Dublin, which was even larger than his father's. The Anglo-Norman administration was placed on a firmer footing; English law was extended to the colony; and the institutions of government in Dublin were refined. In the years that followed, moreover, there was a great expansion in the scale of the English settlement – castles and towns were established, shires created and a hierarchy of local officialdom introduced. By 1300, perhaps as much as two-thirds of Ireland was under English administration. The country was paying its way, and even producing a surplus for the Crown.

In the fourteenth century, however, the English position collapsed. In 1315 Robert Bruce had despatched his brother Edward to conquer Ireland, so as to deprive the English of their base there. Edward enjoyed only brief success before meeting his death in battle in 1318. But the long-term result of his intervention was to undermine English

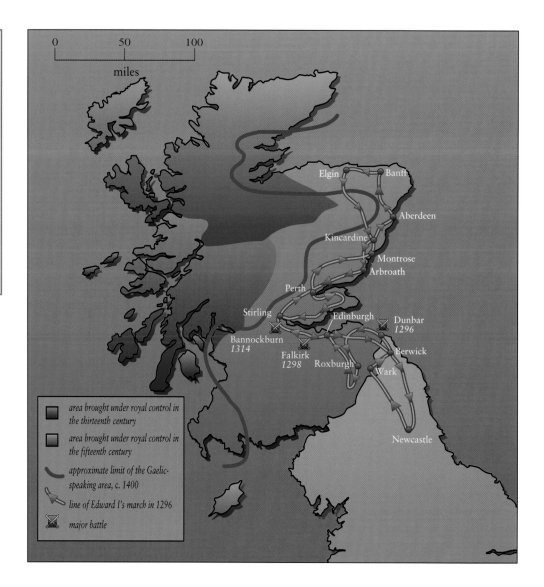

ascendancy and to encourage a revival in Irish self-consciousness. For the remainder of the Middle Ages the English were on the defensive. They became worried about a loss of identity – hence the passing in 1366 of the famous Kilkenny statute, which prohibited the English from marrying native Irish or adopting their manner of dress. And even in the monasteries they felt themselves to be besieged. At Bective, Fore and Althassel the settler monks turned their precincts into fortresses and were terrified to step outside them. Yet because of its commitments elsewhere – in Scotland and in France – the Crown was powerless to lend them assistance.

On the nearer side of the Irish Sea too – in Wales – English power underwent alternate expansion and contraction over the years. In the 1240s it touched a new peak and extended even into the mountainous areas of the interior. But twenty years later, when the war between Henry III and Simon de Montfort undermined the defence of the March, it once again plumbed the depths. In the person of Llewellyn ap Gruffydd the English faced an adversary of great ambition who had succeeded in welding the native principalities into a cohesive unit capable of resisting their designs. Llewellyn won recognition of the title Prince of Wales in the Treaty of Montgomery (1267) and sought to give effect to it by demanding homage from the other leaders of native Welsh society.

CHIRK CASTLE (Clwyd) (NT)
An Edwardian-style fortress built
between 1295 and 1310 for Sir
Roger Mortimer, but probably never
completed: the east and west curtain
walls stop short after the midway
towers

But to a greater extent than he realized his ascendancy depended on English restraint; and as soon as royal authority in England experienced a revival, as it did in the reign of Edward I, then he found himself in difficulties. Disagreements between himself and his brother David led to English intervention in 1277 and subsequently to the loss of the area known as the Four Cantrefs (map 31); and further problems and jurisdictional disputes led to a second war five years later, which resulted in the extinction of the Welsh principality altogether.

Edward's achievement in conquering North Wales was as remarkable as it was comprehensive. For one thing the king's timing was good. He had no commitments elsewhere to distract him: Normandy had been lost three-quarters of a century before, and he was at peace with France. Thus he was able to mobilize the entire resources of his realm and channel them in the direction of Snowdonia. But his organization was exemplary too. His commanders knew exactly what was expected of them; and he ensured

BECTIVE ABBEY (County Meath)
A Cistercian abbey totally rebuilt in
the fifteenth century when the site
was fortified and the massive tower-
house built

through the agency of the wardrobe – the war ministry – that they had the men and the equipment that they needed. In both wars the strategy was the same – to advance westwards along the coast and to cut off Anglesey from the mainland, so as to deprive Llewellyn of his principal supply of grain. In both wars too that strategy was equally successful, and native resistance was overcome.

But North Wales, once conquered, had then to be secured. Edward sought to do this by ringing it with a chain of castles. After the 1277 campaign castles were constructed in mid-Wales at Builth and Aberystwyth, and in the north at Flint and Rhuddlan; and after the 1282 campaign at Conwy, Caernarfon and Harlech, and after the rebellion of 1294–5 at Beaumaris. These were all royal castles, built and paid for by the king and garrisoned by his soldiers. But in addition there was a series of privately owned castles which formed a secondary line of defence – among the most important of them being Ruthin, begun in 1277 for the Greys, and Chirk (NT), begun in 1295 for Sir Roger Mortimer. The function served by these fortresses was everywhere the same: to consolidate the English hold on Snowdonia and to serve as seats of civilian government and administration. At Caernarfon their quasi-imperial role was alluded to in the polygonal towers and bands of differently coloured stone which evoked the Thoedosian wall at Constantinople (Constantine himself was believed to have been born at Caernarfon). Their worth was tested and proved in the crisis of 1294–5 when there was a native uprising, and in the years that followed, as occupation deepened into settlement, they became the nuclei around which the structures of a colonial régime could be

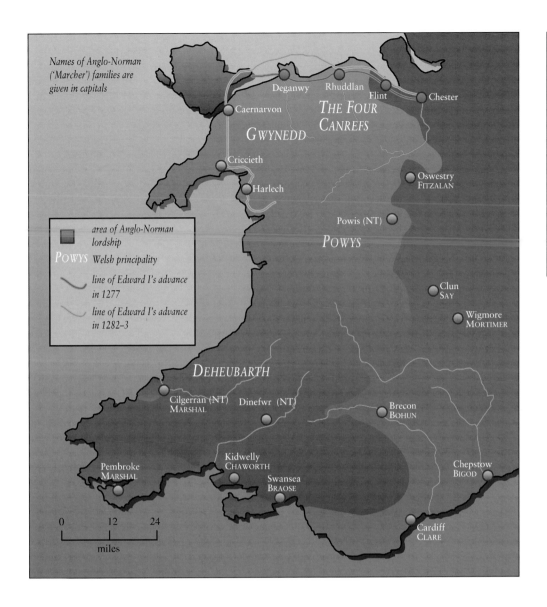

Names of Anglo-Norman ('Marcher') families are given in capitals

Deganwy
Rhuddlan
Flint
Chester
Caernarvon
THE FOUR
CANREFS
GWYNEDD
Criccieth
Oswestry
FITZALAN
Harlech

■ area of Anglo-Norman lordship
POWYS Welsh principality
〜 line of Edward I's advance in 1277
〜 line of Edward I's advance in 1282–3

Powis (NT)
POWYS

Clun
SAY
Wigmore
MORTIMER

DEHEUBARTH

Cilgerran (NT)
MARSHAL
Dinefwr (NT)
Brecon
BOHUN

Kidwelly
CHAWORTH
Chepstow
BIGOD
Pembroke
MARSHAL
Swansea
BRAOSE

0   12   24
miles

Cardiff
CLARE

MAP 31: WALES IN THE THIRTEENTH CENTURY

In 1200 Anglo-Norman colonization was largely confined to the south and east of the country. Further north lay the principalities of native Wales. The ending of Welsh independence was finally achieved by Edward I's two campaigns of 1277 and 1282–3.

established. At Rhuddlan, Conwy, Caernarfon and Harlech boroughs were founded beneath their walls – English boroughs, that is, for the native Welsh population was dispossessed to make way for the new English one. Not surprisingly their establishment was deeply resented by the Welsh. But all the same most of them flourished and took root. Their character can best be savoured today at Conwy, where the walled town acts as the perfect foil to the castle. It is an archetypal Edwardian borough – one of the last and one of the best.

Encouraged by his success in Wales, Edward tried to achieve a similar mastery over the affairs of Scotland. The extinction of the direct line of the Scottish royal family in 1290 gave him the excuse that he needed to intervene; and the establishment on the throne of his ally John Balliol opened the possibility of being able to give a sharper and more specific form to the rather vague feudal overlordship which he and his ancestors had claimed in the past. At first his plans enjoyed a measure of success. But he reckoned without the Scots' response to his heavy-handedness. In 1296 there was a major uprising against him, and in the following year full-scale war broke out.

After a long struggle the Scots emerged victorious. Two factors in particular contributed to their success. The first was the sheer size of their country. Just how big it

'That Worm-Eaten Hold of Ragged Stone'

The Edwardian strongholds of North Wales represent the summit of the castle-builder's art in Britain. They are not only buildings of supreme architectural distinction. They are monuments to the grandeur of Edward's imperial mission in Wales. Never before had power been converted into stone with such mastery, and never would it be again.

In terms of design the Edwardian castles saw the realization of the ideal of an integrated system of defence. The dichotomous two-piece plan of the motte-and-bailey castle was abandoned in favour of a single enclosure or a series of concentric enclosures. No longer was the keep conceived as the ultimate strongpoint, to be held should the rest of the castle fall. After a final appearance at Flint, it vanished altogether. From now on defensive strength was disposed more equally around the walls by the placing of towers – usually drum towers – at regular intervals. These enabled the garrison to fire at besiegers from the flanks; at the same time they also served to knit the castle together into a single cohesive unit.

The regularity of the Edwardian castle is marvellously conveyed at Chirk, the only one of the strongholds that is still inhabited. Chirk lay in the second line of defence, in the Marches, and was built not for the king but for one of his lieutenants, Sir Roger Mortimer. But it formed part of a single defensive system, and its similarity to Harlech and Beaumaris is such that it must be the work of the same architect – that is to say, either James of St George or his chief assistant, Walter of Hereford. Like Beaumaris it was planned as a rectangle with a massive drum tower at each corner and a semi-circular tower midway along each side. Again like Beaumaris, however, it was never completed. The east and west curtain walls stop short after the midway towers; an improvised southern section was built, and in place of a full-scale gatehouse on the lines of Harlech a smaller entrance was cut on the northern side. These modifications remind us of the heavy expense involved in castle-building. During the fifty-year period from 1277 to 1330 some £93,000 was spent on the royal construction programme in North Wales. Yet still it was not enough, and castles were left unfinished.

Such is the fame of the Edwardian castles that it is easy to forget that many of their most characteristic features had already been anticipated. Mural towers had been added to the bailey walls at Corfe (NT) in the early thirteenth century; and the concentric principle had been worked out at Caerphilly ten years before it was taken up at Harlech. Thus there was little that was innovative about the castles built by Edward I. Their claim to fame lies rather in the skill with which these various elements were brought together and welded into a coherent and logically satisfying whole. Indeed, so successfully was this done that the subsequent history of the castle is often written solely in terms of its decline – a falling away from a brittle perfection realized, however briefly, in the mountains of Snowdonia.

But to suggest as much would probably be to mislead. The late Middle Ages saw little slackening of the pace in fortification. In all parts of England, but particularly in the north, existing castles were strengthened and new ones constructed. At Dunstanburgh (NT) on the Northumberland coast a mighty new castle was built by Thomas of Lancaster, probably to provide the local people with protection against the Scots, and himself with a place of refuge in the event of trouble with his cousin Edward II. Not far away at Alnwick a new gatehouse and barbican were added by the Percys to the outer bailey of their already extensive castle. And at Warkworth, another Percy property, in a return to the strategic ideas of the Normans, a tower-house or keep was built in the 1390s which combined the best in residential comfort with a strong defensive capability.

In southern England castle-building was prompted mainly by the need to afford protection against the French. England's navy was neither large enough nor mobile enough to perform the task alone; and in a sense castles were seen as providing a secondary line of defence. Three were built in the late fourteenth century when the threat was at its height: Queenborough and Scotney in Kent, and Bodiam in East Sussex. Of these Queenborough has vanished without trace; Scotney (NT) survives as no more than a fragment; and only Bodiam (NT) has come down to us in anything approaching reasonably complete condition.

Bodiam is a famous castle and justly so. Quite apart from its romantic setting and purity of outline, it is a building of the highest architectural importance. It set new standards of symmetry and integration; and in the disposition of the buildings around the courtyard it struck a near perfect compromise between the rival claims of defence and domesticity. On the northern side, next to the gatehouse, stood the garrison's quarters. On the far side, and furthest from danger, were placed the hall, the kitchen and the buttery. Running north-east from the hall, and accessible from it, were the main residential apartments, the most important of them being on the first floor, as in the great Elizabethan houses. First came the solar, then probably a bedchamber and then beyond that a smaller room with a window looking down into the chapel which enabled the lord and lady to hear Mass without actually descending.

The logic of Bodiam's internal planning is matched by the clarity of its strategic vision. The castle's strength is concentrated in a single rectangle from which a cylindrical tower projects at each angle and to which access is gained by a twin-towered gateway. The gateway is accented less strongly than it was in the Edwardian castles. But it is provided with gunports as well as arrow-slits; and additional protection is afforded by the right-angled approach across an outwork in the moat which exposes the attacker to fire from the garrison within.

Bodiam was concieved as a fortress, then. But it was also something more. It was a status symbol, a power-house. It bore visible witness to the standing in local society of its builder, Sir Edward Dallingridge. Dallingridge was a leading light among the Sussex gentry. He was a JP and many times a knight of the shire (i.e. an MP). His patrons included the Duke of Brittany and nearer home the Earl of Arundel, the greatest landowner in Sussex. Behind him he had an impressive record of service in the wars in France. Indeed, he honoured one of his commanders, Sir Robert Knolles, by displaying his arms on the southern façade of the castle. However, there was just one thing he lacked, and that perhaps the most important – good lineage. Unlike his peers in county society he was not of knightly descent. He was of yeoman stock from Dalling Ridge in the Weald. He owed his success to a mixture of ability and good fortune. A career in service brought him material reward and social advancement; marriage to an heiress gained him a landed estate; and the death without issue of his elder brother allowed him to add his lands to his own. By the 1380s he was rich. He had the money to build, and to build well. So he demolished the old manor-house of his in-laws, and raised a new castle on a fresh site by the River Rother. Its splendour was to bear witness to his standing in county society.

There had never been a time when castles had not been monuments to their builders' ambitions. But this aspect of their character appears to have become more prominent with the passage of time. Gatehouses became bigger, and heraldic displays more grandiose. Castles tended to show off more than they had. Whether or not this amounts to a decline in castles is a moot point. For, oddly enough, the castle's misfortune was that it had become too strong. By the fourteenth century the cost of reducing one had grown so great that alternative ways were sought of resolving struggles – chiefly in the end by resort to pitched battle. Castles, therefore, were made redundant; and henceforward they lived on as stately homes.

BODIAM CASTLE (East Sussex) (NT)
A view from the south-east showing the postern gate and the great hall to its right

*DUNSTANBURGH CASTLE
(Northumberland) (NT)
Dramatically sited on the
Northumberland coast,
Dunstanburgh was built by Thomas,
Earl of Lancaster, in the early
fourteenth century when regular
Scottish raids were endangering the
security of northern England*

*SIZERGH CASTLE (Cumbria)
(NT)
A view of the fourteenth-century
peel tower, to which a residential
wing was added in a later, and more
peaceful, age*

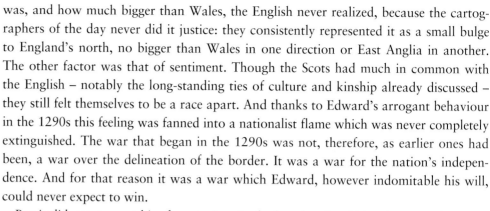

was, and how much bigger than Wales, the English never realized, because the cartographers of the day never did it justice: they consistently represented it as a small bulge to England's north, no bigger than Wales in one direction or East Anglia in another. The other factor was that of sentiment. Though the Scots had much in common with the English – notably the long-standing ties of culture and kinship already discussed – they still felt themselves to be a race apart. And thanks to Edward's arrogant behaviour in the 1290s this feeling was fanned into a nationalist flame which was never completely extinguished. The war that began in the 1290s was not, therefore, as earlier ones had been, a war over the delineation of the border. It was a war for the nation's independence. And for that reason it was a war which Edward, however indomitable his will, could never expect to win.

But it did not prevent him from trying. In the last decade of his reign scarcely a year passed when an army was not sent northwards. Triumphs at Dunbar in 1296 and Falkirk in 1298 suggested that success, if not imminent, might well be possible; and the capture and execution of William Wallace in 1305 deprived the Scots of their one leader of stature. But Scottish resistance was not to be quashed that easily. Within a year of Wallace's death a new leader had come forward in the person of Robert Bruce. Under his inspiration the effort to repel the invader was redoubled, and in 1314 a mighty defeat was inflicted on the English at Bannockburn. Edward II himself was nearly captured, and many of his knights met grisly deaths in the pits which the Scots had dug to ensnare their horses. It was the worst calamity to befall English arms since Hastings.

Edward II returned home humiliated. He could neither disclaim responsibility for the disaster nor offer hope of its early reversal. Heavy indebtedness prevented him from putting another army in the field for three or four years, and in that time the vital border town of Berwick was added to the list of English losses. Until its recapture fifteen years later there was no barrier to Scots' penetration of the northern counties of England, and devastating raids were launched as far south as the Vale of York. The purpose of these was to extract money rather than to inflict destruction. No fewer than eight times, between 1311 and 1327, the people of County Durham were driven to paying the Scots to go away, and it has been estimated that as much as a third of the value of some lands was handed over. This was a heavy price to pay for peace, and before long it was realized that proper security could only be afforded by resort to fortification.

On both sides of the border during this period new castles were built and existing ones strengthened. On the Scots side, Hermitage in Liddesdale was one of many fortified manor-houses that were converted into more forbidding tower-houses. On the English side, Alnwick (Northumberland) and Raby (Durham) were turned from fairly ordinary castles into sprawling great fortresses. On a more modest scale peel towers, like those at Sizergh (Cumbria) (NT) and Dalton (NT) were built by the gentry and clergy to afford a measure of protection for themselves and their servants; and even church towers were rebuilt with an eye to defence. By the mid-fourteenth century the border had become a militarized society – living by war and feeding on war. It replaced the Welsh Marches as the most dangerous frontier area in Britain, and in doing so it developed many of the features characteristic of a frontier society: aggressive militarism, resort to self-help to settle disputes and the build-up of power by the nobility. The rise of the two families of Percy and Neville, whose rivalry was to do so much to influence the future course of national as well as regional history, was a product of the long period of warfare that opened in the 1290s.

THE HUNDRED YEARS' WAR

The experience of fighting in Scotland aroused mixed feelings in the men who made up the English armies. The cause they saw as a worthwhile one, certainly: they were taught to think of the Scots as 'cursed caitiffs, full of treason'; and the blood-curdling tales which were put into circulation of atrocities committed in the northern counties generated in them feelings of bitter hatred towards the enemy. But, on the other hand, Scotland itself was considered an unattractive land; the weather was cold, the terrain difficult and the countryside poor. An incentive to fight was provided by the grants of land in Scotland which Edward I made to many of his captains; but in the wake of Bruce's triumph all these were lost, and the prospect of further material gain was slight.

In 1337 it was with general approval, then, that Edward III switched the thrust of England's attack to France. His claim to the French Crown provided him with the justification that he needed, and in 1338 he crossed with an army to Flanders. Initially he made little headway. But in the 1340s his fortunes changed, and he scored a series of victories which raised the English monarchy to new heights of renown.

Good tactical sense was one reason for Edward's success. He took care to avoid the mistakes that had cost his predecessor so dearly at Bannockburn. Instead of placing the archers behind the knights (so that the latter got in the way), he placed them side by side – the knights usually in the centre, either mounted or dismounted, and the archers on the flanks. When battle commenced and the enemy advanced, the archers would release a hail of arrows to break up the cavalry. In the ensuing melée the knights would then move in to finish the job. The first battle to witness the use of these tactics was probably Morlaix in 1342. They were used again to devastating effect at Crécy in 1346 and Poitiers in 1356 – by which time the English army had won for itself the reputation of being the most formidable fighting force of its day.

It also needs to be said that the organization of war had changed greatly since the time of Bannockburn. No longer was the English army deployed in one great host. It was usually broken into two or three forces, each operating in a different theatre, but conforming to an overall strategy directed by the king and his commanders. The twin objectives were to deprive the French of the initiative and to keep them guessing as to the direction from which the next attack was to come. It was a strategy which reaped particularly rich rewards in 1356. In that year the Black Prince and Duke Henry of Lancaster fielded two separate armies, one to the north and one to the south of the Loire, and between them they teased and diverted the French until the Prince delivered the knock-out blow at Poitiers on 19 September.

The assurance of success undoubtedly made warfare in France a more attractive proposition than warfare in Scotland – a change in perception which was reflected in a greater willingness to participate. The armies of the Hundred Years' War were not always very large (after the Black Death they were necessarily smaller than those fielded before), but they included a fair number of regulars who made a profession of arms and fought on campaign after campaign. For these men warfare was a way of life and a means of gaining a living. It was a calling which offered companionship, excitement and danger. It was the supreme occasion for the display of virtue. And more materially it held out the prospect of financial gain. Peace was viewed by these men as a misfortune not a blessing. It brought unemployment not hope. It obliged them to seek openings elsewhere, in Spain or Italy perhaps, in one of the free companies that ravaged the countryside between campaigns. John Carington, for example, the orphaned son of a

ST MARY'S, WARWICK
The choir, built by Thomas
Beauchamp, Earl of Warwick
(d. 1369), who lies buried with his
wife beneath the tomb in the middle

knight who had served with distinction under the Black Prince, served under Richard II in the 1390s, fled to the continent after his downfall, and found employment with the Visconti dukes of Milan, under whose banner he fought at the battle of Como. John was a veteran campaigner, reluctant to put down roots – just like his father and grand-father before him and his cousin after him. But even young esquires with no family background of service viewed warfare in these practical, unsentimental terms. When two such young men, Nicholas Molyneux and John Winter, set foot in France for the first time in 1421, they made a mutual agreement to secure themselves against possible loss: each committed himself to secure the other's liberation in the event of capture pro-vided that the ransom did not exceed £1,000; if it did, then the other was to become a hostage for up to nine months to allow the prisoner to return home to raise the larger sum. All the gains of war, meanwhile, were to be pooled and sent home; and whichever of the two reached England first was to invest their accumulated capital in land as wisely as he could to their joint profit.

It is evident from this agreement that capture was the disaster which soldiers feared most. Payment of a ransom to secure release could wipe away the profits of a lifetime. For those whose rank earned them a high blood-price it could mean ruination. Robert, Lord Moleyns had to mortgage all his estates to raise the sum of nearly £10,000 demanded by his captors in 1453; and for him there were no gains to set against this massive loss. A knight of humbler rank, Sir John Hadreshull, Edward III's lieutenant in Brittany in the 1340s, was captured two, perhaps even three, times in the course of his long career: first at Bannockburn in 1314 and then again much later in Brittany. But whether in the end he returned home richer than he set out we can only guess.

Over the period of the war as a whole – and bearing in mind that the English won most of the set-piece engagements – it seems likely that the English took more prisoners than the French and that the balance of income therefore flowed in England's direction rather than vice versa. Edward III himself enjoyed the ransom of not one but two kings: David of Scotland and John of France. Nevertheless, fighting in France, as Hadreshull would have affirmed, was always a gamble, and whether or how well it paid off depended partly on luck and partly on rank. It was luck that delivered the King of Scots into the hands of the north country man-at-arms John Coopland at Neville's Cross in 1346; but it was rank that determined how the proceeds of his ransom were distrib-uted. By the fourteenth century no man-at-arms could reckon to pocket the whole of a ransom himself. By general agreement he paid over one third of it to his captain, and the latter a third of that to the king. In the case of the most important prisoners, how-ever, the Crown took over all the ransom rights itself, giving the man responsible for the capture a 'reward' by way of compensation – £500 in Coopland's case.

Because of the existence of these conventions the Hundred Years War in France did much less than is sometimes supposed to promote a redistribution of wealth in late medieval society. Undoubtedly there were some men of humble birth whose fortunes were made by war. One example is Sir Robert Knolles, who is said to have amassed upwards of 100,000 crowns in the 1360s and whose ignoble origins are attested by the reluctance of some of the nobility to serve under him. Another example is his distin-guished contemporary Sir Hugh Calveley. Interestingly, both these men were natives of Cheshire, a county which benefited more than most from the war because of the tenure of its earldom by the Black Prince. From other parts of the country the examples tend to be fewer and less spectacular – suggesting movement within a particular rank of soci-ety rather than a jump from one to another.

ST MARY'S, WARWICK
The Beauchamp Chapel, looking west towards the painting of the Last Judgement. Earl Richard's tomb is in the forefront

War in the Middle Ages was, therefore, much less of a leveller than it was to be in later times. Indeed, it did not so much undermine as reinforce the dominance of the ruling élite – for the simple reason that fighting was their traditional vocation and the function that they were assigned in the three-fold ordering of society. So long as the dominant values of society were militaristic and aristocratic, as they were in England throughout the Middle Ages, then their position was secure. They encountered no criticism from the Church. The Church, indeed, so far from inclining towards pacifism, actually lent its support to war – provided that it was war in a just cause; and in the opinion of the English hierarchy no cause was more just than the war for the French Crown. Thus it is not surprising, but entirely appropriate, that the spirit of the age should be captured most perfectly in one of its churches – St Mary's, Warwick. This is a 'war church', built by one great captain, Thomas Beauchamp, 3rd Earl of Warwick of his line (d. 1369), and sumptuously enlarged by another, Richard Beauchamp, the 5th Earl (d. 1439). It contains the tombs of them both. Earl Thomas' tomb is a large, somewhat mechanical composition, placed centre-stage in the choir. Earl Richard's far finer and more splendid monument is the dominant feature of the chapel which he founded – known today as the Beauchamp Chapel. It consists of a tomb chest of Purbeck marble, topped by a gilded bronze effigy of the earl, on which is centred an iconographic scheme embracing the whole chapel. Its theme is the earl's admission to the kingdom of heaven. His upward ascent is serenaded by a chorus of angels which fills the traceried lights of the windows. From the summit of the east window the golden figure of the Almighty, holding the world in His hand, looks down benevolently. The earl's hands are drawn apart, as if in wonder at this unfolding vision; and his gaze is fixed upwards on the figure of the Virgin Mary carved on the central boss of the vault. The only discordant note is struck by the painting of the Last Judgement on the west wall (and thus safely out of the onlooker's view as he faces the altar). This image apart, there is no sense in the chapel of the terror of the torments of hell which pervaded the art of the twelfth century. But then this virtuous knight had nothing to fear. The causes that he had upheld were God's causes, and the wars that he had fought were God's wars. The store of worldly renown that he had enjoyed would never have been granted him had he not basked in the Almighty's grace. If ever a man's salvation was assured, Earl Richard's was.

Over two centuries earlier, at the death-bed of an even greater knight, the Master of the Templars had said:

God has granted you a great favour, that you will never be separated from Him. He has shown you this in your life, and He will do the same again after your death. In the course of your life you have had more honour than any other knight. When God granted you His grace in this way, you may be sure that He wished to receive you at the end.

These words were spoken in 1219 to the Regent of England, William Marshal, Earl of Pembroke, who, thus reassured, shortly afterwards passed away. But the values that they express were the values of an age. They make as fitting a tribute to Earl Richard as they do to his illustrious predecessor.

RETROSPECT

The face of Britain had been transformed in the five to six millennia or more covered by this book. The countryside had been tamed, the forests cleared and the marshlands drained. Towns had been established, churches founded, manor-houses and castles built and rebuilt, and a network of communications built up along which traders and way-farers could thread their way. There were few areas in which the influence of human endeavour had not made itself felt.

But the pace of advance over the period was neither uniform nor consistent. Some periods were witness to a higher level of activity than others. The late Bronze Age and Iron Age, it is now clear, saw a far greater intensification of arable farming than was once thought possible. The early Saxon period, on the other hand, probably saw a not inconsiderable retreat. The whole business of colonization and settlement was a lengthier, more complex and less even process than was once supposed.

The changing character of British society can be traced in the physical remains that have come down to us. The rapid extension of colonization is hinted at by the mid-third century millennium fields at Scord of Brouster in the Shetlands; the power of the civilizing mission of Rome is suggested by the great villa at Chedworth; the popular concern for salvation is proclaimed by the ruins of the abbey church at Fountains; the desire for higher living standards is affirmed by the comfortable manor-houses of Ightham Mote in England and Kellie in Scotland. The sheer range of experience attested by these buildings is enough to astonish and to command our attention. Britain in the Middle Ages was clearly no backward, mono-cultural society. It was a rich and prosperous land inhabited by peoples as ambitious as they were creative. The foundations that they laid are the ones on which later ages were to build, and on which so much of our civilization rests today.

LATE MEDIEVAL SITES IN THE CARE OF THE NATIONAL TRUST OR THE NATIONAL TRUST FOR SCOTLAND

CASTLES

Bellister Castle (Northumberland)

Bodiam Castle (East Sussex)

Castle Campbell (Central Scotland)

Chirk Castle (Clwyd)

Cilgerran Castle (Dyfed)

Compton Castle (Devon)

Corfe Castle (Dorset)
Croft Castle (Hereford and Worcester)
Dalton Castle (Cumbria)
Dirleton Castle (Lothian), owned by NTS,
    administered by Historic Scotland
Drum Castle (Grampian)
Duffield Castle (Derbyshire)
Dunseverick Castle (County Antrim)
Dunstanburgh Castle (Northumberland)
    (owned by NT, administered by English
    Heritage)
Dunster Castle (Somerset)
Fyvie Castle (Grampian)
Kellie Castle (Fife)
Powis Castle (Powys)
Scotney Castle (Kent)
Skenfrith Castle (Gwent)
Sizergh Castle (Cumbria)
Tattershall Castle (Lincolnshire)

MANOR-HOUSES

Baddesley Clinton (West Midlands)
Boarstall Tower (Buckinghamshire)
Clevedon Court (Avon)
Cotehele (Cornwall)
Great Chalfield Manor (Wiltshire)
Greys Court (Oxfordshire)
Ightham Mote (Kent)
Little Moreton Hall (Cheshire)
Lower Brockhampton (Hereford and
    Worcester)
Lytes Cary Manor (Somerset)
Norbury Old Manor (Derbyshire)
Old Soar Manor (Kent)
Priest's House, Muchelney (Somerset)
Treasurer's House, Martock (Somerset)

URBAN AND VERNACULAR BUILDINGS

Aberconwy House, Conwy (Gwynedd)
Clergy House, Alfriston (East Sussex)
Fleece Inn, Bretforton (Hereford and
    Worcester)
Greyfriars (Worcester)
Priory Cottages, Steventon (Oxfordshire)
St George's Guildhall, King's Lynn
    (Norfolk)
Stoneacre, Otham (Kent)
Tudor Merchant's House, Tenby (Dyfed)

MONASTIC BUILDINGS

Bredon Tithe Barn (Hereford and
    Worcester)
Buckland Abbey (Devon)
Canon's Ashby Priory
    (Northamptonshire)
Cartmel Priory Gatehouse (Cumbria)
Fountains Abbey (North Yorkshire) (in
    guardianship of English Heritage)
Great Coxwell Tithe Barn (Oxfordshire)
Hailes Abbey (Gloucestershire) (in
    guardianship of English Heritage)
Lacock Abbey (Wiltshire)
Middle Littleton Tithe Barn (Hereford
    and Worcester)
Mottisfont Abbey (Hampshire)
Mount Grace Priory (North Yorkshire) (in
    guardianship of English Heritage)
Ramsey Abbey Gatehouse
    (Cambridgeshire)
St Michael's Mount (Cornwall)
Stoke-sub-Hamdon Priory (Somerset)

BIBLIOGRAPHY

Place of publication is London unless otherwise indicated.

PREHISTORY

A number of excellent texts survey British prehistory from the Paleolithic to the Iron Age. A detailed account of the material evidence of British prehistory is to be found in *Introduction to British Prehistory*, J.V.S. Megaw and D.D.A. Simpson (eds) (Leicester, 1979), while an alternative source with a slightly different approach is *British Prehistory: A New Outline*, C. Renfrew (ed.) (1974). A third source, in a more narrative style and with less detail, is T. Darvill, *Prehistoric Britain* (1987). J. Dyer, *Southern England: An Archaeological Guide*, is an excellent guide to the main sites of southern England. Sadly no guide of equivalent stature exists for the monuments of northern England, but for Scotland two compact guides exist in the form of R. Feachems, *Guide to Prehistoric Scotland* (2nd edn, 1977), and E. Mackie, *Scotland: An Archaeological Guide* (1975). For the development of the landscape, a major theme in prehistory, several excellent books exist. *The Environment in British Prehistory*, I. Simmons and M. Tooley (eds) (1981), is an authoritative introduction, while C. Taylor, *Village and Farmstead* (1983) offers a wide-ranging and accessible overview. For primitive temperate-zone agriculture two books in particular are to be recommended: *The Agrarian History of England and Wales, I (Prehistory)*, S. Piggott (ed.) (Cambridge, 1981), which is a sound historical guide, and *Farming Practice in British Prehistory*, R.J. Mercer (ed.) (Edinburgh, 1981), which examines the techniques of how agriculture was conducted. Specialist examinations of each period of British prehistory are also available. S. Piggott, *Neolithic Cultures of the British Isles* (Cambridge, 2nd edn, 1971) is invaluable for the Neolithic, and C. Burgess, *The Age of Stonehenge* (1980) and B. Cunliffe, *Iron Age Communities in Britain* (3rd edn, 1991) equally so for the Bronze and Iron Ages respectively.

ROMAN AND EARLY MEDIEVAL BRITAIN

A brief introduction to Roman Britain, now a little dated, is I. Richmond, *Roman Britain* (2nd edn, Harmondsworth, 1963). Much larger are P. Salway, *Roman Britain* (Oxford, 1981) and S. Frere, *Britannia* (1967). For Boudica's revolt the standard work is G. Webster, *Boudica: the British Revolt against Rome AD 60* (1978). The subject of the Romano-British countryside is dealt with in *Rural Settlement in Roman Britain*, A.C. Thomas (ed.) (1966), and *Studies in the Romano-British Villa*, M. Todd (ed.) (Leicester, 1978). For Hadrian's Wall see D.J. Breeze and B. Dobson, *Hadrian's Wall* (Harmondsworth, 2nd edn, 1978), and for roads, I.D. Margary, *Roman Roads in Britain* (1967). There are several good surveys of the Anglo-Saxon period. The classic account is F.M. Stenton, *Anglo-Saxon England* (Oxford, 3rd edn, 1971), though this is now a little dated. *The Anglo-Saxons*, J. Campbell (ed.) (1982) is a stimulating, well-illustrated survey. The story of the Conversion is told by Bede, whose *Ecclesiastical History of the English People* is available in a number of editions, notably B. Colgrave and R. Mynors (eds) (Oxford, 1969). For Offa and the eighth century see C. Fox, *Offa's Dyke* (1955). Alfred may be approached through the sources in *Alfred the Great*, S. Keynes and M. Lapidge (eds) (Harmondsworth, 1983). For the artistic and creative achievement of the Anglo-Saxons see the catalogues of two exhibitions held at the British Museum, *The Making of England. Anglo-Saxon Art and Culture*, AD 600–900, L. Webster and J. Backhouse (eds) (1991), and *The Golden Age of Anglo-Saxon Art, 966–1066*, J. Backhouse and others (eds) (1984). For archaeological insights see R. Hodges, *The Anglo-Saxon Achievement* (1989), and *The Archaeology of Anglo-Saxon England*, D.M. Wilson (ed.) (Cambridge, 1976). On architecture there are two excellent surveys: H.M. and J. Taylor, *Anglo-Saxon Architecture* (3 vols, Cambridge, 1965, 1978) and, on a smaller scale, E. Fernie, *The Architecture of the Anglo-Saxons* (1983).

MEDIEVAL BRITAIN

For relations between England and the continental possessions of the Crown see J. Le Patourel, *The Norman Empire* (Oxford, 1976) and J. Gillingham, *The Angevin Empire* (1984). The best introduction to the economic history of the late medieval period is J.L. Bolton, *The Medieval English Economy, 1150–1500* (1980). For living standards see C. Dyer, *Standards of living in the later Middle Ages* (Cambridge, 1989). K.B. McFarlane, *The Nobility of Later Medieval England* (Oxford, 1973), and C. Given-Wilson, *The English Nobility in the Late Middle Ages* (1987) consider the lives of the nobility and gentry, a subject also explored from a local angle in N.E. Saul, *Scenes From Provincial Life. Knightly Families in Sussex 1280–1400* (Oxford, 1986). Developments in urban society in the period are explored by C. Platt, *The English Medieval Town* (1976) and S. Thrupp, *The Merchant Class of Medieval London* (Chicago, 1948). There are useful surveys of the political history of the period in M.T. Clanchy, *England and its Rulers, 1066–1272* (1983), and A. Tuck, *Crown and Nobility, 1272–1461* (1985). R. Frame, *The Political Development of the British Isles, 1100–1400* (Oxford, 1990), exceptionally covers the British Isles as a whole. Developments in Wales and Scotland separately are considered by R.R. Davies, *Conquest, Coexistence and Change, Wales 1063–1415* (Oxford, 1987) and A. Grant, *Independence and Nationhood: Scotland 1306–1469* (1984) respectively. For Ireland see J. Otway-Ruthven, *A History of Medieval Ireland* (2nd edn, 1980). The best general survey of the medieval church is R.W. Southern, *Western Society and the Church in the Middle Ages* (Harmondsworth, 1970). For the monasteries see C.H. Lawrence, *Medieval Monasticism* (1984), and for the parish churches, C. Platt, *The Parish Churches of Medieval England* (1981). Architectural history is addressed in a number of books. For church architecture the best guide is now

C. Wilson, *The Gothic Cathedral* (1990); for military architecture see R.A. Brown, *English Castles* (2nd edn, 1970), and M.W. Thompson, *The Decline of the Castle* (Cambridge, 1987). The creative achievement of the period may be savoured in *The Age of Chivalry. Art in Plantagenet England, 1200– 1400*, J. Alexander and P. Binski (eds) (1987). The interaction of culture and society is considered by various authors in *The Age of Chivalry. Art and Society in Late Medieval England*, N.E. Saul (ed.) (1992). For literacy, literature and learning see M.T. Clanchy, *From Memory to Written Record* (1979), and *The Cambridge Guide to the Arts in Britain. The Middle Ages*, B. Ford (ed.) (Cambridge, 1988).

ACKNOWLEDGEMENTS

The General Editor and Publishers gratefully acknowledge permission to reproduce the following illustrations: Page 1: Wiltshire Archaeological and Natural History Society; 6: J. Wymer, *Lower Palaeolithic Archaeology in Britain* (London, 1968); 7: J.G.D. Clark, *Excavations at Star Carr* (Cambridge, 1964); 17: J.M. Coles & B.J. Orme, *Prehistory of the Somerset Levels* (Cambridge, 1980); 31: P. Christie, in *Procs. Prehistoric Soc.*, 1967; 40, 41: B. Cunliffe, *Danebury: Anatomy of an Iron Age Hillfort* (London, 1983); 46: I. Stead, in *Archaeologia*, 1967; 53: from *The British Numismatic Journal*, volume 60, by permission of the British Numismatic Society; 79: Royal Commission on the Historical Monuments of England; 101: British Library Board; 111 and 118: Royal Commission on the Historical Monuments of England; 119: C. Wilson; 120: Royal Commission on the Historical Monuments of England; 126: British Library Board; 132: Dr Malcolm Norris, Monumental Brass Society; 140: Shakespeare Birthplace Trust Record Office, Stratford-upon-Avon; 145: Jim Henderson; 148: National Trust for Scotland; 147: the estate of Canon Ridgway; 159, 160: English Heritage; 164: Aerofilms Ltd; 170, 175, 178, 182: Royal Commission on the Historical Monuments of England; 186: British Library Board; 196: Historical Monuments Commission of Ireland; 202, 204: Vicar and Churchwardens of St Mary's, Warwick. Illustrations of National Trust properties are reproduced by permission of the National Trust.

The General Editor and Publishers gratefully acknowledge permission to reproduce material from the following maps: Page 4: J. Wymer, *Lower Palaeolithic Archaeology in Britain* (London, 1968); 5: *The Mesolithic in Europe*, S. Kozlowski (ed.) (Warsaw, 1973); 20: A. Burl, *The Stone Circles of the British Isles* (New Haven and London, 1971); 21, 33: T. Darvill, *Prehistoric Britain* (London, 1987); 23: Cummins, in *Stone Age Studies*, I (Council of British Archaeology, London, 1982); 27: P. Ashbee, *The Bronze Age Round Barrow in Britain* (London, 1960); 29: R.F. Tylecote, *The Early History of Metallurgy in Europe* (London, 1987); 34: N.O. Johnson, in *The British Later Bronze Age*, Barrett & Bradley (eds.) (London, 1980); 130: R. Glasscock and the Cambridge University Press; 139: *Field and Forest: An Historical Geography of Warwickshire and Worcestershire*, T.R. Slater & P.J. Jarvis (eds.) (Norwich, 1982); 156: B.P. Hindle, *Medieval Roads* (Princes Risborough, 1982); 183: N.I. Orme, *Education and Society in Medieval and Renaissance England* (London, 1989).

INDEX